SHAKESPEARE AND VIOLENCE PREVENTION

Shakespeare & VIOLENCE PREVENTION
A Practical Handbook for Educators

AMANDA GIGUERE

UNIVERSITY OF WYOMING PRESS
Laramie

© 2025 by University Press of Colorado

Published by University of Wyoming Press
An imprint of University Press of Colorado
1580 North Logan Street, Suite 660
PMB 39883
Denver, Colorado 80203-1942

All rights reserved

 The University Press of Colorado is a proud member of Association of University Presses.

The University Press of Colorado is a cooperative publishing enterprise supported, in part, by Adams State University, Colorado School of Mines, Colorado State University, Fort Lewis College, Metropolitan State University of Denver, University of Alaska Fairbanks, University of Colorado, University of Northern Colorado, University of Wyoming, Utah State University, and Western Colorado University.

ISBN: 978-1-64642-722-2 (hardcover)
ISBN: 978-1-64642-723-9 (paperback)
ISBN: 978-1-64642-724-6 (ebook)
https://doi.org/10.5876/9781646427246

Cataloging-in-Publication data for this title is available online at the Library of Congress.

Front cover photographs by Jennifer Koskinen (*top and middle*) and Patrick Campbell (*bottom left and right*). Back cover photographs by Jennifer Koskinen (*top*), Patrick Campbell (*middle*), and Amanda Giguere (*bottom*). All cover photographs © Colorado Shakespeare Festival.

To Holden and Baxter

Contents

Prologue ix

1. Introduction 3

   Interlude: The Tragedies and Violence Prevention 33
2. *Macbeth*: Empathy and Violence 36
3. *Julius Caesar*: Targeted Attacks and Warning Signs 54
4. *Romeo and Juliet*: Suicide and Community Violence 71

   Interlude: The Comedies and Violence Prevention 89
5. *Much Ado About Nothing*: "The Merry War": Rumors, Gossip, and School Climate 91
6. *Twelfth Night*: Bullying and Cyberbullying 104
7. *The Comedy of Errors*: Presence, Breath, and Mindfulness 126
8. *The Taming of the Shrew*: Gender and Relationship Violence 138
9. *The Tempest*: Prospero's "Rarer Action": Forgiveness and Breaking the Cycle of Violence 156
10. Conclusion 179

    Epilogue 192

    Acknowledgments 199
    Appendix A: Macbeth *Materials* 202
    Appendix B: Julius Caesar *Materials* 206

Appendix C: Romeo and Juliet *Materials*   212
Appendix D: Much Ado About Nothing *Materials*   218
Appendix E: Twelfth Night *Materials*   225
Appendix F: The Comedy of Errors *Materials*   230
Appendix G: The Taming of the Shrew *Materials*   238
Appendix H: The Tempest *Materials*   242

References   249
Index   255
About the Author   265

Prologue

A MEMORY FROM 2011

As I sat down at the gleaming table in the conference room, my palms were sweating. The building was brand new (or, at least, newer than the one-hundred-plus-year-old stucco cottage that housed my office down the street). The windows were immense and offered a breathtaking late-afternoon view of Boulder sprawling below: the bustling grounds of Boulder High School, the tree-canopied Boulder Creek Path, the muted browns and greys of campus housing. I felt, in this sealed-off, glassy space above Boulder, like I had been invited into a special place, a room of wisdom, numbers, facts, and a room in which people held the answers. This was my first visit to the Center for the Study and Prevention of Violence (CSPV), housed in a giant building that was a parking lot when I moved to Boulder. I can't quite remember who was in that room for that very first meeting, but if I had to guess, it would be Linda Cunningham, Jane Grady, and Del Elliott, three movers and shakers at CSPV, who would become the early supporters, champions, and collaborators who helped me shape the program that I now write about more than thirteen years later.

At that first meeting, with my nerves vibrating, my voice shaking, and my face reddening as it often does when meeting with authority figures, I began to explain an idea my colleagues and I at the Colorado Shakespeare Festival (CSF) had about pairing Shakespeare plays with an anti-bullying lesson for children. We wanted to tour an abridged performance of *Twelfth Night* to local schools, and we thought it would be a good opportunity to tie it into a conversation about bullying. When I had mentioned the idea to my colleague Jeanne McDonald in CU Boulder's Office for Public and Community-Engaged Scholarship, she had encouraged me to sit down with Dr. Del Elliott, who ran the Center for the Study and Prevention of Violence. I had never heard of the center, even though it was, as I learned on my brief walk to the building, a mere half block away from my own office on the CU Boulder campus.

I assumed that these violence-prevention experts, who spent their days researching trends and thinking about how to reduce violence, would listen with kind smiles and then send me on my way with a fact sheet or an article to read. But that spring afternoon in 2011, as I started to explain *Twelfth Night*'s subplot about the prank involving Malvolio, a letter, and yellow stockings, the CSPV staff members seemed truly interested in the story. They pointed out the connections between the anonymous letter and cyberbullying; they noticed that the story Shakespeare wrote aligned with what they knew about the cycle of violence. By the time I'd finished explaining what happens in the play, and Malvolio's final promise to seek revenge, these violence-prevention experts were genuinely excited about the overlaps between our disciplines, and so was I. Shakespeare's play, it seemed, aligned with their research into how bullying works in the cycle of violence. And I was learning a lot about the definition of bullying, as they jumped in with explanations and anecdotes. They wanted to partner with CSF to shape this program. They believed that a play might offer an engaging way to share research with young people. That was the birth of the Shakespeare & Violence Prevention program.

By the end of the meeting, my sweating palms had cooled, my nervous system had settled, my eyes sparkled with connection, and I felt at ease with this supportive group of collaborators; I felt that I had value, and that I was no longer an outsider in this building but that I belonged.

I begin with this personal story because it highlights one aspect of this book: the ways in which two disciplines may seem to have nothing in common, but when there is an opportunity for the knowledge from different disciplines to come together, the overlaps become clear. I was nervous to reach out to another discipline outside the familiar territory of theatre-making, but I am so glad I did. Theatre-based knowledge and violence-prevention knowledge have much in common, and combining these disciplines has resulted in innovative programming that neither discipline could accomplish independently. And while this book is about bridging research with practice, it is also, like most stories, about human beings, gathering together, and connecting their shared experiences.

NOW

Shakespeare seems to be everywhere these days, not only in classrooms, rehearsal halls, and performance venues worldwide but also in daily life. We might see Shakespeare's work as the topic of a Final Jeopardy answer, featured in a magazine ad, analyzed on a podcast, or appearing as a film on a streaming platform. Despite the plays' origins in a particular time and place, Shakespeare's work has myriad applications beyond its original early modern English context. Cultures continually remake Shakespeare in their own images and reinterpret the plays through the lens of the present day. No matter the topic, Shakespeare's plays, it seems, have something to say. Esther Cloudman Dunn, a Smith College professor in the 1930s, noted Shakespeare's ability to connect with any time period: "The genius of Shakespeare is extraordinarily sensitive to the hour and the age. Into his book, each age has peered, as into a mirror, to see its own face. The images in that mirror fade and are replaced as the decades go by. But the mirror is not discarded" (Dunn 1939, 247–48). Dunn is not alone in the observation that Shakespeare's meaning is ever evolving and dependent on the times. Jonathan Bate, author of *The Genius of Shakespeare*, offers that "Because he was hardly ever narrowly topical in his own age and culture, Shakespeare has remained topical in other ages and cultures" (Bate 1998, 221). The openness and subjectiveness of the plays invite readers and audience members to step in as meaning-makers. As scholar Emma Smith writes in *This is Shakespeare*, Shakespeare's "works hold our attention because they are fundamentally incomplete and unstable; they need us" (Smith 2020, 4).

There is a growing interest among practitioners, educators, and scholars to explore how Shakespeare's plays inform other areas of study outside their traditional homes in literary or theatrical disciplines. Theatre companies continue to produce these plays, and students continue to study these plays in classrooms, but more and more, thinkers, educators, artists, and citizens are pushing back against the inherited boundaries about how Shakespeare's works might serve our world now. What other applications might these early modern plays offer? What elements within the plays are best discarded? What wisdom within Shakespeare's plays might be applicable to other disciplines? How might interdisciplinary approaches to Shakespeare help tackle practical twenty-first-century problems?

At my home institution of the University of Colorado Boulder (CU Boulder), a professional certificate in applied Shakespeare draws teachers, professionals, artists, and enthusiasts together to learn about the way Shakespeare intersects with their own disciplines. Although the field of applied Shakespeare is still in formation, one might define it as *an application of Shakespeare's plays to another field, discipline, or topic to address a particular issue, question, or problem.* As burgeoning applied Shakespeare programs continue to develop, experts in the field are investigating the ways in which Shakespeare's plays resonate with other areas, and often reinforce the wisdom of many disciplines.

Just as Shakespeare practitioners are applying the work to other fields, a similar phenomenon is underway in contemporary violence-prevention research. As violence grows in the United States, prevention scientists call for multidisciplinary approaches to addressing the public health issue, relying on knowledge from a range of disciplines (CDC 2024h). This is not the time for siloed knowledge, and experts agree that violence is a complicated issue that will require innovative and collaborative solutions. How can violence-prevention researchers harness knowledge from other disciplines to translate research into practice, and how can we bridge the gap between research and the daily lives of real people?

Enter Shakespeare.

SHAKESPEARE AND VIOLENCE PREVENTION

1
Introduction
Shakespeare and Violence Prevention:
A Practical Handbook for Educators

This handbook is an exploration of a selection of Shakespeare's plays through the lens of contemporary youth violence-prevention research. It is aimed at educators, theatre practitioners, and teaching artists seeking ways to anchor Shakespeare in a curriculum guided by best practices in violence prevention, and to help improve school climates, deepen empathy, and enhance connectedness within the classroom or rehearsal room. The book is rooted in this question: *How can live, performance-based approaches to Shakespeare's plays reinforce violence-prevention skills in school-aged children?* In this handbook, you'll discover how Shakespeare's plays can provide opportunities for students to witness problematic behavior in performance and strategize their own peaceful solutions through roleplaying. While reinforcing the twenty-first-century skills of creativity, collaboration, and communication, a performance-based approach to Shakespeare in the classroom simultaneously lays the groundwork for many goals of violence prevention, including empathy-building, teamwork, and revealing the possibilities of change. Exposure to Shakespeare's plays can also equip individuals with important social and emotional skills, including the ability to slow down, reflect on human behavior, and observe the connectedness of people, by both watching and making theatre.

This book emerges from grounded experience with the Shakespeare & Violence Prevention program, an interdisciplinary project based in

Boulder, Colorado. The project is a collaboration between the Colorado Shakespeare Festival (CSF), a professional theatre company in association with the University of Colorado Boulder, and the Center for the Study and Prevention of Violence (CSPV), a research center housed in the Institute of Behavioral Science at CU Boulder. This unique partnership has led to an innovative way to connect Shakespeare's plays with a violence-prevention curriculum. This book is an attempt to share some of the best practices and findings from this particular outreach project and to make some of these practices and ideas more widely accessible to educators interested in this kind of work in the classroom and to practitioners interested in applied Shakespeare.

The results from more than a decade of Shakespeare & Violence Prevention performances and workshops qualitatively suggest that this work is effective in translating violence-prevention research into practice. While thousands of students in Colorado experience the Colorado Shakespeare Festival's live Shakespeare & Violence Prevention program each year, my hope in writing this handbook is to expand the reach of this project by supporting you, the reader, in undertaking similar projects in your community. CSF's program is limited by the number of places the troupe can visit each year and the number of miles the CSF van can travel in a school year; if more artists and educators are empowered to take on the work of teaching violence prevention through the arts, the impact can be so much greater.

You do not need to be a violence-prevention expert or a Shakespeare scholar to explore these lessons with your students. I hope that this book helps translate some of the violence-prevention research for educators everywhere and makes it a little more accessible to integrate a violence-prevention lens in educational approaches to Shakespeare. I also hope this handbook encourages more research in the field, so we can continue to harness the arts to translate violence-prevention research. If viewed through a violence-prevention lens, Shakespeare's plays have some lessons embedded within them that can help you explore critical concepts with your students as we work, collectively, toward a more peaceful world.

SHAKESPEARE AND VIOLENCE

Shakespeare may seem a surprising choice as a tool to prevent violence because, on the surface, his plays seem to reinforce the very actions one may wish to prevent in real life. In a recent post-show violence-prevention workshop about *Julius Caesar*, a middle school student asked, "Why are we watching a play about people killing each other?" It's a good question; one that I recommend turning back over to the students in the room. What *does* happen when we watch a play in which characters plot harm, carry out that harm, and then respond to the consequences of that harm? How does it make you feel to watch this happen? How does watching a play in which a lot of violence and mistreatment occurs impact the way you think about violence in our world? In bringing students into the conversation about the impact of staging violence, we begin to use Shakespeare as a tool to understand ourselves, our peers, and our communities. This idea is key to the work of Shakespeare and violence prevention; in the approach laid out in this book, the plays of Shakespeare are tools we can use to explore our world. They are not historic relics to be revered but rather media to be manipulated, stretched, altered, questioned, and experimented with as we work to understand the patterns of violence—and the opportunities to disrupt those patterns—in our own world.

A play does not always represent an ideal world; that would not only make for static theatre but it would also make for an experience devoid of conflict or struggle. A play is rooted in conflict. *Agon*, the Greek term for conflict, struggle, debate, or contest, is at the heart of the theatrical experience (and *agon* is where we get words like "agony," "protagonist," and "antagonist"). When we watch a play, we see struggle and conflict onstage, we see characters hurting others, we see misbehavior and people who make mistakes so that we can gain insight without having to experience these things in reality. A play provides us with critical distance through fiction and metaphor, and theatre can help us purge some of the harmful things about our world, while exploring what it means to be human. To be human, as we often see in Shakespeare's plays, is to be in a constant process of change and growth. Shakespeare's plays can serve as a way to engage students in critical conversations and activities around how violence operates in a community and how we can work to prevent violence in our own communities.

Throughout Shakespeare's plays, across the comedies, tragedies and histories, there is an undercurrent of violence that can be an effective entry point to bridge the distance between the plays and our own time. Violent acts serve as the inciting incidents in the plays. Cruel mistreatment, whether physical, verbal, or emotional, can be traced throughout the canon. Characters are embroiled in wars, acts of revenge, plots, overthrows, conflicts, arguments, and physical fights. Without violence, we would not have Shakespeare's plays. It fuels the action, sparks the passion, and drives the conflict that is so essential to a good play. When we read or watch a Shakespeare play, we are reminded that violence, like so many aspects of the human condition, is not unique to our time.

However, Shakespeare's use of violence is rarely gratuitous. Instead, the violent acts hold meaning; they are nestled in thought, surrounded by soliloquies, and have a deep impact on the plot and characters. Should I kill the king? Should I betray my friend? Should I confess what I have done? We see characters wrestle with choices, engage (sometimes) in violence, and we see the later impacts down the road. These are not violent plays but plays about violence, composed by a playwright who seems to be quietly and continually urging the audience to consider the ramifications of violence within a community.

In *Shakespeare and Violence*, scholar R. A. Foakes explores the acts of violence in the plays and tracks the playwright's evolving approach to violence. While Shakespeare's early plays seem to reinforce the heightened, gratuitous treatment of violence that drew early modern audiences to the theatre, the history plays led him to consider the role of violence more thoughtfully, and Foakes suggests the playwright's "growing uneasiness with violence" by the end of the major history cycles. By the late plays, Foakes suggests, Shakespeare was beginning to seek solutions to violence: "Whereas his previous plays brought home the tragic consequences of deeds of violence, Shakespeare's late plays accept violence as an inescapable part of the natural world and of human society, and are more interested in ways to moderate, control or atone for it" (Foakes 2003, 183). Foakes's work unpacks the patterns of extreme violence, from murder and suicide to assassination and war, connects the plays to our own attraction to violence in media, and tracks Shakespeare's development as a writer in relation to violence. For a deep dive into the treatment of violence throughout Shakespeare's literary canon, I recommend Foakes's compelling and eloquent work.

This handbook, by contrast, focuses on the nuances of violence, the moments upstream of the more extreme acts, particularly as these moments pertain to youth violence. Looking at the less overt acts of violence, such as bullying, mistreatment, and verbal abuse, that occur within the canon can help us explore the parallels between Shakespeare's plays and some of the more recognizable and frequent types of violence that youth experience, particularly in schools. These subtler acts of mistreatment often lay the groundwork for larger, more extreme violence.

Theatre is an especially appropriate site for grappling with questions about violence. In *Henry V*, the chorus asks the audience to forgive the actors for daring to perform "on this unworthy scaffold" (*Henry V* Prologue). While in this usage, *scaffold* refers to the theatrical stage; in other Elizabethan uses, the *scaffold* was the site of a public execution, which was a highly theatrical event, enacted before an audience. Unlike in a public execution, there is an element of safety to the violence depicted within the boundaries of a stage. Audience members may attend the theatre to see other people feel and experience things onstage, and then the audience members, if only subconsciously, feel purged and relieved. Bessel van der Kolk, author of *The Body Keeps the Score*, points out theatre's role as a functional part of a community: "Theatre involves a collective confrontation with the realities of the human condition" (van der Kolk, 336). Theatre can serve as a space in which a society may witness what it means to be human and face its most difficult questions, much like the way Shakespeare's character Hamlet describes the purpose of art: "To hold, as 'twere, the mirror up to nature" (*Hamlet* III.ii.23–24). Through the enactment of a broad spectrum of human experiences in public, a theatrical performance allows audience members to vicariously experience the highs and lows, pleasures and pains, joys and griefs of humanity without risking physical harm.

Aristotle thought the theatre had some healthy side effects, enabling spectators to purge unhealthy emotions without harming others, and experience *catharsis*, the feeling of release at the end of a moving performance. Centuries later, Augusto Boal identified Aristotle's system of tragedy as coercive, because the audience was not an active agent in the narrative but rather a passive spectator unable to shape the outcome. Boal recognized theatre's potential use as a tool to actively engage spectators in their own liberation, if they were able to step into the action and reshape the narrative. Boal defines the main objective of his Theatre of the Oppressed: "To change the people—'spectators,' passive beings in the theatrical phenomenon—into subjects, into actors, transformers of the dramatic action" (Boal 2019, 97). In Boal's vision, theatre can be used as a way for individuals to "train for real action." He suggests "the theatre is not revolutionary in itself, but it surely is a rehearsal for the revolution" (Boal 2019, 98). Boal developed Forum Theatre as an exercise in his Theatre of the Oppressed, in which participants view a scene and are able to step into the action to replace an actor in order to try out a solution. Boal says of this method: "It is not the place of the theatre to show the correct path, but only to offer the means by which all possible paths may be examined" (Boal 2019, 119).

Shakespeare would have been no stranger to violence in his own time. Street fighting was common in early modern England (that is, late sixteenth- and early seventeenth-century England), though the monarchy issued proclamations against it. Public executions were frequent and included beheadings, drawing and quartering, hanging, and burning. After an execution, the offender's remains were displayed as a warning to citizens. Bear-baiting was a popular pastime in which bears and dogs fought to the death. Dueling was technically illegal but still occurred to settle matters of honor. Shakespeare's fellow playwright, Ben Jonson, was imprisoned for killing another actor in a duel, and playwright Christopher Marlowe died in a 1593 tavern brawl. This was a culture in which fights broke out in the streets, animals were killed for entertainment, and London was lined with traitors' heads.

When we consider Shakespeare's plays through the lens of violence prevention, it is important to recognize the difference between our contemporary definition of violence and how Shakespeare used the term. The Oxford English Dictionary defines violence as "the deliberate exercise of *physical force* against a person, property, etc." (my emphasis; Oxford English Dictionary n.d.). The Centers for Disease Control and Prevention define youth violence as "the intentional use of *physical force* or power to threaten or harm others by young people ages 10–24" (my emphasis; CDC 2024e). These definitions consider violence a physical phenomenon rather than a structural, systemic, or emotional event. In Shakespeare's plays, however, violence is not always a physical occurrence.

The root of the word "violence" comes from the Latin adjective *violentia*, which means vehemence, impetuosity, also from *violentus* (full of might). Violence is frequently framed, in Shakespeare's work, as chaos, motion, and activity. Shakespeare's canon includes seventy uses of the word "violence" and its variations. But these uses don't strictly refer to physical harm. Shakespeare's "violence" refers to passion, exuberance, and strong activity. Iago describes Desdemona's love for Othello as follows: "Mark me with what violence she first loved the Moor" (*Othello* II.i.242). Here, we may assume that Desdemona's violence of love was not about physical force or enacted harm but perhaps about emotional intensity. *All's Well That Ends Well* includes a reference to "the violent speed of fire" (*All's Well* III.ii.120). In this instance, it is the speed, not the fire, that is violent.

If Shakespeare's conception of violence is one of chaos and motion, then the opposite of violence, for Shakespeare, is peace: the calm, auspicious seas Prospero promises; the quiet balance of Oberon's "bank where the wild thyme blows" (*A Midsummer Night's Dream* II.i.257); the "flights of angels" that are conjured to sing Prince Hamlet to his rest (*Hamlet* V.ii.398). Although Shakespeare's plays are deeply concerned with violence, they are just as deeply (if not more) concerned with peace. Compare, for example, the canon's seventy uses of "violence" to the 488 uses of the words "peace" and "peaceful."[1] Violence seems pervasive throughout the canon and offers us the conflict and struggle that provides for entertaining art, but there is, simultaneously, a deep undercurrent of peace as a possibility. Just as violence researchers focus on what positive climates look like, and recognize the possibility of change, so Shakespeare continually returned to moments of peace, when the dust settles, when the war ends, when the action comes to a close. Lurking behind the violence that seems to dominate, there is always the possibility of peace.

Many Shakespeare plays reveal a continued pattern of characters talking through difficult moments. When faced with challenging circumstances, a character will turn to the audience in an attempt to

---

1 It should be noted that "peace" also doubles as a command for someone to quiet down (as in, "prithee, peace!"), which may explain the abundance of the word in Shakespeare's canon.

work through the situation. Shakespeare, as a playwright, frequently returns to this pattern of language as a healing force. This notion aligns with contemporary research around social and emotional learning (SEL). The Collaborative for Academic, Social and Emotional Learning (CASEL) defines SEL as "the process through which all young people and adults acquire and apply the knowledge, skills, and attitudes to develop healthy identities, manage emotions and achieve personal and collective goals, feel and show empathy for others, establish and maintain supportive relationships, and make responsible and caring decisions" (CASEL n.d.). Putting one's thoughts into words, speaking up about emotions, and communicating effectively are all important aspects of SEL, and we see the characters in Shakespeare grappling with how to speak up about their challenges. "Give sorrow words," Malcolm urges Macduff, when he is facing the trauma of losing his wife and small children to cruel violence, because "the grief that does not speak / Whispers the o'erfraught heart and bids it break" (*Macbeth* IV.iii.246). Hamlet's soliloquies are a chance to "unpack [his] heart with words" as he copes with his father's murder and his mother's hasty remarriage (*Hamlet* II.ii.614). By the end of *King Lear*, the characters still left standing are challenged to "speak what [they] feel, not what [they] ought to say" (*King Lear* V.iii.393). In *Richard III*, when faced with deep grief and loss, Elizabeth reflects on the healing power of words: "Let them have scope; though what they will impart / Help nothing else, yet do they ease the heart" (*Richard III* IV.iv.134–5). The Countess in *All's Well That Ends Well* says, "Grief would have tears, and sorrow bids me speak" (*All's Well* III.iv.44). Humans will continue to harm one another, violence will continue to occur in our world, but, in Shakespeare's canon, language is placed in direct relationship with violence and is presented as a path *through* it. Shakespeare was not the only early modern playwright to notice this connection. As Thomas Kyd wrote in *The Spanish Tragedy*, "Where words prevail not, violence prevails" (Kyd II.i.108). If language is not harnessed, violence will continue, and words can often ease the heart, even if they cannot change the circumstances. Language, Shakespeare seems to remind us in play after play, is a way of coping with life's difficulties—and, possibly, the path toward prevention and healing.

Shakespeare's plays can provide contemporary audiences with a fictional landscape, heightened language, and a slight remove from our own time. That distance between our world and the world of the play can help audiences see things a little more clearly; this metaphorical distance can invite curiosity in ways that might not be possible if a play is too deeply rooted in our own location, time, and language. Shakespeare's plays can give audiences the safety of metaphor and critical distance. In classrooms, this distance can be just what we need to avoid putting students on the spot; often, it is easier to talk about someone else's story than to be vulnerable about our own experiences.

When an actor stands on an empty stage and delivers any piece of Shakespeare's text, let's say, Hamlet's "to be or not to be," a curious thing happens. The past collides with the present. These words, written over four hundred years ago, have been spoken countless times. The audience members in the theatre have probably heard the words before and seen the play before. The actor playing Hamlet may have played the role before. Although there have been hundreds, thousands of Hamlets before this one, there has never been this particular Hamlet in this particular moment, responding to this particular group of people in the audience, with the given circumstances of the present moment. Theatre is a time-based art form, embedded with lessons about impermanence and presence.

One of the most common things I tell young actors working with Shakespeare is to think in the moment, to discover the thought as you speak the words; the words are predetermined, but your job is to put these words into the present with your body and voice. It can be highly engaging to watch Shakespeare's plays performed by an actor who is extremely present, connected to what is truly happening, letting the thoughts unfurl authentically, and who brings an element of "nowness" to the performance, rather than the too-easy element of "pastness," in which the delivery is predetermined and overrehearsed. The catch, of course, is that in order to create a deep sense of presence and "nowness," a lot of rehearsal and practice is required. Engaging with a play requires one to be fully present; whether you are in the play as an actor or watching the play as an audience member; you experience the story in real time alongside fellow humans. This work is not only beneficial in training actors but also in building self-awareness and mindfulness, both important components of health and well-being.

The presence we experience when we watch a play could be used as another connection to violence prevention. When we are in the present moment, attuned to our bodies and the people around us, we can deepen our awareness and respond to what is, as opposed to what has been or what will be. In contrast, when we are not in the present moment, when we are not aware, when we are caught in past trauma and harm, we cannot see the present moment clearly. Studies have begun to explore the ways in which a mindfulness practice may reduce violence (Morley et al. 2019; Gillions et al. 2019). Incorporating a live performance event into a violence-prevention curriculum can subtly give students the experience of being in the present moment—a key building block to preventing violence.

In order to play a specific role, an actor uses empathy to imagine what it is like to be this character. In preparing a role like Iago, an actor must approach the role not as if the character is a villain—after all, people rarely see themselves as the "bad guy"—but from inside Iago's mind and body, and with consideration of Iago as a full, complex human being. This practice of considering the world from someone else's perspective is a muscle that working actors exercise daily. What motivates my character? What has happened in the past to my character that might impact this scene? What does my character want? What stands in my character's way? These questions, which actors ask regularly when preparing a role, exemplify cognitive empathy; this regular practice of perspective-taking helps actors embody a wide variety of characters. A recent study explored the link between empathy levels and cyberbullying, suggesting that higher empathy is associated with lower rates of cyberbullying others (Hinduja and Patchin 2022). All of these empathy-building activities we see in the theatre can be harnessed to reduce violence; putting ourselves in someone else's shoes makes us more likely to take action to help them.

A play, of course, is fictional, and the characters in a play are not real people. They are temporary roles, inhabited by an actor for a short time, and then the actor releases that role and moves on to the next one. This habitual practice of roleplaying is another helpful tie-in to understanding violence. Just as an actor steps into many roles throughout a career, so a person plays many roles in real life, and the roles can change. Someone may behave as a bully in one moment but is targeted by another person in a different situation. No one is born a bully, and no one is destined to forever be a bully because they behaved as a bully in one moment of their life. People can change and take on new roles. Change is always happening. This practice of role-playing becomes a helpful framework for the way violence-prevention researchers talk about the roles in violence prevention. Focusing on the behavior, or the actions, and talking about the roles people play, as opposed to assigning them a fixed identity based on behavior, is yet another commonality between theatre and violence prevention, and noting this parallel can serve you as you approach a violence-prevention curriculum through Shakespeare's plays.

VIOLENCE PREVENTION RESEARCH

Contemporary violence-prevention research reveals that there are a lot of hurting kids in our world. The Centers for Disease Control and Prevention (CDC) describe youth violence as a public health problem that can have a long-term impact on health and well-being. According to the 2021 Youth Risk Behavior Survey, 18.3 percent of high school students have been in a physical fight, 15 percent of high school students have been bullied on school property, 19.9 percent of high school students have seen someone get attacked, beaten, stabbed, or shot in their neighborhood, and 22.2 percent of high school students have seriously considered suicide (Youth Risk Behavior Survey n.d.). Homicide is the third leading cause of death for young people ages ten to twenty-four and the leading cause of death for non-Hispanic Black or African American youth. Youth violence is an adverse childhood experience (ACE) that can have a negative impact on health and well-being (CDC 2024e). Youth violence is not a stand-alone, isolated problem but instead a complex and interconnected issue that overlaps with other types of violence, which often share the same root causes (Wilkins et al. 2014).

We are seeing the cumulative impact of overlapping types of violence in the United States. In schools, places of worship, marathon finish lines, parades, cinemas, dance clubs, yoga studios, concert venues, grocery stores, and LGBTQ clubs the nation is witnessing violent acts unfold. In 2020, there were 45,222 firearm-related deaths in the United States—that's about 124 people dying from a firearm-related injury each day. More than half of firearm-related deaths were suicides and more than four out of every ten were firearm homicides (CDC

2024g). Systemic racism, bias, and discrimination; economic instability; concentrated poverty; and limited housing, education, and healthcare access drive health inequities, such as violence. Communities of color experience these negative conditions at disproportionate rates, leading to poor health outcomes and higher homicide rates (CDC 2024b). Violence itself is also a risk factor for multiple negative outcomes, including mental health problems, injury, disease, unemployment, and poverty.

Experts are banding together to recommend the nation address the public health crisis of violence, particularly youth violence. We know that youth violence is common, deadly, and costly (CDC 2024e). The CDC formed the Division of Violence Prevention in 1993, and in 1996 the World Health Assembly declared violence "a leading worldwide public health problem" (CDC 2022). Violence prevention researchers specialize in unpacking the patterns and root causes of violence, and their findings intersect with numerous fields, including law enforcement, public health, and education. Experts recognize that violence, like a disease, is preventable, and they research the risk and protective factors related to violence as well as how racist and white supremacist beliefs and systems contribute to the conditions that fuel violence (Kingston et al. 2021). Although it might seem to be an unlikely combination, these key themes from contemporary violence-prevention research reinforce what Shakespeare wrote centuries ago about humanity's relationship with violence.

It can be helpful to break violence into two broad categories: direct violence and structural (or indirect) violence. Direct violence is physical and intentional harm to a person or a group of people. There are many types of direct violence: racial violence, domestic violence, hate crimes, child abuse, elder abuse, and gender violence. And many different types of violence share risk factors, including social isolation, economic stress, and family conflict (Wilkins et al. 2014). This book, based on guidance from a comprehensive public health approach, takes a broad view of violence, exploring the common denominators, rather than attempting to focus on all the nuances of specific types of direct violence. Structural violence refers to the systemic ways in which people are harmed, including poverty, lack of access to medicine, and redlining practices. Although structural violence isn't intentionally caused by a person or group of people, it nevertheless creates inequities and limits people's access to basic needs. The inequities created by structural violence can lead to conditions that spark direct violence.

Beyond direct and indirect violence, another category has emerged in recent years. Otto Scharmer's concept of *attentional violence* means not being seen for one's full potential:

> On a surface level there is *direct violence*. One person is the victim, one is the perpetrator. News reports rarely go below this level. One level deeper, there is *structural violence*. The perpetrators of violence are not people but structures (examples are systemic racism and other mechanisms that exclude particular groups from opportunity). In just about all conflicts around the world there is an interplay between direct and structural violence. A third form of violence in many cases gives rise to the other two: *attentional violence*. Attentional violence means not to see the other in terms of who they really are. (Scharmer 2023)

Attentional violence—not being seen for who you are and who you could be, your future highest possibility—may be at the source of the vicious cycles of violence and trauma that plague our world.

Violence can exist in the attitudes we hold, the beliefs that shape our actions, and in the ways we do or do not see the people around us as fully realized humans. As you read this book, I invite you to expand your understanding of violence beyond the physical harm we often use to frame violence. In this book, we are interested not only in acts of violence but also in the root causes of violence, and we will explore examples that may not seem like violence to you. Sometimes violence is physical, but sometimes it's verbal, sometimes it's structural, and sometimes it's very subtle. We are interested in all the ways humans harm one another and experience harm, whether with weapons, words, or systems. We are going to look upstream and think about the root causes of harm and the attitudes that shape how we respond to violence.

KEY THEMES OF VIOLENCE PREVENTION

This handbook aims to distill some key themes that emerge in twenty-first-century violence-prevention research in order to translate those themes into an interactive, embodied classroom approach. These violence-prevention themes are not exhaustive, and my approach to this conversation stems from a theatre background rather than a public health background. I attempt to explore what matters most in violence prevention, drawing on expertise from CU Boulder's Center for the Study and Prevention of Violence (CSPV) and the CDC, in order to shape a practical tool for readers to apply to Shakespeare's plays in the following chapters. Violence prevention research reveals several common themes:

1. Violence is preventable
2. Explore root causes
3. Address risk and protective factors
4. Build a positive school climate
5. Upstanders make a difference

These five major themes will help us establish a lens through which to examine Shakespeare's plays in later chapters.

1. VIOLENCE IS PREVENTABLE

My colleague, Dr. Beverly Kingston, director of CSPV at the University of Colorado Boulder, often says that if we could apply what we know works, we could prevent 30 percent of the violence in our world. We have plenty of research around the patterns and root causes of violence and tested effective programs that are proven to prevent violence (Blueprints for Healthy Youth Development n.d.). Putting that research into practice is another thing. It is important to acknowledge that violence is not a predetermined inevitability; we can change the course of action through what we know works. Just as we would treat any medical condition, a comprehensive public health approach to violence involves looking at risk and protective factors, developing and testing prevention strategies to address those factors, and assuring widespread adoption of the proven violence-prevention strategies and programs. Just as we work to prevent heart disease, we can work to prevent violence. If you take nothing else away from this chapter, take away this: violence is not inevitable, and our society does not have to be this way.

2. EXPLORE ROOT CAUSES

In order to understand violence, we must address the root causes of violence. What is going on beneath the surface? Dr. Kingston often employs an iceberg analogy to explain violence. When a violent act occurs and attracts media attention, many people sit up and take notice—and they pay attention to the tip of the iceberg. That tip of the violence iceberg is where events like mass shootings, homicides, and suicides take place. Although these events are hard to ignore, we will never prevent violence by only examining the iceberg's tip. We must also consider the deep, dense base below the surface of the water that makes the violence possible. That is where we find concerning behaviors like physical fights, bullying, and suicidal ideation. Deeper under the surface, we find underlying conditions such as structural racism, poverty, and collective trauma. If one endeavors to understand how violence is possible, it is important to examine not only the iceberg's tip but also the large foundational layers beneath it.

In the 2021 book *What Happened to You? Conversations on Trauma, Resilience, and Healing*, co-written by Oprah Winfrey and trauma expert Bruce D. Perry, the authors frame an alternative model for understanding challenging behavior. Instead of asking "What's wrong with you?" we could instead ask "What happened to you?" Our individual actions are directly related to our past experiences. Although a violent act takes place in the present between individual humans, there are also many unseen forces outside of the present moment (below the tip of the iceberg, as it were), which influence the ways individuals behave. Trauma is passed along from one generation to the next, and often the manifestations of this generational trauma result in acts of violence. Thinkers like Joy DeGruy (author of *Post Traumatic Slave Syndrome* [2017]), Resmaa Menakem (author of *My Grandmother's Hands* [2017]), and Thomas Hübl (author of *Healing Collective Trauma* [2020]) acknowledge that the pain and grief we carry in our individual bodies is connected to an intergenerational legacy. Some of the violent behavior we see in our world is a result of pain that is carried from centuries of trauma and ancestral pain.

Violence does not occur in a vacuum, and if we are to address the violence in our world, we must also address the unhealed wounds of the past. We need to become curious about what factors and past experiences are impacting present behavior. We have to go back in time to unpack and heal these cycles. Experts like DeGruy, Menakem, Hübl, and Perry reinforce the concept that deepening our awareness of past trauma can help build a more resilient, more peaceful, and freer future in which we are able to be present rather than stuck in history.

3. ADDRESS RISK AND PROTECTIVE FACTORS

A comprehensive public health approach to violence involves looking at the risk and protective factors. A risk factor increases the risk of something occurring, while a protective factor reduces or buffers the risk. Some risk and protective factors are two sides of the same coin. For example, one risk factor for violence is engaging with antisocial peers, while the protective factor is, essentially, the other side of the coin: engaging with prosocial peers. We want to consider the malleable (changeable) risk factors and consider how we can reduce the occurrence of those risk factors while building up the protective factors.

Some risk factors for violent behavior are individual, such as low IQ, history of exposure to violence, antisocial attitudes, poor behavioral control, and low social emotional learning (SEL) skills. Some are family risk factors, such as low parental involvement, authoritarian parenting, and poor supervision of children. Some are community risk factors, such as poverty, transiency, and low levels of community participation.

On the flip side, protective factors include strong SEL skills; prosocial attitudes; connectedness within one's family, peer group, and community; and access to trusted adults. When kids are isolated, victimized, lacking in social and emotional skills, and without a network of caring adults, they are at a higher risk of experiencing violence. When kids have a strong, caring, and connected family, peer group, and community, they are more protected against experiencing violence. Although a risk factor does not necessarily lead to violence, the presence of one or more risk factors in a young person's life makes it more likely that they will experience violence.

The CDC's online resource outlines some of the risk factors for violence (CDC 2024i). I encourage educators to review this list of risk factors and invite students to map out areas in which we see examples of these occurring in the play being studied.

Over and over, connectedness is found to be a key protective factor. If kids have healthy relationships, strong, prosocial bonds with peers and/or trusted adults, and a sense of belonging and connectedness in their surroundings, this leads to protection from many kinds of violence. Feeling safe and secure in your identity, in your community, and in your relationships contributes to a lower likelihood you'll experience violence. This is not only about reducing direct and structural violence but also reducing attentional violence; ideally, we are building opportunities for all people to be seen for who they really are. Wherever we can work to build connectedness at the individual, peer, family, and community levels, we are simultaneously building protection from violence and cultivating opportunities for people to thrive at their fullest potential.

4. BUILD A POSITIVE SCHOOL CLIMATE

The Secret Service has conducted several studies about preventing targeted school violence and found that one of the most important preventive measures is in building a sustained positive school climate. The Secret Service encouraged schools to "create and promote a safe school climate built on a culture of safety, respect, trust, and emotional support for students. Encourage communication, intervene in conflicts and bullying, and empower students to share their concerns" (National Threat Assessment Center 2019). The National School Climate Center defines school climate as "the quality and character of school life," while a positive climate "fosters youth development and learning necessary for a productive, contributing and satisfying life in a democratic society" (National School Climate Center 2021). The school climate is the "way we do things" or the air we breathe. A climate is made up of the collection of individual and group behaviors and actions. The climate and culture shape our attitudes around what our community values, how we feel about violence, and what behaviors are ignored, addressed, and rewarded. In trainings with the actors in the Shakespeare & Violence Prevention program, CSPV's Dr. Kingston often compares climate to a fish tank. Climate is everywhere; it's the water you swim in, it surrounds you, and there is no escaping it. The fish don't know they're swimming in dirty water, but if you change the water and clean the tank, the fish will begin to thrive. Awareness of our own internal climate is a key part of improving that climate. In a positive school climate, all members of the community feel safe, feel valued, and feel a sense of belonging. Becoming more aware of the climate is one way of understanding the foundation of the iceberg, the root causes of violence, and the forces influencing the behaviors within a community.

A deepened awareness of school climate can help students make better choices about how to keep their school safe. Theatre is a valuable way to explore a climate because it establishes a fictional world—a climate with a wide array of different characters, each with a complicated subject position—and invites you to observe this fictional world.

In order to sustain a positive school climate, many schools utilize a multitiered system of support (MTSS) to meet the needs of every student. A school's MTSS should involve universal prevention for all students, targeted intervention for students with identified risks, and intensive intervention for the students with high-risk behaviors. As part of this comprehensive approach to building a positive climate, staff should be trained on how to watch for and report concerning behavior, and students should be educated about bystander awareness and how to report concerns (Kingston et al. 2018).

5. UPSTANDERS MAKE A DIFFERENCE

An upstander is someone who takes action to help prevent mistreatment, bullying, violence, or other types of harm. Unlike a bystander, an upstander decides not to stand by and let things unfold and instead chooses to act on behalf of someone being mistreated. What the research shows in study after study is that upstander behavior is effective in preventing violence. More than half the time, when a bystander becomes an upstander, bullying ends almost immediately (Hawkins, Pepler, and Craig 2001). This is a powerful piece of information for young people to know: their actions as upstanders could make a tangible difference and could stop many instances of bullying before they escalate. Furthermore, in 81 percent of targeted school attacks, someone other than the perpetrator was aware of the threat (US Secret Service and US Department of Education 2004). This tells us that when dangerous behavior, violence, or mistreatment is about to occur, many people hold information but don't always speak up to prevent harm. There are many reasons people do not become upstanders. Sometimes it's a fear of being seen as a snitch. Sometimes it's a lack of awareness about proper reporting channels. Sometimes it's a worry that it might be unsafe to step in. All of these reasons are real barriers that prevent people from taking action, and these concerns should be addressed in order to encourage a culture of upstanders.

There are many ways of being an upstander. One strategy is direct confrontation, like telling someone who is bullying a peer, "Hey, that's not cool." Other strategies are indirect, like telling a teacher or a trusted adult about something concerning. Someone might employ a distraction strategy, like changing the subject or spilling some water in a situation that feels uncomfortable. Kim Scott amplified the 5D approach to upstander behavior, introduced by Right to Be, in her (2021) book *Just Work*. The 5Ds are: Direct, Distract, Delegate, Delay, and Document (Right to Be n.d.). Not all strategies are right for everyone, and not all strategies are right for every situation.

Sometimes anonymous reporting is an appropriate upstander strategy. Colorado, for example, has an online, anonymous reporting tool for individuals to report dangerous behavior called Safe2Tell. Many areas have similar systems, so you may want to investigate the tools available to you and your students for reporting dangerous behavior. It's important to emphasize that it is no less courageous to report concerns anonymously.

With this information, how can we bridge that distance between a culture of bystanders and a culture of upstanders? How do we normalize upstander behavior? Most of the time, young people are aware of dangerous situations in a school before adults are, so how do we get young people more comfortable implementing upstander strategies with their peers?

The field of violence prevention faces challenges about how to translate research in meaningful ways for the general population. Live theatre can be an engaging way of translating some of the key messages from violence prevention and can help bring the research to life. Watching a play in which characters mistreat others, in which people make mistakes, and in which mistreatment ripples through a community may resonate with young audiences in ways that a lecture, PowerPoint presentation, or schoolwide discussion may not.

SHAKESPEARE AND VIOLENCE PREVENTION IN COLORADO: CASE STUDY

This handbook has emerged from practical experience, and throughout the book I refer to a specific Shakespeare & Violence Prevention program in action. In 2011, the Colorado Shakespeare Festival (CSF), a professional theatre company in association with the University of Colorado Boulder (CU Boulder), began a partnership with the Center for the Study and Prevention of Violence (CSPV), a research center housed on the CU Boulder campus. The result of this collaboration is the Shakespeare & Violence Prevention program, which has reached more than 136,000 Colorado schoolchildren as of this book's publication. With examples from this case study, my aim is to support theatre practitioners, teaching artists, and educators interested in pursuing similar models, replicating the CSF program, or innovating new models in which Shakespeare's plays are used as a tool to address youth violence.

The Shakespeare & Violence Prevention program pairs live Shakespeare performance with a violence-prevention curriculum and provides a model of how these two disciplines intersect and reinforce one another. In the program, a troupe of three or four professional actors performs an abridged Shakespeare play onsite at a school, highlighting the moments of violence and mistreatment and guided by expertise in violence-prevention research.

CSF strives for a forty-five-minute performance for middle and high school audiences (grades 6–12) and a thirty-minute performance for upper elementary school audiences (grades 3–5). This may feel heretical to Shakespeare enthusiasts, scholars, and artists, but keeping the run time short allows the play to fit neatly into a school assembly period, thus increasing the ease of a school hosting a visit. A graduate student we worked with studied the attention of the audience in our school performances and noted an increase in wiggles with elementary audiences after the thirty-minute mark, while middle and high school audiences had a slightly longer wiggle-free endurance of forty-five minutes (Goldfarb 2017). I don't disagree that students can and should watch full-length Shakespeare performances; I simply imagine that with a clear focus on violence prevention within the plays, a tighter cutting can increase the chances of the play actually being seen, and significantly reduce the burden on community partners to fit the program into a standard school day without overly disrupting their schedule.

CSF touring productions are designed for three or four actors. This is a practical decision, as a small company reduces costs, which is a legitimate consideration for any theatre company. The small cast size also serves to underscore some important tenets of violence prevention, in that we see actors working as a tight team, and we see them embodying change as they rapidly transition between characters. In an abridged production in which actors play multiple roles, we have found costumes to be a helpful storytelling device, and it's exciting for audiences to watch three actors transition seamlessly from one character to the next.

The performances are held in gyms, auditoriums, cafeterias, libraries, and multipurpose classrooms; the set and costumes are simple, all designed to fit in a minivan. The actors play multiple roles, quickly switching from one character to another with a swift donning of a cape, a vest, or a hat. The performances typically integrate Spanish-speaking characters, and often include live music, and plenty of direct address. Incorporating music into the play can be an engaging on-ramp for audiences to connect to the play and can hook in young audiences. CSF often hires actors with musical abilities, singing and/or playing instruments that are easy to tour with. Ukuleles, for example, are a very portable and acoustically helpful tour favorite. In whatever form it appears, music becomes a more dynamic way to break up the performances. The productions experiment with gender to support the specific actors in the company. Many of Shakespeare's characters are written as male, and performed by male actors, but in these touring productions, especially because actors play multiple roles, character genders are routinely changed to serve the company.

In these touring shows, CSF aims to incorporate audience involvement whenever possible. Much like the original audiences at an Elizabethan playhouse, young audiences connect more deeply to the play when the actors talk directly to them, make eye contact with them, and involve them in unexpected ways.

Following the performance, the actors lead audience members through a reflection on the play's violence and opportunities for prevention and intervention. What examples of mistreatment did the students observe? Who in the play could have taken action to prevent harm? How can one person prevent harm in their school? The actors are often joined by a staff member from the hosting school, who helps contextualize the conversation for their specific community.

This post-show Q&A aims to prepare students to experience interactive roleplaying exercises (the workshops).

After the schoolwide Q&A, the actors lead interactive roleplays in breakout groups, in which students rehearse their own strategies about how they would take action to prevent the harm depicted in the play—in other words, how could the students be upstanders instead of bystanders in the situation? These roleplays, typically limited to no more than thirty students at a time, function as an engaging, embodied way to teach violence prevention through Shakespeare, and they are influenced in part by Augusto Boal's work and in part by violence-prevention research about upstander behavior effectiveness. Students are invited to step into a moment in the play (upstream of the major mistreatment) and enact their own strategies.

The Shakespeare & Violence Prevention program consistently reports positive results from students and teachers. Of the students participating in post-show roleplays, 89 percent report they are likely to take action to help the next time they witness mistreatment, while nearly unanimously teachers say this program deepened their students' understanding of Shakespeare and knowledge of violence-prevention skills. Year after year of this program being run in schools, nearly all teachers who respond to post-visit surveys say they would recommend the program to other schools.

Actors involved in the Shakespeare & Violence Prevention program are highly experienced performers who have an impressive facility with Shakespeare's text but are also trained by violence-prevention experts and coached in workshop facilitation. Over the years of building the program and touring it in Colorado schools, I am continually reminded that that this work could be applied in classrooms across the globe. Now I wish to share the work of the CSF model with a wider audience, in order to support this work in classrooms everywhere. This program is not perfect, but it seems to be working in Colorado, and I wonder if you might take up this work of exploring violence prevention through Shakespeare too.

THE CSF METHOD

The Colorado Shakespeare Festival (CSF) method is rooted in the idea that we can rehearse the behavior we know works to prevent violence. Just like we rehearse all sorts of important skills, we can rehearse upstander behavior. Violence prevention experts repeatedly point to the effectiveness of upstanders. Bystanders hold a lot of information and can prevent violence before it occurs by acting as upstanders. To that end, the CSF method focuses on the upstander strategies of the students in the room and gives them the opportunity to practice their ideas in the safety of a classroom. The Shakespeare play sparks their imagination, invites them to witness human behavior, and gives them a shared experience in which teamwork, empathy, and change are on full display. After watching the performance, the same actors who performed in the play then unpack a moment from the play in which characters are making harmful choices. In these short scenes, students are invited to step into the scenario as themselves to try to change the outcome. This model emphasizes that change is possible, because students can change the outcome of a scene; it also emphasizes the importance of teamwork, as students strategize their solutions together; it emphasizes empathy, as students are invited to think about why a character might be behaving in a harmful way. The model is simple and can be easily replicated by any classroom teacher, regardless of acting chops or access to a professional theatre troupe. The idea behind the CSF model is that students engage with a fictional scenario from a Shakespeare play and then draw connections between the fiction and their own world as they imagine stepping into the scenario as themselves to alter the outcome. This emphasizes hope and connectedness, because students can discover how one action can have a ripple effect on others. Although no solution will be perfect or will stop all the violence, practicing our behaviors in advance enables us to feel more equipped to try them in real life. Students are encouraged to play themselves in these roleplays and to treat the activity as a rehearsal for real life. Just as we practice important life skills like tying shoes, doing multiplication tables, and driving cars, we can also practice our upstander strategies before we need them.

It's important that teaching artists using this model don't get too prescriptive about solutions; the students will have their own strategies, and what works for one student may not be comfortable for another. The teaching artist is there not to be an expert on Shakespeare or violence prevention but to facilitate the activities and remain curious about the knowledge and wisdom in the room.

This method helps remind us that change is possible. Although a Shakespeare play is already written, and the ending is determined, our narratives are not predetermined. We can step into the narrative, practice an upstander strategy, and change the outcome. Just as violence-prevention research emphasizes that violence is preventable, the CSF method is a way to physically embody change and give students a way to experience what change looks, feels, and sounds like.

SHAKESPEARE AND WHITE SUPREMACY

Shakespeare has a problematic history as part of a system centering whiteness, and it is important to recognize the ways in which Shakespeare is used to harm and silence BIPOC bodies and voices. As our culture collectively takes an honest look at the racism, white supremacy, and anti-blackness that we have been steeped in for centuries, it is important to apply rigor and curiosity to our approaches to Shakespeare. My CSF colleagues and I are continually examining how these plays speak to our present moment, especially from the perspective of marginalized audiences, and I encourage you, as you seek to apply Shakespeare to a violence-prevention curriculum, to do the same.

By way of example: since 2016, all productions in the Shakespeare & Violence Prevention project have included an element of Spanish-speaking. This is usually one or two characters who speak primarily in Spanish but also sometimes includes code-switching between the two languages, depending on how it fits the production concept and the actors' language abilities. Since making this decision to incorporate Spanish in the plays, we have prioritized hiring at least one actor who is fluent in Spanish with each touring company. The incorporation of another language can expand the audience's understanding of what Shakespeare is and can be. Colorado has a high population of Spanish-speaking families, and we have noticed that when Spanish is incorporated seamlessly into the performance, people lean forward to listen a little closer regardless of language skills. We often see students who may not speak Spanish turning to their peers who do and asking them what's going on. We often see the faces of Spanish-speakers light up with recognition when a character speaks in Spanish. This kind of normalization of Spanish-speaking within Shakespeare's plays can not only better represent the population we serve in schools but also deepen a respect for different cultures and languages. Although subtle, the incorporation of other languages in addition to English can support a violence-prevention curriculum. By representing diverse languages on the stage, we are expanding the understanding of whose stories matter and whose stories get to be told. The more respect and appreciation we have for differences in our communities, the more connected we become, and connectedness is a protective factor against violence.

Below are some foundational beliefs and guiding principles that shape the work we do in CSF's education programs:

- Shakespeare belongs to all of us.
- Shakespeare's work is a tool to help us understand ourselves, our fellow humans, and our world.
- Shakespeare does not belong on a pedestal. The work invites engagement, not uncomplicated adoration.
- There is no single or correct meaning in Shakespeare. The work is open to interpretation, and meaning is fluid.
- We have permission to (and a responsibility to) root out racist and harmful language in the plays.
- Engagement with Shakespeare should be student-centered—the aim is to seek the wisdom in the room, encourage students to share their own ideas and responses to the plays.

This work of dismantling racism in Shakespeare is ongoing. I encourage you to do the following:

- Decolonize the language in the plays that is harmful to BIPOC communities.
- Cast plays and hire employees with intention and awareness and strive to support BIPOC individuals in your learning and working environments.
- Deepen your awareness of what is shaping the space and whose voices are centered.
- Work from a place of respect for one another and with the knowledge that we are each fully human, irreplaceable, and deeply knowledgeable.
- Create a space in which the knowledge is collective and located in the room (virtual or otherwise) and all voices are heard and valued.

HOW TO USE THIS BOOK

I have collaborated with some amazing, talented, empathetic actors and teaching artists over the years in the Shakespeare & Violence Prevention program, but you do not need to be a classically trained actor or a social scientist to engage in the work of unpacking the violence in Shakespeare. That's why I wanted to write this book: to enable you, the reader, to learn about the opportunities held within Shakespeare's canon to integrate a violence-prevention curriculum and to harness Shakespeare's deep influence on contemporary culture to address a critical social need. Many students are exposed to Shakespeare in academic and cultural settings. Why not look for the opportunities in the plays to address the patterns of violence? I hope you'll find this handbook helpful, whether you are a seasoned Shakespeare educator or a newcomer to Shakespeare. These plays (and many more) can be used to help students rehearse upstander strategies, develop empathy, and analyze social climates—all of which are important practices for reducing violence. We know that violence prevention requires not just one solution but multiple partners working together to achieve change. The CSF model demonstrates one way that the arts and creativity can be harnessed as part of the solution.

WHAT IS A VIOLENCE-PREVENTION LENS?

This book proposes a violence-prevention lens to explore Shakespeare's plays. By this I mean a lens that holds an awareness of some of the key themes of violence prevention listed above, including root causes, risk and protective factors, school climates, and upstander behavior. A violence-prevention lens begins with the knowledge that violence is preventable and considers these key questions:

- **LOOK UPSTREAM:** What moment(s) upstream of the violence led to the event? What are the root causes?
- **LOOK AT THE RISK AND PROTECTIVE FACTORS:** Where do we see risk factors and where do we see protective factors? What is hurting the situation and what is helping?
- **LOOK AT THE CLIMATE:** What behaviors, actions, practices in the climate led to the violence? What are the norms around violence in this climate? What is the mood of this climate?

- **LOOK FOR UPSTANDERS:** Who could have taken action to prevent it? Who did take action and how did that turn out?
- **LOOK IN THE MIRROR:** What might my upstander strategy be in that situation? How can I break the cycle of violence?

A violence-prevention lens, when applied to a Shakespeare play, can help us analyze how violence moves through the fictional world, how it impacts a community, how it impacts relationships between individuals, how it impacts individuals (which we see play out in soliloquy), and how it impacts the audience. Using this violence-prevention lens can help translate the lessons learned from violence-prevention research into a practical, hands-on approach to use in conversations about both Shakespeare and real life. The more we practice using this lens, the more skilled we will become in noticing the opportunities to break the cycle of violence—not only in Shakespeare's plays but also in our own lives. Engaging in this work is not just about interrupting violence in the present moment; it can also lay the foundation of a less violent society for generations to come.

CHAPTER BREAKDOWN

Each of the following chapters focuses on a different Shakespeare play and provides the tools you need to introduce the play to your students through a violence-prevention lens. The chapters include a plot synopsis, connections to play-specific violence-prevention research, and reflections about how to produce the play for or with young audiences. In the discussions of each play, the pronouns reflect the genders of the characters as written by Shakespeare, but when working on the play with students, remember that these characters can be played by performers of any gender, and if it serves your students to adjust the character's gender, please do not hesitate to do so. The focus of your work should be on supporting your students. All quotations from Shakespeare's plays in this book come from Folger Shakespeare Library's digital editions (folger.edu). In the appendixes of this book, readers will find a sample lesson plan for each play along with additional discussion questions and activities. I encourage you to jump directly to the chapter you are most interested in based on your classroom needs. There is no need to move through this book sequentially. You may want to return to this introduction to review the violence-prevention themes, because they will be referenced throughout chapters 2–9.

We begin with the tragedies and explore some of the more overt examples of violence. The plays in this section (*Macbeth*, *Julius Caesar*, and *Romeo and Juliet*) are recommended for middle and high school students. In chapter 2, we look at *Macbeth*'s regicide and the relationship between empathy and violence. Chapter 3 explores *Julius Caesar*'s planned attack and deaths by suicide. In *Romeo and Juliet* (chapter 4) we see a world consumed by violence and its impact on the community's youth population.

We then shift the discussion to the comedies, which explore the subtler, more upstream examples of violence. We begin with *Much Ado About Nothing* (chapter 5), a play about rumors, gossip, and public shaming that works well with middle and high school audiences. Chapters 6–8 focus on comedies that work well with upper elementary audiences (grades 3–5): the bullying of Malvolio in *Twelfth Night* (chapter 6); physical mistreatment and impulsivity in *The Comedy of Errors* (chapter 7); and gender and relationship violence in *The Taming of the Shrew* (chapter 8). We close with *The Tempest* (chapter 9), sometimes considered a comedy and more commonly considered a romance (a late play that deals with reconciliation, magic, and healing) and consider Prospero's choice between vengeance and forgiveness in the wake of his own mistreatment.

Chapter 10 concludes with thoughts about the role of hope and peace as it pertains to violence in Shakespeare and raises questions about Shakespeare's role in facilitating a healthier world for young people. I end with a call to action for other artists, educators, parents, administrators, researchers, and caregivers to integrate the tenets of violence prevention into their own work and to commit to learning more about how to cultivate connectedness, empathy, and change in their work with young people. Whether through Shakespeare or other forms, humanity is capable of bringing about real, tangible change and cultivating a safer, healthier world for future generations.

Shakespeare will always offer more each time we return to a play, and this handbook is meant to launch initial conversations about the patterns of mistreatment and the cycle of violence within the play. Ideally, each activity leads to further creative action, in which students feel empowered to positively impact their communities. I analyze eight plays in this book and have selected these plays because they are titles CSF has adapted for the violence-prevention touring program, but I believe that more Shakespeare plays can be explored through the lens of the cycle of violence. I encourage you to familiarize yourself with the method in each chapter and then dive into plays not included in this text.

TIPS ON TEACHING SHAKESPEARE

Shakespeare can be a daunting subject for educators; my advice is to seek the wisdom in the room and be curious about the topic right alongside your students. You do not need to be the explainer but rather a fellow learner, and there is no right way to teach these plays, because the plays do not hold a single, stable, fixed meaning. For further information about how to approach Shakespeare in the classroom, I recommend Thompson and Turchi's (2016) *Teaching Shakespeare with Purpose* and Fiona Banks's (2014) *Creative Shakespeare*. Malone and Huber's (2021) *Cutting Plays for Performance* could be a resource for you if you decide to generate your own cuttings (a practice I highly recommend!).

I suggest that you approach Shakespeare's plays as you would approach Play-Doh: something you can experiment with rather than revere. Shakespeare is a tool you can use to question, analyze, and comprehend your own world, rather than something worthy of unexamined praise. The plays are for you and your students to grapple with, wrestle with, and play with. There is no single, authoritative meaning to any Shakespeare play. Have fun!

SOME TIPS:
- **EMBODY IT:** Put it in your body and voice: speak it aloud, act it out with a group. Remember, use your own voice, not some voice that sounds "Shakespearean" to you.
- **PARAPHRASE IT:** When looking at text, try to put it in your own words. How would you say this in your own voice?
- **WATCH IT:** See a performance (if possible, live) or stage it with your students.
- **GET CREATIVE:** When tackling a play, think about how it resonates with you. Does it inspire you to draw pictures? Rewrite the play as a poem? Create a graphic novel? Design a video game? Write a song? Make up a dance? There are many ways to interpret

a play, and the act of engaging with the text can lead to some really great creations. I remember seeing a group of students stage *Much Ado About Nothing* as the film *Mean Girls* many years ago, and they performed it for our actors when the troupe arrived to perform our forty-five-minute *Much Ado*. The imaginations of young people are amazing, and the possibilities for creative engagement are endless.

ONE FINAL NOTE

As the author of this text, I wish to acknowledge my investment in the CSF model. I co-created the Shakespeare & Violence Prevention program in my role as a staff member at the Colorado Shakespeare Festival, in collaboration with several valued colleagues along the way, including CSF artistic director Timothy Orr, CSF managing director Wendy Franz, CSF assistant director of outreach Dr. Heidi Schmidt, CSPV director Beverly Kingston, and CSPV research assistant Laurie Keith. Now, more than thirteen years into this robust program, and having witnessed the program's evolution, I wish to share these findings with a larger audience beyond the thousands of Colorado schoolchildren who have experienced it live. While I do have a deep affinity for this work, I strive to approach a balanced viewpoint, as much as possible, in order to disseminate the creative and research-based work of this project. I do hope that other scholars, educators, and artists take on this question of the overlaps between Shakespeare's plays and violence prevention and how a theatrical approach to the plays might affect tangible change in communities facing violence.

Shakespeare's plays, which have endured for more than four hundred years, hold valuable lessons that intersect with the research of leading violence-prevention experts in the twenty-first century. I believe these plays have a tremendous amount to teach us about how to live our best lives, be our bravest selves, and realize our greatest potential as individuals, and also as a collective community. If you join me in peering into the plays through the lens of violence prevention, you may find creative, imaginative pathways to dive into the complexity of how violence operates on individual, relational, and community levels . . . and how we can carve out opportunities to rehearse alternatives to violence.

Interlude
The Tragedies and Violence Prevention

Shakespeare's tragedies often reveal the worst-case scenarios of what can happen when violence is enacted and not interrupted. Whereas the comedies, which will be explored in chapters 5–9, frequently deal with moments upstream of major violence and feature more subtle types of mistreatment and harm, the tragedies tend to depict more overt acts of violence, and these acts are typically quite far downstream of the original conflict, leaving characters with little room to turn the ship around. Macbeth rationalizes his continued violence: "I am in blood / Stepped in so far that, should I wade no more, / Returning were as tedious as go o'er" (*Macbeth* III.iv.168–70). Because he has already committed so many violent acts, Macbeth rationalizes that he might as well keep going. When connecting these plays to a violence-prevention curriculum it is important to emphasize that there is always a choice, that change is possible, and that violence is preventable.

Shakespeare's tragedies depict not only acts of violence but the consequences that ripple downstream as the cycle of violence escalates and rips a wider path of destruction. The following three chapters explore *Macbeth*, *Julius Caesar*, and *Romeo and Juliet* through a violence-prevention lens, meaning we pay attention to root causes, risk and protective factors, the climate in which the violence occurs, and upstander behavior, and we consider how we might respond in similar situations.

https://doi.org/10.5876/9781646427246.c002a

I focus on these three tragedies for two reasons: First, they are widely taught in middle schools and high schools across the United States, and second, they are titles the Colorado Shakespeare Festival has toured in the Shakespeare & Violence Prevention program, so I have observed how these plays operate in an applied context. I encourage the reader to consider additional plays through a violence-prevention lens, and I hope these chapters can be used as a framework to apply to other titles. Although *Macbeth*, *Julius Caesar*, and *Romeo and Juliet* work especially well with middle and high school groups, and the suggested exercises in chapters 2–4 use that age range as the intended audience, educators can use these plays with a variety of ages to great success, with some age-appropriate tweaks.

The Centers for Disease Control and Prevention define violence as "intentional use of physical force or power to threaten or harm others" (CDC 2024e). This definition, as discussed in chapter 1, focuses on physical acts, and our contemporary use of the term likely conjures up images of murder, homicide, brutality, and domestic violence. In other words, we frequently link violence to the body and use the term violence to describe the physical harm that is intentionally enacted on other people. Shakespeare provides abundant examples of physical violence, and it seems that as a playwright he learned how to grapple with violence throughout his career. In an early play like *Titus Andronicus*, which was heavily influenced by the popular revenge-tragedy style of playwriting, Shakespeare presents a nightmarish world of cruelty, retaliation, and brutality. He hadn't yet developed a way to offer characters the space to process, reflect on, and share the impact of that violence through the powerful soliloquies and scenes he so deftly employs in later plays. In the following three chapters I will focus on three tragedies that reveal how Shakespeare provides a space to unpack violence and examine the ripples it sends through the world. In the discussion of each play, I'll explore some central connections to violence-prevention research and describe how CSF adapted each play to tour to middle schools and high schools in Colorado.

The tragedies pose some different questions for young people to grapple with than the comedies do, and they often reveal situations pushed to the extreme in a series of worst-case scenarios. In touring the shows, we often talk with middle and high school students about how to bridge the gap between a Shakespearean tragedy and their real lives. While we hope students today are not facing the extreme situations that Macbeth, Brutus, Romeo, and Juliet are facing, what is the equivalent of something that might happen in school today? Maybe it's not life or death, but can you draw connections between the play and your own life? And if we think through the extreme situations depicted in the play, might it help us think through what we might do in those hypothetical situations? Theatre doesn't always show us an ideal world. It can show us a world we don't want for ourselves, and it can help us witness that world from a safe distance without getting physically hurt. As we approach the tragedies through a violence-prevention lens, we can safely imagine unhealthy realities, so we can make our reality something better.

While Shakespeare's narratives are already written and the words have been on the page for more than four hundred years, the action of the play is not inevitable. What occurred in any play did not have to be the only outcome. In a play there are a series of choices, and if we point out all the tiny choices made along the way, we can see the ways in which these actions are preventable and malleable, rather than fixed and predetermined. And because the Shakespeare narrative ends one way, that does not mean that our own narratives have predetermined paths. Young people need to know that they have the tools, creativity, and right to rewrite their narratives.

Hope is a powerful thing in a tragedy. Although tragedies often end in death, they also end with a sense of hope, a new world order moving in, or a deepening of the cultural consciousness. In *Macbeth*, a new king is crowned and will take over, having rooted out some of the violent urges within the community. In *Julius Caesar*, Cassius and Brutus, whose assassination of Caesar sparked more violence, both die by suicide, and a new leader assumes control. In *Romeo and Juliet*, we have the promise of peace between the families. The plays are forward-leaning and ushering in the promise of something new. This reminder that hope is ever-present is a salient connection to violence prevention, underscored by the belief that change is possible and violence is preventable. Equipped with research about what works in preventing violence, we can consciously and intentionally strive to do better than the Montagues, Capulets, Macbeths, and the plotters in *Julius Caesar*. We can make different choices with a deeper awareness of the consequences of violence.

2
Macbeth
Empathy and Violence

First performed in 1606, Shakespeare's *Macbeth* was written during the reign of James I of England, who also ruled Scotland as James VI. Like his predecessor Elizabeth I, James was a supporter of the arts; he was the patron of Shakespeare's company, the King's Men. Likely as a hat-tip to his monarch and patron, Shakespeare's *Macbeth* is set in Scotland, and features witches, which were a particular topic of fascination for James. This play, with its depiction of the witches, its rhythmic language, and its exploration of opposing forces (fair vs. foul, fate vs. free will) is a highly engaging way to explore Shakespeare with young audiences.

As discussed in the introduction, a violence-prevention lens considers root causes, risk and protective factors, the climate, upstander behavior, and our own upstander strategies. If we peer beyond the play's magical elements and look through a violence-prevention lens, we see that *Macbeth* also depicts what happens when power interferes with human connection, when empathy is limited, when people try to control outcomes by taking matters into their own hands using violence, and how quickly the cycle of violence can metastasize. These themes make *Macbeth* an especially relevant play for kids ages twelve to eighteen, because at this age, we are learning how to cope with pressure, be a responsible and principled member of society, and manage difficult emotions. A violence-prevention approach to the play might focus on the connection between empathy and violence, the impact of power on human behavior, and the role of language in the face of violence.

This play's exploration of power, language, and empathy is all deeply connected to some core questions about human behavior. How do we share power? How do we communicate? How do we connect with another person's emotional state? The kind of connectedness that can come from shared power, language, and emotions can deepen ties within a community. Set in a distant past against the backdrop of a magical realm, and featuring extreme stakes of life and death, perhaps this play gives middle and high school audiences enough metaphorical and critical distance from the present time and place to cultivate the right environment for a safe exploration of these questions.

PLOT SYNOPSIS

On their journey home from war after a victory in battle, Scottish warriors Macbeth and Banquo encounter three witches. The witches predict that Macbeth will become king, and that Banquo's descendants will also be kings. After the witches' earlier predictions prove accurate, this kingly prediction gets inside Macbeth's head, and he tells his wife about it. Lady Macbeth encourages her husband to speed fate along by murdering King Duncan, Scotland's current ruler, and claiming the crown. While Duncan is a guest in their home, the Macbeths murder him in his sleep, framing his guards for the crime. Afraid for his safety, Duncan's son and heir, Malcolm, flees to England, which leaves the path to the throne clear for Macbeth.

Once crowned, Macbeth isn't satisfied. He becomes distrustful and secretly kills anyone he perceives as a threat (including Banquo). As the murders pile up, Macbeth no longer sees other people as human but as obstacles in his rise to power. He turns off his feelings in order to commit heinous acts and finds himself tormented with guilt. "O, full of scorpions is my mind," he confesses to his wife (*Macbeth* III.ii.41). Lady Macbeth falls into a hallucinatory state, haunted by Duncan's blood.

Macduff, a Scottish nobleman, finds Malcolm in exile, and together they raise an army to remove Macbeth from the throne and reinstate

Malcolm as rightful heir. Macbeth learns his wife is dead just as the battle begins. He is killed by Macduff, as the witches predicted, and Malcolm is crowned King of Scotland.

VIOLENCE PREVENTION CONNECTIONS TO *MACBETH*

As with many of Shakespeare's tragedies, *Macbeth* is an example of the cyclical nature of violence. We know that violence leads to violence, and it can often seem nearly impossible to break that cycle. While this extreme situation, in which an individual gains power through murder, seems set on an inevitably destructive course, the research tells us that violence is preventable. If we can learn to recognize and respond to warning signs and cultivate connected communities, much of the violence we see in our world can be stopped. Violence prevention research underscores the steady heartbeat of a repeated idea: it doesn't have to be this way.

Look Upstream: Root Causes

Let's consider some of the root causes of the primary violent act of the play: the murder of Duncan. What are the events that occurred before Duncan's murder, and what are some of the underlying behaviors and norms that may have contributed to that crime? Duncan's murder is not, in fact, the first violent death in the play. In act 1 scene 2, we learn that Scotland is at war and that Macbeth has "unseamed" a man "from the nave to the chops" (*Macbeth* I.ii.24) in battle and mounted his head on the battlements. King Duncan then orders the execution of the rebellious Thane of Cawdor, resulting in Macbeth's promotion. Shakespeare keeps these murders offstage, though these violent deaths that occurred upstream of Duncan's murder are just some examples of the root causes. One might presume that the violence that occurs in the first scenes of *Macbeth* was preceded by countless other violent acts before the play begins. In Macbeth's community, the war has a direct impact on the citizens' lived experiences and likely contributes to the regular occurrence of violence.

Look at Risk Factors

As discussed in the introduction, risk factors for violence increase the likelihood of violence; some are changeable (malleable), and some are not changeable (fixed). Looking at risk factors can help us understand more about how and why violence occurs. The CDC's online resource outlines some of the risk factors for violence (CDC 2024i). Encourage your students to review these risk factors and observe where they occur in *Macbeth*.

On an individual level, Macbeth engages in several antisocial relationships throughout the play. His relationship with his wife, at least during the period in which the events of the play occur, seems rooted in a power struggle and appears to be highly conditional. Lady Macbeth encourages her husband to murder the king and manipulates him through peer pressure. When Macbeth has doubts about committing the murder, Lady Macbeth questions his manhood. "When you durst do it, then you were a man" (*Macbeth* I.vii.56). When Macbeth shares his concerns, he is shamed and shut down. This kind of disconnection can be isolating, and a lack of prosocial bonds in an individual's life can contribute to a higher risk of violence. Macbeth also engages in antisocial relationships with the witches and the murderers, characters who encourage and support Macbeth in his quest to harm others—or, in the witches' case, perhaps just plant the seed to see what Macbeth will do with the information about his future. These are relationships that revolve not around mutual respect but around dominance, power, and planned harm.

Another risk factor is high emotional distress. Throughout the play, Macbeth behaves in increasingly erratic ways. He grows suspicious of Banquo, whose friendship is ostensibly the sole prosocial bond Macbeth experiences during the play. Macbeth is tormented by sleeplessness, which leads to further disruption in his nervous system—"Macbeth shall sleep no more" (*Macbeth* II.ii.57)—and begins having mental health challenges. "O, full of scorpions is my mind" (*Macbeth* III.iii.41), he confides to his wife.

At a family level, the Macbeths have also experienced trauma; the play alludes to the loss of a child. Lady Macbeth, when persuading her husband to follow through on his promise to murder the king, conjures a violent image in her rhetoric:

> I have given suck, and know
> How tender 'tis to love the babe that milks me.
> I would, while it was smiling in my face,

> Have plucked my nipple from his boneless gums
> And dashed the brains out, had I so sworn
> As you have done to this.
> (*Macbeth* I.vii.62–67)

The juxtaposition of an image of maternal love with the murder of a child is jarring, and this intermingled image suggests a past that is laced with violence. This moment, in which a domestic image is interrupted by a violent one, might be a clue to the personal traumas the Macbeths may have endured, perhaps in their own childhoods as well—and we know that adverse childhood experiences (ACEs) can have long-term negative impacts. In addition to personal hardships, both Macbeth and Lady Macbeth may have been scarred by Macbeth's experiences as a seasoned war veteran in the household. Macbeth's most recent combat, alongside a presumed long career in Duncan's army, would likely affect the way he relates to the people around him, the way he responds to situations, and the way his nervous system functions. The background activity of an ongoing war is a community risk factor, and Macbeth's direct experience with war violence largely shapes his behavior. We know that exposure to violence increases the risk of more violence, both for individuals and at a community level.

While none of these risk factors directly cause the violence, collectively they make eventual violence more likely. As a suggested activity with your students, encourage them to try swapping out some of the risk factors in the play (antisocial bonds, disconnection, war trauma) with protective factors. What would happen if Lady Macbeth heard and respected Macbeth's concerns about killing Duncan in a prosocial way? What would happen if Banquo reported his concerns about his friend's erratic behavior to an authority figure? What would happen if Macbeth were working with a mental health professional to unpack his war trauma? Swapping risk factors for protective factors can help unearth alternatives to the violence in the play.

Look at Protective Factors: Empathy and Connectedness

Empathy could be defined as feeling with someone, putting oneself in someone else's shoes, and seeing the world from another person's perspective. There are different types of empathy, but I use cognitive empathy when relating it to a violence-prevention curriculum: "understanding others' feelings," which involves not necessarily taking on a person's emotions but thinking critically and imaginatively about how they might be feeling. In this way, we are not encouraging students to feel exactly what someone is feeling, or to suffer alongside them, but to *think about* how they might feel; it is more about deepening awareness than encouraging students to change their emotional states to match their peers' emotional states.

The cultivation of empathy can be a protective factor against violence because it builds connectedness, while encouraging individuals to explore perspectives beyond their own. A recent study of fifth-grade students conducted in South Korea found that an empathy-focused violence-prevention curriculum had a significant effect on students' empathy and attitudes toward violence, while other studies have found that the lower the empathy level in an individual, the more the aggressiveness and violence (Kang et al. 2022). When individuals in a community regularly practice empathy, violence becomes a less likely occurrence.

On the flip side, a lack of empathy makes violence a more likely outcome. Lady Macbeth worries that her husband won't follow through with his plan to murder Duncan because he is "too full o' th' milk of human kindness" (*Macbeth* I.v.17). She worries that Macbeth's natural tendency toward kindness and connectedness—an existing protective factor—will prevent him from harming another human. In order to be able to harm another, that "milk of human kindness" must be turned off.

The play becomes a useful vehicle to think about empathy and its connection to violence. Lady Macbeth begs for her inherent tendencies to be removed in order to kill Duncan:

> Come, you spirits
> That tend on mortal thoughts, unsex me here,
> And fill me from the crown to the toe top-full
> Of direst cruelty. Make thick my blood.
> Stop up th' access and passage to remorse,
> That no compunctious visitings of nature
> Shake my fell purpose, nor keep peace between
> Th' effect and it. Come to my woman's breasts
> And take my milk for gall, you murd'ring ministers,
> Wherever in your sightless substances
> You wait on nature's mischief. Come, thick night,

> And pall thee in the dunnest smoke of hell,
> That my keen knife see not the wound it makes,
> Nor heaven peep through the blanket of the dark
> To cry "Hold, hold!"
>   (*Macbeth* I.v.47–61)

Lady Macbeth knows she cannot commit this unnatural harm without suppressing the very things that make her human. The protective factors of compassion and empathy must be turned off in order to practice violence on others.

Although empathy and connectedness may seem like subjective terms, these concepts can be measured, and studies continue to find a correlation among high empathy levels, interconnectedness, and reduced violence. In the *Handbook for School Violence*, Michael J. Karcher suggests that violence may stem from a lack of empathy: "Violence, both physical and verbal, reflects the dominance of one's own needs and wants over another's. Violence is, therefore, evidence of limited perspective taking (Selman et al. 1992). This may be due either to an unwillingness or an inability to consider and respect others' points of view" (Karcher 2004). Perspective-taking can help strengthen bonds within a community. When we can put ourselves into the shoes of another, we are more likely to recognize that person as a full human, and more likely to watch out for them. When we are unable to take the perspective of another person, and we put our own needs ahead of the needs of others, we are more capable of harming others. Our ability to enact violence, therefore, may be tied up in the degree to which we recognize the full humanity of the people around us.

When individuals feel deep ties to the people in their lives, they become more resilient. According to a 2021 Colorado Healthy Kids survey, 68.5 percent of youth in Colorado experienced poor mental health during the COVID-19 pandemic, but the same study revealed that significant protective factors were also at play, with 64.7 percent of youth reporting they felt like they belonged at their school, while 54.7 percent of youth reported that they could talk to a friend about their feelings most of the time or always (Colorado Department of Public Health and Environment n.d.a). This kind of connectedness, bonds within the community, prosocial relationships, and a sense of belonging can build resilience in children and protect against violence, even as they move through challenging times.

As we see in the play, the more Macbeth turns away from other people, the more capable he is of harm. On the flip side, if young people can regularly practice empathy, perspective-taking, and turning toward others, these behaviors can deepen their feelings of connectedness and encourage them to see themselves as belonging in their community. Karcher concludes: "Promoting connectedness in the lives of adolescents is critical to violence prevention in many ways. Beyond the role of alienation and disconnection as precursors to violence, promoting connectedness also is key to successful violence prevention" (Karcher 2004). When young people gain a stronger sense of the ways their actions affect the well-being of others, and how the actions of others impact their own well-being, the often-invisible ties that comprise a community become more pronounced. Deepening an awareness of our interconnectedness through empathy and perspective-taking can make our communities more resilient against violence.

Look at the Climate: Targeted Violence

Targeted violent acts often come with red flags and warning signs. According to a Secret Service study, in 81 percent of planned attacks in schools, someone other than the perpetrator was aware of the plan. Studies continue to find that prior to violent incidents, plotters leaked their plans and gave signals that they were in trouble. We see this play out in the climate of *Macbeth*, where red flags and warning signs are pervasive. The Macbeths form their plan together, and although they don't directly communicate their plan to anyone else, Banquo grows suspicious of his comrade's concerning behavior: "Thou hast it now—king, Cawdor, Glamis, all / As the Weïrd Women promised, and I fear / Thou played'st most foully for 't" (*Macbeth* III.i.1–3). Banquo is concerned, and although he may not be able to clearly articulate his concerns, he senses something is wrong with his friend. In this moment, the murder of Duncan has already occurred, but in many situations, the warnings are also sent in advance of a planned attack. Learning to recognize and speak up about warning signs can make a difference in preventing violent incidents. We can use *Macbeth* as a way to examine warning signs with our students. Often, when a plan is leaked about a violent attack in a school, it is leaked to a peer rather than to an adult. If we can train young people to be aware of erratic behavior and watch for warning signs, we can empower them to be active upstanders in building safer communities.

Macbeth is initially on the fence about the plan to murder Duncan and shares his concerns with the audience. Macbeth seems on the cusp of deciding against the murder, but his wife convinces him to follow through. What might have happened if Macbeth had stood his ground or reached out to another trusted person about his struggles? We can use the play as a way to connect students to contemporary resources for reporting targeted violence. How might things have turned out differently if a bystander had submitted an anonymous tip to local law enforcement, for example? How might things have been different if someone had heeded the warning signs and taken action to prevent the murder of Duncan?

Look at the Climate: Power and Violence

The climate of *Macbeth* is filled with instability related to power; a person in power can be quickly toppled, as we see with the Thane of Cawdor, and many characters operate under the assumption that a good life is a life of power over others. The relationship between power and violence is a complicated one, and although people in power (especially characters in a Shakespeare play) may resort to violence to maintain power, that is not the sole dynamic between the two concepts. Brené Brown, a researcher focused on shame, vulnerability, and leadership, describes power as a neutral concept: "What makes power dangerous is how it's used. Power over is driven by fear. Daring and transformative leaders share power with, empower people to, and inspire people to develop power within" (Brown 2020).

In *Macbeth*, we see that power becomes a dangerous influence on the main character. He learns from the witches that he will become king. Rather than wait out the situation to see what unfolds, Macbeth and his wife take the situation into their own hands. After the murder of Duncan, Macbeth is crowned king, and he becomes increasingly focused on holding power over others. According to Brown, a leader operating in a "power over" framework believes that power must be hoarded, not shared; uses dehumanizing language and fear-based practices; and sees power as finite. In the play, Macbeth starts to see his fellow humans as obstacles to his power as king. His comrade

Banquo shifts from a trusted friend to a dehumanized threat, which must be neutralized. Macbeth's fixation on power blinds him to the humanity of the people around him. This idea will be explored further in the following chapter's analysis of *Julius Caesar*, as the title character must be turned into an abstract concept in order for Brutus to contemplate his assassination. As you work through *Macbeth*, encourage your students to track how power operates in the climate of the play. Who holds power throughout the play? How does each character define power? How does the concept of power impact the violence within the play? What would it look like if Macbeth's concept of power shifted from a "power over" framework to a leadership model in which power was shared, humanity was recognized, and a high value was placed on empathy and connection? Understanding the nature of power within the play can also help your students explore what kind of climate shapes the characters' actions. How might a different climate change the outcome?

Look at the Climate: Language

As we see in many of Shakespeare's works, several moments throughout *Macbeth* highlight the role of language in violence prevention, and the importance of giving voice to your concerns, your griefs, your fears. When you can put something into words, it becomes less scary, while the things we cannot name have power over us. In a moment of horrific trauma, facing the loss of his family, Macduff is speechless. Malcolm tells him: "What, man, ne'er pull your hat upon your brows. / Give sorrow words. The grief that does not speak / Whispers the o'erfraught heart and bids it break" (*Macbeth* IV.iii.245–47). In other words, we must give words to our pain, or our hearts will break. This is an idea Shakespeare continues to return to: the importance of putting things into words and of connecting with our fellow humans through language. We see, repeatedly, that in order to process and cope with difficult experiences, one's pain must be translated into words. When Macduff loses his family, he is advised to "give sorrow words" because otherwise the grief will consume him. In the midst of a play about violence and power, we also see some glimmers of hope, as characters turn to one another for support, and reach out across the chasm of despair to connect through language. Violence prevails when words are absent. Language is a necessary path out of violence.

In the climate of the play, some characters use language to move through violence, as we see in act 4 scene 3 with Malcolm and Macduff. Macbeth tries to sort through his fears about killing Duncan in act 1 scene 7, but after he has committed the murder, he turns away from language, stops confiding in the audience, stops confiding in his wife, stops confiding in Banquo. He leaves language behind, turns away from his loved ones, and commits to further violence. If this climate normalized language as a way through violence, and placed value on speaking up, sharing difficult emotions, and offering appropriate reporting channels, perhaps the violence could have been prevented.

Look for Upstanders: Banquo

Macbeth is not alone when the witches offer up their first prediction. He is accompanied by Banquo. The witches tell Macbeth that he shall become king, and that Banquo's children shall be kings. When staging or discussing the play with your students, you might emphasize the power of a prosocial bond, and the ways in which friendship can be a protective factor against violence. Banquo is one of the first characters to act as an upstander, although his efforts do not prevent the eventual violence from occurring. When Macbeth and Banquo hear the witches' predictions, Banquo warns Macbeth not to read too much into what happened: "But 'tis strange. / And oftentimes, to win us to our harm, / The instruments of darkness tell us truths, / Win us with honest trifles, to betray's / In deepest consequence" (*Macbeth* I.iii.134–38). In performance, this interaction offers an opportunity to exemplify the friendship between Banquo and Macbeth, and to establish Banquo as a trusted support person. It is an opportunity to reveal the prosocial bond and the natural kindness between them, as well as Banquo's concern for his friend. Often, our friends can be important resources for us to test out our ideas, and to keep us anchored to ourselves. Perhaps Macbeth's natural "milk of human kindness" is put on display in his relationship with Banquo. After encountering the witches, Macbeth encourages Banquo to "think upon what hath chanced, and at more time, / The interim having weighed it, let us speak / Our free hearts each to other" (*Macbeth* I.iii.170–73). These are close friends who value communication and whole-hearted connection. Based on this language, one might assume that Macbeth and Banquo have had many conversations in the past in which they spoke their "free hearts" to each other. This seems a balanced, rational, and authentic reply, from one friend to another. The stronger the bond, the harder it is for Macbeth to turn off his affections for his friend when he orders Banquo murdered. In ordering that murder, Macbeth is turning away from his empathy, turning away from his natural "milk of human kindness" and turning toward violence and power. This is an opportunity to discuss Banquo's upstander strategy. Could he have employed other strategies to prevent the eventual harm? Who else could have been an upstander in the play?

PERFORMING THE PLAY FOR YOUTH AUDIENCES

Macbeth deals with many complicated issues surrounding mental health, planned attacks, and relationships. The play also depicts several moments in which violence could have been prevented, inviting young audiences to think about how we recover from our mistakes and how we can help others do the same. Attending a live performance can serve to spark the imaginations of young audience members and encourage them to consider the complicated ways in which people are impacted by violence in the play.

In CSF's touring Shakespeare & Violence Prevention program, students watch a forty-five-minute version of *Macbeth* as part of a violence-prevention curriculum, followed by post-show activities to invite empathy and to strategize upstander ideas. Since not all educators have access to local theatre companies that offer touring or school matinees, it may be difficult to arrange for your students to see a live production of *Macbeth*. Below, I share some of the considerations that went into CSF's staging of *Macbeth* through a violence-prevention lens. My hope is that these reflections may encourage theatre companies to produce the play for local schools, while also guiding educators who undertake staging student performances in the classroom. Perhaps you decide to coach your high school students to perform the play for younger students at a nearby middle school, and lead follow-up workshops with them. Any way you get the play up on its feet, whether performed by professional actors or by the students in your class, live performance can offer young people a way to engage with the concepts in an embodied way.

CSF toured an abridged performance of *Macbeth* in 2018–19 with a three-actor cast, directed by Kevin Rich. In developing the cutting, we explored the nature of planned violence, the relationship between empathy and violence, and the notion that violence is preventable. The casting breakdown for the three-actor abridged version of *Macbeth* was as follows:

> **ACTOR 1:** Macbeth, 3rd Witch
> **ACTOR 2:** Duncan, Banquo, Macduff, 1st Witch
> **ACTOR 3:** Malcolm, Lady Macbeth, Murderer, 2nd Witch

All three actors played the witches and wore long, hooded cloaks. The transitions between the witches and the other characters were rapid and theatrical, often accomplished with the flourish of a cloak, or an actor spinning in a circle to remove a hood. If you don't need to double roles for economic reasons, I encourage the separation of these roles, which would make it easier to accomplish scenes in which the witches speak to Banquo and Macbeth. But if doubling is more practical, the rapid switches onstage can be theatrically pleasing to watch, and these moments serve as another chance to underscore the message that we are always capable of changing roles and behaviors in real life, just as we watch actors transforming before our eyes.

To establish a violence-prevention lens, CSF's touring productions often incorporate a prologue to set the stage, introduce the characters, establish key themes, and prime the audience to think about the play's violence. Our production began with the following introduction (most of which are Shakespeare's words but arranged by director Kevin Rich and myself):

> **ACTOR 2:** How can fair be foul?
>   How can foul be fair?
> **ACTOR 1:** How can a person,
>   Full of the milk of human kindness,
> **ACTOR 3:** Make the choice to
>   Harm,
>   Hurt,
>   Wound,
>   Kill?
> **ACTOR 2:** As our story begins, (*Macbeth steps forth*)
>   Macbeth is fair, full of wit and promise.

What a piece of work is a man, how noble in reason, how infinite in faculties!
And his true love (*Lady Macbeth steps forth*) is his equal. Age cannot wither her,
nor custom stale her infinite variety.

LADY MACBETH: My bounty is as boundless as the sea, my love as deep
The more I give to thee, the more I have, for both are infinite.

MACBETH: What you do
Still betters what is done. When you do it, sweet,
I'd have you do it ever. When you do dance, I wish you
A wave o' the sea, that you might ever do
Nothing but that.

ACTOR 2: But soon, too soon, delightful measures are changed to dreadful marches.

(*Actors transform to witches.*)

FIRST WITCH: Roses have thorns, and silver fountains mud.
THIRD WITCH: Clouds and eclipses stain both moon and sun.
SECOND WITCH: And loathsome canker lies in sweetest bud.
ALL WITCHES: All men have faults.

Throughout this production, we thought about the role of the witches as the witnesses to humanity, the watchers of society, and the observers who notice the violence unfolding in the world. They reminded us a little of the violence-prevention researchers we partner with at CSPV. The witches hold information, know what will unfold, and try to give information to the humans when they request it. In creating the adaptation, we thought about the witches as a neutral voice. They are not encouraging violence but offering up what they know. The witches are curious about humanity, and they notice the contradictions inherent in being human—"Fair is foul, foul is fair" (*Macbeth*, I.i.12). Perhaps there is a sense of hope that the people will use the information responsibly, and perhaps a sense of disappointment when they don't.

The witches spoke multiple languages in our production (English, Spanish, and Arabic). This multilingual approach helped to underscore that the witches were a collective of voices rather than a single voice. Whether or not students understand all of these languages, we do find that a multilingual production encourages audience members to lean in, listen more intently, and invest more in the story. It requires the actors to rely on body language and clarity in storytelling. When we weave multiple languages into a play, I believe we are subtly underscoring Shakespeare's ability to cross boundaries and connect people regardless of language.

LOOK IN THE MIRROR: UPSTANDER ROLEPLAY EXERCISE

A key part of a violence-prevention lens is the opportunity to think about how we might respond to a situation. How could we break the cycle, act as upstanders, and change the outcome depicted in the play?

One moment in particular stands out as a powerful opportunity to connect with a violence-prevention curriculum and to explore how an upstander might have made a difference. In act 1 scene 7, Macbeth faces a choice, and he's left alone onstage for a soliloquy:

> MACBETH: If it were done when 'tis done, then 'twere well
> It were done quickly. If the assassination
> Could trammel up the consequence, and catch
> With his surcease success; that but this blow
> Might be the be-all and the end-all here,
> But here, upon this bank and shoal of time,
> We'd jump the life to come. But in these cases
> We still have judgment here, that we but teach
> Bloody instructions, which, being taught, return
> To plague th' inventor: this even-handed justice
> Commends the ingredients of our poisoned chalice
> To our own lips. He's here in double trust:
> First, as I am his kinsman and his subject,
> Strong both against the deed; then, as his host,
> Who should against his murderer shut the door,
> Not bear the knife myself. Besides, this Duncan
> Hath borne his faculties so meek, hath been
> So clear in his great office, that his virtues
> Will plead like angels, trumpet-tongued, against
> The deep damnation of his taking-off;
> And pity, like a naked newborn babe,
> Striding the blast, or heaven's cherubim, horsed
> Upon the sightless couriers of the air,
> Shall blow the horrid deed in every eye,
> That tears shall drown the wind. I have no spur

> To prick the sides of my intent, but only
> Vaulting ambition, which o'erleaps itself
> And falls on th' other.
> > (*Macbeth* I.vii.1–28)

Macbeth has the chance to make a choice that would prevent violence and break a cycle. The speech is filled with hesitation, ruminating, and turning an idea over and over. Macbeth is on the fence, and it's not a foregone conclusion that he will agree to the plan to murder Duncan. If he could get it over with without any consequences, he'd do it in a second, but he knows there will be consequences. The murder won't be done once it's done. The act will ripple through the fabric of the community, and he knows that what goes around comes around. He sees the many reasons not to kill Duncan; and yet, Macbeth's ambition (or his thirst for power over others) is the main reason to follow through with the murder. This is a moment of choice, in which any number of scenarios could play out. Just after this speech, Lady Macbeth enters and persuades Macbeth to follow through with the murder. What if she acted as an upstander instead? What if Macbeth followed his instincts to let fate unfold naturally and decided that murder was not the right choice? What if a witness to this speech pulled Macbeth aside and asked him more questions? This kind of present-moment thinking is key to exploring the play. None of it, although written by Shakespeare centuries ago, should feel like a predetermined outcome. If we can stage these moments, bring them to life in the classroom, and consider that these events are happening in real time, we can begin to understand how the events unfold. What makes Macbeth decide what to do? How might an upstander have changed the outcome?

CSF's touring production of *Macbeth* focused on the above speech in post-show activities. As with all the upstander roleplays in the Shakespeare & Violence Prevention project, students are invited to step in as themselves, because those are the roles they will play in the real world. This speech is a powerful candidate for a roleplay because it is upstream of the violence, when the thought is still a thought, not yet enacted. What if you witnessed this moment? How would you take action as an upstander?

When we toured the production and taught the workshops (as outlined in the lesson plan in appendix A), students came up with a great variety of upstander strategies:

- I would tell Macbeth that a crown is temporary, but guilt is forever.
- Talk it through. Ask why. Ask questions. Give Macbeth space.
- Encourage Macbeth to go to Duncan about concerns around leadership.
- Report it to the Scottish authorities.
- Temporarily distract Macbeth with something else (puppies, baby goats).

Macbeth's soliloquy is one of those moments in which the concept of violence is nestled in thought, and in which an opportunity for prevention exists. A space opens up here, an on-ramp to dive into conversations about how you'd act to prevent harm if you were aware of this. But as yourself, not as Macbeth or Lady Macbeth. In this scene, as a main character reflects on the choice to enact violence, we find an opportunity for intervention.

Often students working on this scene want a magical solution that fixes everything. A student might offer up the idea that perhaps Lady Macbeth changes her mind and decides not to convince Macbeth to murder the king, or perhaps that Macbeth has a change of heart and decides to forget about murder. In those kinds of solutions, we are relying on a quick, magical fix outside of our own behaviors. But what if it's really just you in a situation like this? What can you do, knowing you can't wave a magic wand and make people change? Within the confines of this situation, and these given circumstances, what are your solutions?

You will find the lesson plan for the *Macbeth* upstander roleplay in appendix A. As you try it out with your students, I encourage you to give a bit of resistance for your students to work against. If your students try out direct confrontation, what if Macbeth doesn't give in so easily to their solution? What if it's actually really hard to talk Macbeth out of the plan to harm Duncan? What if he still plans to enact harm? The scene depicts a high-stakes situation. What if the stakes were lower, and this occurred in your school? Perhaps you overheard someone planning to harm another student at your school. How might you respond?

It is powerful to give young people the chance to try out their own solutions as themselves, which doesn't usually solve all the problems or prevent all the violence. There is no right solution, but here is a chance to practice upstander behavior. Practicing these behaviors before we need them in the real world is an opportunity to rehearse what these strategies feel like in our bodies and voices.

In appendix A, you will find suggested discussion questions to accompany your viewing or staging of *Macbeth* with your students. Please expand upon this list and develop questions that encourage your students to consider the upstander opportunities, the roles involved in the violence, the climate in which the events occurred, and their own strategies for preventing events like the ones depicted in the play.

TAKEAWAYS FROM *MACBETH*

When educators approach *Macbeth* through a violence-prevention lens, there are opportunities to dig deeper to understand the risk factors that appeared, while engaging in conversations about the role of empathy in violence prevention. Had the "milk of human kindness" not been stopped up, had more upstanders taken action, had the Macbeths remembered the full humanity of the people around them, things might have turned out differently. The elements of magic in the play can provide students with metaphorical distance in order to safely approach conversations of how to interrupt harm when they are aware of it in their own communities. Although infused with elements of magic and high-stakes situations, *Macbeth* offers students a real-world lesson: things do not have to be this way.

3
Julius Caesar
Targeted Attacks and Warning Signs

> "Incidents of targeted school violence at school rarely are sudden, impulsive acts. Prior to most incidents, other people knew about the attacker's idea and/or plan to attack."
> —Secret Service Study 2004, Final Report and Findings of the Safe Schools Initiative

> "For I believe they are portentous things
> Unto the climate that they point upon."
> —*Julius Caesar* I.iii.31–32

The action of Shakespeare's *Julius Caesar* centers on a planned violent attack. Although the play is named for the assassination's victim, it more closely follows the storyline of Brutus, one of the plotters. Caesar is killed at the beginning of act 3. While the first half of the play depicts the planning and execution stages of the attack, the second half focuses on the destructive consequences of assassinating a political leader. The play raises questions about how to function as a society, how to respond to leaders we disagree with, and how planned acts of violence impact a community. How many opportunities were there to prevent the violence? How did one act of violence quickly lead to more? How does mob mentality affect one's ability to see others as fully human? Although written in Elizabethan England and set in Ancient Rome, this story is a gut punch in the way it tackles pressing concerns of our time. How do we in the twenty-first century prevent planned attacks, read and respond to warning signs, and address the ripple effects of violence throughout a community?

Violence prevention researchers examine the ample red flags that are present leading up to most violent incidents. If community members deepen their awareness of and learn to recognize warning signs and red flags, many planned attacks can be prevented. In performance, *Julius Caesar* can provide an embodied and emotional exploration of the impact of planned violence, and follow-up activities can help middle and high school students strategize how to speak up and take action when they are aware of planned violence. In the aftermath of the January 6 attack on the Capitol building in 2021, a play about planned violence at the Capitol takes on a contemporary resonance that should not be ignored. Applying a violence-prevention lens to *Julius Caesar* that looks upstream, considers risk and protective factors, examines the climate, analyzes upstander behavior, and invites our own upstander strategies can enrich this play in the classroom and can become an avenue to wrestle with a complex text, while identifying and analyzing some of the prevention opportunities depicted within that text.

PLOT SYNOPSIS

Julius Caesar's power in Rome is growing, and some Romans are worried. What dangers might Rome face with a leader whose power is limitless? What should the citizens do to preserve Rome's republic? Several Romans who are dissatisfied with their present leader choose to address the problem through violent means. Cassius persuades Brutus, Casca, and others to join a plot to kill Julius Caesar. Despite many warning signs to Roman citizens that trouble was brewing, the plotters succeed and murder Caesar in the Capitol on the Ides of March. After the assassination, Mark Antony rouses an angry mob against the conspirators. Rome is plunged into civil war, and political, personal, and social problems escalate. In the midst of a losing battle, Brutus and Cassius both find themselves in a seemingly hopeless situation, and they die by suicide. Antony is left to pick up the pieces of a collapsed Rome.

VIOLENCE PREVENTION CONNECTIONS TO *JULIUS CAESAR*

Julius Caesar was written hundreds of years ago, but it aligns in surprisingly relevant ways with the work researchers have done on targeted violence in schools, patterns in the behavior of plotters, and the importance of reporting tools and information gathering. Widely taught in secondary schools as an introduction to Shakespeare, this play can do double duty as an introduction to some findings from violence-prevention research.

Look Upstream: Root Causes

Before the play begins, Caesar defeated Rome's former leader, Pompey, and is now becoming more and more powerful in Rome. This earlier overthrow of a leader suggests an ongoing instability of power that likely influences the action of the play. Additionally, Cassius, one of the key conspirators, holds a grudge against Caesar before the play begins. A 2019 Secret Service report found that in targeted attacks 83 percent of attackers were retaliating for a grievance, and 63 percent of the time the grievance was with a classmate, often due to bullying (National Threat Assessment Center 2019). Personal feuds, grudges, and grievances with peers are a common part of growing up but can also lead to significant acts of violence if they appear among a constellation of other concerning behaviors. Cassius confides in Brutus about his frustration with their leader: "You gods, it doth amaze me / A man of such a feeble temper should / So get the start of the majestic world / And bear the palm alone" (*Julius Caesar* I.ii.135–38). Exploring this with your students would be worthwhile. Why might Cassius be frustrated with Caesar? What supports might be offered to both characters to help avoid the violence which occurs? How might earlier interventions have helped?

Julius Caesar depicts an assassination, but well before the crime occurs, the play is steeped in history and peppered with references to earlier wrongs. The country has been at war; Cassius has been snubbed. Rome likely is experiencing social inequity and class struggles, as is suggested in the opening scene. Invite your students to think about what earlier events might have impacted what happened in the play? Where might Rome be experiencing systemic root causes of violence, such as poverty and disenfranchisement?

Look at Risk Factors

We see several risk factors depicted in the play, which, in real life, could be cause for intervention, including Cassius's antisocial behaviors. Caesar observes:

> I do not know the man I should avoid
> So soon as that spare Cassius. He reads much,
> He is a great observer, and he looks
> Quite through the deeds of men. He loves no plays,
> As thou dost, Antony; he hears no music;
> Seldom he smiles, and smiles in such a sort
> As if he mocked himself and scorned his spirit
> That could be moved to smile at anything.
> Such men as he be never at heart's ease
> Whiles they behold a greater than themselves,
> And therefore are they very dangerous.
> (*Julius Caesar* II.i.210–20)

Individuals who go on to commit violent crimes often display warning signs, such as cruelty toward animals, violent behavior, violent threats, and a history of aggressive behavior. While Caesar is not reporting any violent behavior, he still notices Cassius's lack of connectedness, enjoyment, and ease in his identity; all of this seems concerning to Caesar. Paying attention to risk factors can help us see how some of the larger acts of violence occur within the play.

As we will see in *Romeo and Juliet*, *Julius Caesar* depicts some of the risk factors that contribute to a higher likelihood of suicide, including sleeplessness, hopelessness, and disconnection. After they murder Caesar, both Cassius and Brutus grow more and more erratic and distraught, and, at first aligned in purpose through the assassination, they are soon at odds:

> CASSIUS: Do not presume too much upon my love.
>   I may do that I shall be sorry for.
> BRUTUS: You have done that you should be sorry for.
>   (*Julius Caesar* IV.iii.72–74)

Brutus is visited by Caesar's ghost, which may be a metaphor for being haunted by his past actions. The situation grows more desperate as Cassius and Brutus find themselves in a losing battle. They begin miscommunicating and misreading one another; later, a series of misunderstandings lead to their deaths by suicide. Another risk factor for violence is a lack of connectedness; toward the end of the play, both Cassius and Brutus begin in-fighting, and they have isolated themselves from their support networks. Brutus's wife dies by suicide, and the two friends grow more antagonistic. There are resources for people experiencing suicidal ideation, including the newly established 988 Lifeline in the United States. A classroom discussion of *Julius Caesar* can emphasize the lack of resources and connectedness for the characters within the play but that there are many resources available to twenty-first-century people dealing with and surviving suicidal despair.

Look at Protective Factors

While the climate of *Julius Caesar*'s Rome seems filled with risk factors for violence, from a steady exposure to violence, sleeplessness, and a lack of communication and connectedness, there are also examples of connectedness and hope in the play. These moments of connection, empathy, and humanity function as small cracks in the climate of violence, which allow for small sparks of light to shine through the darkness of "a mourning Rome, a dangerous Rome" (*Julius Caesar* III.i.315). Caesar's wife, Calphurnia, offers a safe space for her spouse to open up and share vulnerability, and she, in a moment of partnership and connection, expresses her concerns. She has a bad feeling and urges her husband to stay home. At first, Caesar refuses to let cowardice keep him home, but Calphurnia is persistent:

> Alas, my lord
> Your wisdom is consumed in confidence.
> Do not go forth today. Call it my fear
> That keeps you in the house, and not your own.
> We'll send Mark Antony to the Senate House
> And he shall say you are not well today.
> (*Julius Caesar* II.ii.52–57)

Calphurnia recognizes that Caesar is not thinking clearly, and she advocates for his well-being when he will not. In offering herself as the reason for his absence, she allows him to save face with his followers. She trusts her intuition and acts on behalf of the safety and well-being of another. Caesar agrees to stay at home.

This safe bubble is violated when Decius enters and mocks Caesar for listening to his wife. Decius asks, "If Caesar hide himself, shall they not whisper, / 'Lo, Caesar is afraid?" (*Julius Caesar* II.ii.105–6). In this moment, despite the protective factor of a connected and prosocial relationship between spouses, another person plays to Caesar's fear of ridicule and persuades him to go to the Capitol, despite his promise to Calphurnia. What if more of the relationships in the play were rooted in connectedness over competitiveness?

Portia is likewise a safe person for Brutus. When he is sleepless and silent with her, she urges him, "Make me acquainted with your cause of grief" (*Julius Caesar* II.i.276). She invokes their marriage contract, and charges him to share his worries: "By all your vows of love, and that great vow / Which did incorporate and make us one, / That you unfold to me, your self, your half, / Why you are heavy" (*Julius Caesar* II.1.293–97). Portia reminds Brutus of their connectedness; she shares in his joys and sorrows, and what happens to him also happens to her. We presume, perhaps, that in an offstage scene Brutus does confide in Portia, as he promises to do. A strong, caring, loving relationship focused on connection and belonging can strengthen resilience, making individuals better able to withstand difficult circumstances, knowing there is a trusted support person to offer acceptance no matter what.

Look at the Climate

"This is a mourning Rome; a dangerous Rome."
—*Julius Caesar* III.i.315

In *Julius Caesar*, as with many of Shakespeare's tragedies, characters resort to violence to solve their problems. In this Rome, there is an unspoken but palpable idea that violence is an acceptable solution. When a community normalizes violence, it becomes difficult to see it as a problem. They are unhappy with their leader? Kill him. Antony is mad they killed Caesar? Stir up rebellion. Brutus and Cassius feel hopeless? Threaten suicide. Violence, whether directed toward others, the nation, or the self, is seen, within this Rome, as an acceptable reaction to difficult situations. The climate is not one in which all members of the community are safe, valued, or feel a sense of belonging. This climate has a profound impact on the individuals within it, just as the fish in a fish tank are affected by the condition of the water they inhabit.

A recent study on thwarted school shootings revealed some common factors in many of the prevented attacks, and we can draw direct lines between the results of the study and *Julius Caesar*. In many of the prevented attacks, the date of the event was somehow significant, or held a particular meaning for the perpetrator(s). We see this in *Julius Caesar*, in which the date takes on great significance; the soothsayer repeatedly warns Caesar to beware the Ides of March. Later, the date is called back as a reminder between Cassius and Brutus: "Remember March; the ides of March remember" (*Julius Caesar* IV.iii.19). As Cassius prepares to die by suicide, he reveals that the day of his death is also his birthday. In many acts of violence, plotters select a date that holds meaning for them. The same study demonstrated, as many studies continue to reveal, that more than one person was aware of the planned violence. In *Julius Caesar*, several plotters participate in the assassination, and some ancillary figures grow suspicious: Portia, Calphurnia, the soothsayer, Artemidorus. Many people hold information, and had they pooled their knowledge, the violence might have been prevented.

After the 2013 shooting at Arapahoe High School in Colorado, in which a high school gunman shot seventeen-year-old Claire Davis, who later died from gunshot wounds, a study conducted by the Center for the Study and Prevention of Violence found twenty-seven missed opportunities to prevent the shooting because of siloed information and inadequate reporting (Woodward and Goodrum 2016). This is a common occurrence in studies conducted in the aftermath of planned attacks. Speaking up when we are aware of dangerous situations can help connect the dots, inform the adults, and get help to the people who need it.

The red flags in *Julius Caesar* suggest things are not okay in Rome, from the sky raining down fire to a lion wandering the streets of Rome, not to mention all the signs, omens, warnings, and gut feelings sprinkled throughout the play. Despite these warning signs, Caesar heads to the Capitol, and is murdered by a group of conspirators. Hindsight, of course, provides greater clarity, and although we as audience members can see the impending tragedy in Shakespeare's play, the warning signs in real life are not always so clear-cut. The play can become a useful opportunity to apply violence-prevention research about red flags and warning signs to a classroom discussion. Although the warning signs in *Julius Caesar* are more metaphorical than literal, these can all be opportunities to discuss the prevalence of warning signs prior to a planned violent incident. Perhaps the warning signs in real life will not be as obvious as lions birthing in the street or fire raining from the skies, but if we learn to pay attention, we'll get better at recognizing warning signs, just as we recognize foreshadowing in an early modern play.

Act 3 scene 3, one of the most powerful scenes in *Julius Caesar*, takes place after Antony has incited the mob of citizens. A group of Romans encounter Cinna the poet, and, in a case of mistaken identity, they kill him because he shares a name with one of the conspirators. The scene is short, and it's often cut from full productions. This scene is an excellent opportunity to explore some key questions with your students, because it highlights the dangers of a society in which people don't think for themselves and other people aren't seen as humans but as threats, and it speaks to the rushed, impulsive nature of violence. While much of the play is about a planned attack, it's important to see that violence can also be thoughtless and unplanned when people aren't thinking clearly, aren't taking the time to slow down, listen to others, and recognize the humanity of the other.

Look for Upstanders

Several characters in *Julius Caesar* could have stepped in as upstanders, and in fact, some of them actually tried to take action. In the play, one of the most recognizable lines is, in fact, a warning from a well-intentioned upstander. The soothsayer tells Caesar, "Beware the ides of March" (*Julius Caesar* I.ii.21), which means beware the middle of the month, or March 15. Caesar ignores the soothsayer's advice—an upstander who is aware of impending harm and attempts to intervene. Although most of us lack the clairvoyance of the soothsayer, it's important to speak with young people about their gut feelings. Sometimes you just have a sense about someone or something and get a feeling that something might be off. Learning to speak up when you have a bad feeling about something can be an important preventive tool.

The words of the soothsayer are not the only spoken warnings in the play. Caesar asks his team of augurs to make a determination about his best course of action. In ancient Rome, the practice of augury was a way of interpreting omens in the natural world in order to ascertain the will of the gods. An augur (or the more archaic term "augurer," which is used in the play) might be called on to help a leader make an important decision. Just as one might assemble an advisory board to weigh in from their various areas of expertise and offer counsel, an augur, in the ancient world, gave a leader insight to assist with making an informed decision. In this instance, Julius Caesar's servant reports: "They would not have you to stir forth today. / Plucking the entrails of an offering forth, / They could not find a heart within the beast" (*Julius Caesar* II.ii.41–43). In the world of augury, this is a bad sign. Despite the warnings, Caesar, not wanting to be considered a coward, ignores the signs and proceeds to the Capitol, which, we soon learn, is fatal to him and destructive for Rome. How often do we ignore warning signs because they are inconvenient, embarrassing, or we doubt them?

Calphurnia acts as an upstander when she begs Caesar to avoid the Capitol. Prior to the assassination, Artemidorus tries to give Caesar a letter, warning of the planned violence. Even Casca, one of the Romans involved in the plan to kill Caesar, shares concerns with Cicero, a fellow Roman, about some worrying events he has observed:

> Are not you moved, when all the sway of earth
> Shakes like a thing unfirm? O Cicero,
> I have seen tempests when the scolding winds
> Have rived the knotty oaks, and I have seen
> Th' ambitious ocean swell and rage and foam
> To be exalted with the threat'ning clouds;
> But never till tonight, never till now,
> Did I go through a tempest dropping fire.
> Either there is a civil strife in heaven,
> Or else the world, too saucy with the gods,
> Incenses them to send destruction.
> (*Julius Caesar* I.iii.3–13)

In the above speech, Casca admits that he has experienced frightening events before; he has seen the wind tear thick oak trees from the ground, and he has seen the ocean's waves reach as high as the clouds, but he has never lived through such a storm as the one he is currently experiencing, in which fire is falling from the skies. This turbulent weather makes Casca wonder if the gods are angry with the world. This is a similar warning sign to *Hamlet*'s "Something is rotten in the state of Denmark" (*Hamlet* I.iv.100). We do not need to have precise knowledge of what is wrong in order to know when a climate is off. Sometimes we just know, based on erratic behavior or other unspoken signs, that something is not quite right. Casca is, of course, aware of the planned assassination, though he may not consciously connect the concerning weather patterns with the impending murder of Caesar. Here, the raining fire serves as a metaphorical and loud warning sign, but often, the warning signs in real life are more subtle. Following this speech, Cicero asks his friend to expand on his concerns:

> CICERO: Why, saw you anything more wonderful?
> CASCA: A common slave (you know him well by sight)
>   Held up his left hand, which did flame and burn
>   Like twenty torches joined; and yet his hand,
>   Not sensible of fire, remained unscorched.
>   Besides (I ha' not since put up my sword),
>   Against the Capitol I met a lion,
>   Who glazed upon me and went surly by
>   Without annoying me. And there were drawn
>   Upon a heap a hundred ghastly women,
>   Transformèd with their fear, who swore they saw
>   Men all in fire walk up and down the streets.
>   And yesterday the bird of night did sit
>   Even at noonday upon the marketplace,
>   Hooting and shrieking. When these prodigies
>   Do so conjointly meet, let not men say
>   "These are their reasons, they are natural,"
>   For I believe they are portentous things
>   Unto the climate that they point upon.
>   (*Julius Caesar* I.iii.15–33)

Casca has witnessed concerning sights indeed. Take a moment to envision all of these separate images: an enslaved man wandering Rome with his hand aflame but unhurt, a lion roaming the streets, a hundred terrified women, reported sightings of men on fire, and a nocturnal bird shrieking in the middle of the day. Something is rotten in Rome. Casca is worried and doesn't want his friend to dismiss these events as normal. In this scene between two friends, one of whom (Casca) will later help assassinate Caesar, we find an opportunity for intervention. What might happen if Cicero noticed his friend's disturbed state and took his concerns more seriously? What if Cicero went to the authorities, concerned for his friend's mental health? What if Cicero asked Casca more questions? As with most instances of planned violence, multiple characters in the play are aware of the planned assassination of Caesar. We know that Brutus has second thoughts about the attack, and we might imagine that other plotters are second-guessing their actions. What if just one of the plotters decided against it and submitted an anonymous tip to Caesar's security detail? Might the attack have been prevented? All of the characters listed above are potential upstanders, and their actions could likely have changed the outcome.

PERFORMING THE PLAY FOR YOUTH AUDIENCES

The Colorado Shakespeare Festival has toured three productions of *Julius Caesar* as part of the Shakespeare & Violence Prevention initiative, all of which have been directed by Wendy Franz, CSF's managing director. In the most recent production during the 2021–22 school year, which was shared in the aftermath of an actual planned act of violence at the US Capitol building on January 6, 2021, the play acquired additional contemporary relevance. In conceptualizing the 2021 production, Franz used images from the actual footage of the Capitol insurrection to influence the costuming and staging of the citizens in *Julius Caesar*, and the play echoed many of the images shared in the media about the riot at the Capitol. It was a clear way of seeing how one Shakespeare play can take on new meanings based on the changing circumstances of the world in which the play is staged.

In adapting the play, we focused on the planned assassination and the downward spiral of the conspirators. The script was cut down to forty-five minutes and focused on the warning signs throughout the play. We retained the soothsayer's warning, Portia's expressions of concern, and Calphurnia's pleas with Caesar to stay home—all three characters exemplify what it looks like to speak out when we see concerning behavior, and they can provide fodder for students to consider how they might have responded more effectively in order to prevent the violence.

The play includes references to suicide, some onstage, some offstage. Based on conversations with Colorado's Office of Suicide Prevention, the team opted for abstract rather than realistic approaches to staging the suicides. We know that suicide is never inevitable, so in working with the actors in staging these moments, we strove to make the deaths by suicide feel like a decision in one specific moment, not a predetermined given. Most suicidal thoughts *do not* result in suicide, and it's important that suicidal thoughts don't always lead to suicide in media representations, including theatrical performances. Talking about suicide does not plant the idea of suicide in a young person's mind; on the contrary, when caring adults can have calm and regulated conversations about suicide prevention, it's a signal to young people who may be experiencing suicidal ideation that they are safe people to talk to. In creating the study guide, we included materials from Colorado's Office of Suicide Prevention, equipping the teachers with tools about how to talk about suicide with young people, and we trained our actors in youth suicide prevention. We included the following content warning in the materials shared with schools prior to the performance:

> *Julius Caesar* is a play about a planned attack in a public setting, and the storyline involves the deaths of characters by suicide. This content may be triggering to some members of your school community. We encourage you to have conversations with your students prior to the performance, particularly students who may have been personally impacted by recent trauma. Please work with your students to make the most appropriate decisions for them regarding viewing the performance and participating in post-show workshops. If you are concerned about a student, below are some resources.

We also shared local and national suicide-prevention resources. I recommend partnering with a local suicide-prevention organization for advice on recommended resources to share with young people viewing the performance, and in crafting your own content warning.

CSF touring productions of *Julius Caesar* incorporated Spanish-speaking characters. In one production, Brutus's spouse spoke primarily in Spanish, and Brutus understood Spanish but spoke primarily in

English. In another production, the soothsayer communicated only in Spanish and gave Caesar the Ides of March warnings in Spanish, but Caesar couldn't understand the language. If you incorporate languages beyond English, I recommend considering how it affects the storytelling, and what changes should be made to help the choice make sense in the context of the play.

In each of the *Julius Caesar* tours, we cast a female-identifying actor as Brutus, playing the role as a woman, with she/her pronouns; we did not change the character's name. Casting a woman in a position of political power can have an immense impact on young people watching the play. When making a gender decision about a character, I encourage you and your students to consider how the change affects the meaning and message in the play overall. Do we feel differently watching a female Brutus than a male Brutus? Why? Gender changes in a production can serve as an excellent way to deepen awareness of how meaning ripples throughout a play. This kind of attention to gender can also subtly reinforce some important violence-prevention lessons, as we expand the definition of whose stories belong onstage and how gender intersects with the way people are treated in a community.

Look in the Mirror: Upstander Roleplay Exercise

The play might better be titled *Brutus* rather than *Julius Caesar*, because it is Brutus's struggle, his grappling with the decision to kill his leader, and his eventual decline that we track in the play. Caesar dies at the mid-point of the play, and appears briefly as a ghost toward the end, but is otherwise an absent eponymous figure, and this is Brutus's story. Let's explore one key moment of choice Brutus faces.

Brutus is approached by the conspirators early in the play. Cassius tries to convince him to join them in taking down Caesar. Brutus knows something isn't right with Caesar in charge. But does he agree that it's best to take matters into his own hands? Should brute force outweigh the proper channels of procedure when leading a country? Does Brutus have any reason to kill Caesar? As a friend, no. But what about as a leader? Brutus recognizes he needs to turn off his personal feelings toward Caesar in order to take action on behalf of Rome. In a violence-prevention curriculum, the moment in which Brutus confides in the audience to express his reservations can be an effective roleplay opportunity. Brutus is on the fence about whether he'll agree to Cassius's plan. When a character is on the fence, this is a prime opportunity to dig into the character's present moment and to engage in a roleplaying exercise. Invite your students to practice speaking up or taking action, as if they overheard this scene. In the full scene, Brutus is left alone with his thoughts. He confides in the audience:

> It must be by his death. And for my part
> I know no personal cause to spurn at him,
> But for the general. He would be crowned:
> How that might change his nature, there's the question.
> It is the bright day that brings forth the adder,
> And that craves wary walking. Crown him that,
> And then I grant we put a sting in him
> That at his will he may do danger with.
> Th' abuse of greatness is when it disjoins
> Remorse from power. And, to speak truth of Caesar,
> I have not known when his affections swayed
> More than his reason. But 'tis a common proof
> That lowliness is young ambition's ladder,
> Whereto the climber-upward turns his face;
> But, when he once attains the upmost round,
> He then unto the ladder turns his back,
> Looks in the clouds, scorning the base degrees
> By which he did ascend. So Caesar may.
> Then, lest he may, prevent. And since the quarrel
> Will bear no color for the thing he is,
> Fashion it thus: that what he is, augmented,
> Would run to these and these extremities.
> And therefore think him as a serpent's egg,
> Which, hatched, would, as his kind, grow mischievous,
> And kill him in the shell.
>   (*Julius Caesar* II.i.10–36)

There is a lot to understand here. This soliloquy is a strong example of what I mean when I say that in Shakespeare, violence is often nestled in thought. Here we have a character thinking about killing another person. Look at the way the thoughts tumble out, intersect, and bleed together. This is a character whose brain is going a million miles a minute, and he uses his time alone onstage to unpack his heart, sort through the thoughts, and make meaning with his confidantes, the audience members.

In the above speech, Brutus comes to believe that the only way to stop Caesar's growing power is through his death. The problem is, Brutus has nothing personally against Caesar, but he is worried about what might happen, hypothetically, if Caesar grows too powerful. There are rumors he will be crowned, and Brutus fears that Caesar might become dangerous if he has unchecked power. Based on what he imagines might happen, he reasons that it's better to kill him now, before he hurts anyone, as one might kill a serpent before it grows into a threat. In short, this murder is preventive, according to Brutus. It is a way to avoid further danger and harm. Here, Brutus is not treating Caesar as a friend or a fellow human, but as a threat; the irony is in Brutus's line, "The abuse of greatness is when it disjoins remorse from power" (*Julius Caesar* II.i.19). In this moment, though he is weighing Caesar's potential power and hypothetical lack of remorse, Brutus could be describing himself. He is in a position of power over Caesar because he holds information about the assassination and has already started to "disjoin" remorse for his friend. This act of dehumanization will eventually lead the way to the choice of violence. A few moments later, Brutus confesses:

> Since Cassius first did whet me against Caesar,
> I have not slept.
> Between the acting of a dreadful thing
> And the first motion, all the interim is
> Like a phantasma or a hideous dream.
> The genius and the mortal instruments
> Are then in council, and the state of man,
> Like to a little kingdom, suffers then
> The nature of an insurrection.
> (*Julius Caesar* II.1.64–72)

This growing sense of unease, restlessness, and emotional volatility is common for people planning harm. Brutus describes his body and his mind as experiencing an insurrection, like his country shortly will. Then the conspirators enter, and they make a plan to kill Caesar. They discuss who else to include in the plan, and whether to kill only Caesar, or anyone else. Cassius argues that Mark Antony should die too, but Brutus persuades them to stick to only Caesar, otherwise "our course will seem too bloody" (*Julius Caesar* II.i.175).

This is a powerful moment to roleplay, because, while extreme, it is upstream of the major violence. The assassination hasn't happened yet, civil war has not yet broken out, and the suicides have not occurred. Although we hope our young people will not be privy to conversations about planned violence, rehearsing how we might respond to try to prevent harm can lead to more preparedness in the real world.

When introducing the scene to your students, discuss the extremity of this situation's stakes. What if we lowered the stakes and brought it down to the everyday level of your school? Imagine that you overheard someone encouraging Brutus to fight Caesar after school. What would you do? Whom could you approach for help? This exercise can be an opportunity for students to share aloud the names of their trusted adults. A lesson plan about upstander roleplays related to *Julius Caesar* appears in appendix B, and I encourage you to use this outline as a post-show activity after your students read, watch, and/or stage their own production of *Julius Caesar*. When CSF actors led these workshops after our performances of *Julius Caesar*, students consistently came up with similar solutions. Here are a few examples:

- Report it to Caesar, go to the authorities (go covert).
- Talk with Brutus and Cassius, ask questions (be direct).
- Distract the plotters and temporarily pause the plans through distraction (with cute puppies, spilled water, asking them for help with something unrelated, etc.).

The aim of the upstander roleplay activity is not to identify a single solution that will stop it all. How can you use this opportunity to practice solutions that feel accessible to you?

It is important to link this material to the real world, in which students may well hear of plans that adults are unaware of. I have already mentioned that 81 percent of the time in planned attacks, someone other than the perpetrator knew their plan, but the more compelling statistic is that most of the time it was a peer who was aware. It can be helpful to remind students that they have trusted adults they can go to, that prevention is possible, and that normalizing and practicing upstander behavior is a healthy way to build preparedness.

TAKEAWAYS FROM *JULIUS CAESAR*

Shakespeare's plays are always shape-shifting in terms of their relevance; what resonates today with a play may not resonate in the same way a year from now. In the aftermath of the January 6 insurrection on the US Capitol, the planned attack in *Julius Caesar* was no longer hypothetical, or a stretch of imagination, but rather something we witnessed in the news. In thinking about how to adapt this play for the present times through the lens of violence prevention, this play can help middle and high school students talk about the importance of information-sharing, the importance of paying attention to red-flag behavior in our peers, and the importance of speaking up and taking action when we are aware of potential harm.

4
Romeo and Juliet
Suicide and Community Violence

Although *Romeo and Juliet* is frequently touted as one of literature's greatest love stories, when viewed through a violence-prevention lens the play is rife with opportunities to reflect on widespread community violence. The play depicts how community violence impacts the lives of everyone within a society, and the especially devastating effect it has on young people. Verona, the city in which the play is set, is a society consumed by an ancient grudge between its two prominent families, a grudge that, although rooted in the past, continues to negatively impact its citizens in the present. The play contains pervasive fighting, a frustrated leader, and unnecessary deaths. In this unsafe climate, trusted adults don't act in the best interest of young people, citizens resort to violence to solve problems, and Verona's youth population, in the absence of healthy, regulated adult role models, lacks coping skills to navigate difficult situations. The play moves quickly, and the speed at which the action plays out provides opportunities to underline connections between violence and impulsiveness. Most of the characters in the play are trying to do their best, but because they lack the time and space to breathe and think, the go-to solutions are usually based in violence and secrecy. The play depicts the deaths of young people—some by suicide, some by homicide—and a world that is ripped to shreds by the time of its conclusion, when the older generation must face rebuilding. By the play's end, the community of Verona hits rock bottom, loses many of its youth to violence, and must face the difficult question of how to start over and do better. To call it a love story is to miss the play's warnings about the consequences of community violence.

This play is widely read in high schools across the United States and is often a student's first introduction to Shakespeare. Rather than focusing on themes about star-crossed lovers and emphasizing the actions of its eponymous couple, educators have the opportunity to take a broader view of the play by deepening their students' awareness of the backdrop against which this story is set and examining the systemic ways in which violence pervades the climate. In bringing a contemporary understanding of community violence to the study of *Romeo and Juliet*, we can use Shakespeare's text to spark discussions about how to build healthier, safer, more resilient communities.

Romeo and Juliet offers opportunities to pose vital questions to students: How does violence affect young people in a community? How do we learn to cope with difficult situations? How can communication de-escalate conflict and prevent further violence? How can we build our own resilience to prevent the kind of violence we see in the play? In tackling *Romeo and Juliet* with middle and high school students, we can use empathy for the characters to examine our own choices in similar situations while simultaneously analyzing the broader climate to deepen our awareness of what community resilience might look like.

PLOT SYNOPSIS

Two prominent families of Verona, the Montagues and the Capulets, are sworn enemies. When their feud sparks yet another public brawl, the Prince of Verona, tired of the ongoing violence, threatens death to anyone who disturbs the peace. Meanwhile, the lovestruck Romeo Montague is infatuated with Rosaline, and sneaks into a party hosted by the Capulets, hoping to catch a glimpse of her. Instead, he meets Juliet Capulet, a member of the rival family. The two fall in love, profess their mutual affection, and make plans to marry the following day. Romeo's mentor, Friar Lawrence, weds the young couple, believing it might heal the family feud.

Shortly after the secret marriage, Romeo encounters Juliet's cousin, the fiery Tybalt, but refuses to fight him. Romeo's friend Mercutio, surprised by Romeo's sudden compassion for a Capulet, steps into the fight and is killed by Tybalt. In an act of revenge, Romeo murders Tybalt. As punishment, the prince banishes Romeo from Verona.

Aided by Juliet's nurse, Romeo and Juliet spend their first—and last—night together as a married couple before Romeo departs to live in banishment. Juliet learns that her parents have arranged for her hasty marriage to a family friend, Paris. She seeks advice from the friar, who gives her a drug to induce a death-like state. This, he hopes, will buy her time to escape the arranged marriage and reunite with her legal husband. The friar promises to send word to Romeo, informing him of the plan. The scheme goes awry when the friar's message to Romeo remains undelivered. Romeo learns of Juliet's "death" and visits her tomb. Believing her truly dead, he swallows poison. Juliet awakens when her drug wears off, sees Romeo dead, and fatally stabs herself. The two families learn, too late, of the love between Romeo and Juliet, and they vow to bury their grievances.

VIOLENCE PREVENTION CONNECTIONS TO *ROMEO AND JULIET*

Look Upstream: Root Causes

This play speaks volumes about the impact of violence on a community. It begins with a prologue that summarizes the play's major events and establishes Verona as a city steeped in violence: "Two households, both alike in dignity / In fair Verona where we lay our scene / From ancient grudge break to new mutiny /Where civil blood makes civil hands unclean" (*Romeo and Juliet* prologue 1–4). This ancient grudge between these two families results in present, real, youthful blood. By the play's end, we will see this grudge between the Montagues and the Capulets, the source of which is unrevealed in the play, lead to the deaths of Mercutio, Tybalt, Paris, Romeo, and Juliet. Violence is so common in Verona, that after the prologue, the first scene depicts a street brawl between the servants of the warring households. What begins as a fight between servants soon escalates into a communal fight, involving even the heads of the households, Lord Montague and Lord Capulet. By opening the play with the citizens of Verona publicly brawling, Shakespeare establishes from the start that *Romeo and Juliet* is a civic story. The stage is set, not simply in fair Verona, but in a city dominated by violence. When the prince breaks up the fight in the street, his language reveals that this fight is not the first of its kind, but is part of a repeated problem:

> Three civil brawls bred of an airy word
> By thee, old Capulet, and Montague,
> Have thrice disturbed the quiet of our streets
> And made Verona's ancient citizens
> Cast by their grave-beseeming ornaments
> To wield old partisans in hands as old,
> Cankered with peace, to part your cankered hate.
> If ever you disturb our streets again,
> Your lives shall pay the forfeit of the peace.
> (*Romeo and Juliet* I.i.91–99)

Three big fights have recently occurred in public, and the fights are breaking out over nothing substantial (an "airy word") and are causing even Verona's elderly citizens to bear arms. Lots of people are hurt by the fighting, not just the heads of the families. If we scratch the surface of Verona, we find the root cause of so much of the violence in the play is this grudge between the two families.

Look at Risk Factors

One prominent risk factor featured in *Romeo and Juliet* is the absence of trusted adults. Juliet's parents don't know how to talk to their teenage daughter about her feelings. Lady Capulet needs backup in the form of the nurse when she tries to broach the topic of marriage with Juliet. Both Capulet parents try to push their daughter into an arranged marriage to Paris when she's grieving the death of her cousin Tybalt—excessively, they believe—rather than talking through their shared trauma of losing a loved one. Early in the play, Lord Montague dodges a conversation with his son Romeo, instead foisting the duties onto the shoulders of Benvolio, Romeo's cousin. With absent and uncommunicative parents, the young people in the play don't have easy access to adult family members who model calm, prosocial behavior; on the contrary, when a young person faces difficulty, the adults behave impulsively. When Tybalt is troubled by Romeo's presence at the Capulets' private party, Lord Capulet shames his nephew and tells him to keep his concerns to himself. Tybalt, who has been raised by a generation of Capulets and trained to believe that Montagues are enemies, insists that he can't "endure" Romeo being at the party. Rather than listening, calmly reflecting, and offering guidance to this struggling young person, Capulet mocks Tybalt for his presumption of authority. "He shall be endured. / What, goodman boy? I say he shall. Go to. / Am I the master here or you?" (*Romeo and Juliet* I.v.86–88). When that doesn't settle his nephew's anger, Capulet resorts to threats: "Be quiet or . . . for shame, I'll make you quiet" (*Romeo and Juliet* I.v.98–99). The behaviors modeled by the adults in the play have the effect of teaching some unhealthy habits to the younger generation about coping with difficulty and managing emotions. According to the examples modeled by the adults in Verona, young people should navigate challenging situations and uncomfortable emotions through the use of anger, shame, silence, and threats.

Substance abuse is another risk factor in youth violence (CDC 2024i) and appears in *Romeo and Juliet*. When the friar offers up a drug to sedate Juliet in order to mimic death, this should raise a red flag for contemporary readers. Romeo has access to poison, secured through the apothecary, and he uses that poison to die by suicide at Juliet's side when he believes, erroneously, that she is dead. We might imagine how the action of the play would be changed if drugs—or weapons, for that matter—were not available to the characters. How might things have turned out differently? Additional risk factors for violence are disconnection and isolation; the Montagues and the Capulets are divided, disconnected, and full of enmity.

The young people, despite the occasional glimpses of connectedness, ultimately lack coping skills. They have learned, by swimming in the waters of their families' feud, to respond to difficult situations rashly. When Tybalt sees Romeo crashing the party, he vows revenge. When Romeo learns he's banished, he becomes furious with the friar and threatens self-harm. When Juliet learns she must marry Paris, she likewise threatens suicide in the friar's presence. When things get difficult for these young people, they respond with violence, either to others or to themselves. They have seen no alternative way modeled by the adults in their lives. Some of the situations these young people face are extraordinarily difficult and are in fact a direct result of the longstanding feud between families. The solutions offered up by the friar, while not as violent, still involve deception and secrecy. With the odds stacked against them, is it any wonder that young people do not thrive in Verona?

In *Romeo and Juliet*, the main characters are teenagers. Juliet is not quite fourteen years old, and Romeo, although his age is not specifically identified in the text, may be slightly older. Over the course of the few days in which the play is set, both characters undergo potentially traumatic events: a knife fight between Mercutio and Tybalt in which both are killed, Romeo's banishment, a forced marriage plan, parental abuse, suicidal ideation, and death by suicide. Considering the prevalence of violence in Verona, we may presume that they have experienced additional traumas prior to the events of the play.

Adverse childhood experiences (ACEs) are potentially traumatic events that occur in childhood between the ages of zero and seventeen. ACEs may include experiencing or witnessing domestic or community violence, experiencing or witnessing neglect or abuse, and/or experiencing the death of a loved one. ACEs, especially when children experience multiple events, can have a long-term deleterious impact on well-being, can result in long-term chronic illness, and can negatively impact many aspects of an individual's life, from employment opportunities to involvement in harmful activities. According to the CDC, ACEs are very common: "61% of adults surveyed across 25 states reported they had experienced at least one type of ACE before age 18, and nearly 1 in 6 reported they had experienced four or more types of ACEs" (CDC 2024a).

Romeo and Juliet concludes with two deaths by suicide, both of which were preventable. The two title characters experience hopelessness in their final moments in the tomb. Romeo arrives, believing (incorrectly) that Juliet has died, because he did not receive the message from the friar. He is unaware of the plan for Juliet's feigned death, and therefore does not know that her seeming death is not real. On top of that, Romeo is sleep-deprived, and he has committed his second murder just moments earlier (first Tybalt on the streets of Verona, then Paris in the tomb). With all of the stress of this moment, his nervous system dysregulated, and his brain unable to process the situation clearly, Romeo is likely in the midst of a mental health crisis as he makes the decision to end his life. He dies by suicide by swallowing poison at Juliet's side. Moments later, the friar enters the tomb and realizes that Romeo is dead. Juliet wakes up, and the friar informs her of Romeo's death, then tries to remove her from the tomb and usher her to safety. She refuses and sends the friar away.

Concerned by the sounds of people approaching, the friar leaves Juliet alone. This moment is likely rushed, impulsive, and full of adrenaline. When Juliet is alone, she realizes that Romeo has died by swallowing poison. She tries to kiss the poison off his lips, but none remains. Juliet hears a noise, realizes she doesn't have much time, so she stabs herself with Romeo's dagger and dies.

A lack of sleep is a risk factor in youth violence, and sleeplessness can also be a risk factor for suicidal ideation. The whole action of the play unfolds in just a few days. Romeo goes several days without sleep, and by the end of a sleepless few days, he dies by suicide. His sleeplessness is not the sole cause of his death by suicide (or Juliet's for that matter), but what might the action of the play look like if Romeo and Juliet were both well rested, and let their relationship unfold over several weeks or months? What would the play look like if they heeded the friar's advice to go "wisely and slow. They stumble that run fast" (*Romeo and Juliet* II.iii.101)?

There are so many ways these deaths could have been prevented: if the friar hadn't provided the drug to induce Juliet's deathlike state; if Romeo had received the message warning of the plan; if the friar had stayed with Juliet in the tomb; if the families had resolved the feud; if the marriage hadn't been kept a secret. . . . Looking at the alternative outcomes can help young audiences understand that suicide and violence are not inevitable but preventable.

When approaching this play through a violence-prevention lens, it's key to consider current best practices and recommendations from public health experts about suicide prevention, and to approach the topic with care. CSF's Shakespeare & Violence Prevention program has been supported by guidance from the Colorado Office of Suicide Prevention, with expertise from Dr. Lena Heilmann, the current director of that office. Some facts about suicide can help spark conversations with your students and help you approach these conversations.

First of all, as discussed in chapter 3, experts agree that talking about suicide with young people does not plant the idea in anyone's mind. If you do encounter a young person whom you suspect may be in suicidal crisis, you may ask directly and calmly if they are having thoughts of suicide. This won't give them the idea; if anything, it will show that person that you are a safe and trusted adult who is willing to have difficult conversations. Experts recommend talking openly about suicide in a calm, regulated way, so young people know you are someone who can handle these conversations (Colorado Department of Public Health and Environment n.d.b). Be mindful of the language you use when discussing the deaths of *Romeo and Juliet*. Phrases like "commit suicide" or "take one's life" stigmatize, criminalize, and assign blame to the person who has died, so experts recommend using the phrase "die by suicide" when speaking about a suicidal death. To describe a "death by suicide" is also to acknowledge that a human life has ended, which is a grievous loss, as is any death, regardless of the cause.

It is important to recognize that death is not the only outcome of suicidal ideation. Stories of survival and resilience in the aftermath of suicidal thoughts or attempts are crucial. While many people struggle with suicidal thoughts, many people can also, with support, move through these challenging experiences, and not only survive but thrive. According to the Suicide Prevention Resource Center, for every one adult death by suicide in the United States, 267 people have had serious thoughts of suicide in the past year (Suicide Prevention Resource Center n.d.). When approaching this play through the violence-prevention lens, I encourage you to explore with your students many of the alternative ways the play could have ended. Death by suicide is never a predetermined outcome, and it is preventable.

There is never one single reason for suicide. Every situation is different and there are often intersecting factors. Feelings of connectedness, a relationship with at least one trusted adult, and a sense of belonging are all protective factors. As you discuss the play, you can examine the various reasons for the outcomes we see in the play: lack of sleep, disconnection, violence in the community, access to drugs, access to weapons, or emotionally unavailable family members, for example. Exploring the myriad reasons for death by suicide in the play can help unpack not only the complexity of Shakespeare's plot, but also the complicated nature of suicide.

In staging the violence and representations of suicide in the play, it is important to emphasize hope, pay attention to the opportunities for this not to have happened, and stage it in a way that does not glorify the deaths or depict them in overtly realistic ways. As you work through the play, I encourage you to find ways for your students to recognize the ways in which everyone is worthy of support within the play, and to become aware of whether the characters receive individualized support. How were Juliet's needs met in the play? How was she supported? How were her needs not met, and how was she unsupported? We can ask the same about everyone in the play in order to explore the climate and characters more fully.

For further resources around suicide prevention, I recommend connecting with your local health department for resources closer to home. Colorado's Office of Suicide Prevention is a valuable resource and partner in handling the topic in CSF's Shakespeare & Violence Prevention program and in training our actors. When touring *Romeo and Juliet* to local schools, we also share information about Colorado Crisis Services, a crisis call and text line that provides immediate support for people in crisis. You may also explore national resources, such as the Suicide Prevention Resource Center. Additionally, the Applied Suicide Intervention Skills Training (ASIST) through Living Works (www.livingworks.net) is one of the leading trainings that equips caregivers with the skills to respond to someone in crisis. As of July 2022, the National Suicide Prevention Hotline in the United States was assigned a three-digit line, 988, and rebranded as the Suicide and Crisis Lifeline. Just as we encourage people in the US to contact 911 for any emergency, we can train young people to contact 988 with any suicidal crisis.

Look at Protective Factors

One protective factor against violence is a feeling of connectedness. Though none of the characters seem to hold a sense of connectedness within the larger Verona community, the two families, perhaps, hold an internal sense of belonging, though it's hard to say whether the family bond comes from a feeling of connectedness as a family or a feeling of antipathy toward their enemies. However, we do see a strong, supportive connection in the burgeoning relationship between Juliet and Romeo. When they meet, they listen deeply to one another, reflect back, through language, what they are hearing, and they collaborate as co-creators, co-equals. Their first conversation forms a complete sonnet, and we get the sense, at least through the language, that this relationship is something rare in Verona. It seems akin to Prospero's description of Miranda and Ferdinand in *The Tempest*, which will be explored in chapter 9: "Fair encounter / Of two most rare affections"

(*The Tempest* III.i.89–90). "Rare," as we will see in *The Tempest*, means more than simply "uncommon," connoting also a sense of sacredness, transcendence, and purity. When it comes to protective factors, sometimes all you need is one prosocial relationship in which you are truly seen, supported, and valued—that rare relationship can make all the difference.

Look at the Climate

A production of *Romeo and Juliet* is an opportunity to put a climate on the stage for all to see, analyze, and understand. Remember the fish tank analogy posed by Dr. Kingston of CSPV? Verona is like a dirty fish tank, in which the water is unclean but the fish are oblivious to the negative effect the water has on them. They don't know any other way of being.

In the community of Verona, violence is the norm. And even though the prince speaks out against it, he himself uses threats of violence to try to calm the violence. We can learn a lot about a community based on the kind of behaviors that occur within it, and the kinds of behaviors that are normalized. In a healthy climate, individuals know that they are valued, they are safe, and they belong. By contrast, Verona depicts a climate in which animosity runs deep and citizens are not safe from danger. In this climate, individuals are not recognized, valued, or truly seen. I get the sense, when reading and watching the play, that the Veronese citizens spend so much time fixating on the feud that they are not awake to and present in their lives. Shakespeare omits the source of the grudge between the Montagues and the Capulets, so we, as readers and as audience members, are left to wonder why these families are at odds in the first place. How far back does this ancient feud go? Did it start with Lords Capulet and Montague? Did it start with their parents? Their grandparents? Is it inherited by each generation, passed along through the bloodlines without giving much thought to the origin, or do the youth get taught about the grudge intentionally by their parents?

The climate of Verona lacks a strong sense of safety: public fighting could break out at any moment, the prince is at a loss for how to handle it, and he threatens death to anyone who engages in violence. The climate of Verona lacks respect; individuals are judged based on their family allegiance, and seen as Capulets or Montagues, rather than as individuals. The climate of Verona lacks emotional support: the young people are not helped in working through their emotions, and the adults are largely absent as the young characters navigate living within a community in conflict. Taking a close look at the climate, and the backdrop against which the action is set, can reveal some of the forces acting on the characters and can help us understand where the eventual violence in the play comes from.

According to the Centers for Disease Control and Prevention, "community violence happens between unrelated individuals, who may or may not know each other, generally outside the home. Examples include assaults or fights among groups and shootings in public places, such as schools and on the streets. Research indicates that youth and young adults (ages 10–34), particularly those in communities of color, are disproportionately impacted" (CDC 2024b). While the violence in the play primarily stems from the feud between the Capulet and the Montague families, it has begun to impact the whole community of Verona. Sick of the fighting, the prince (leader) of Verona threatens death to anyone who reignites the feud.

The prevalence of violence within a community, as we see depicted in *Romeo and Juliet*, has harmful effects beyond those directly impacted by the violence, including physical injuries, depression, anxiety, and chronic diseases (CDC 2024b). When young people are raised in a community in which violence is a regular occurrence, the cumulative effects of this perpetual violence threaten not only a person's physical safety but also one's ability to grow, thrive, and develop a sense of connectedness within their community, resulting in long-term effects on individual well-being and happiness.

Look for Upstanders

Although we see a lack of upstander behavior in the play, there are many opportunities for upstander interventions. We know that trusted adults make a difference in supporting youth safety and preventing violence. The parents of Romeo and Juliet could have been upstanders by paying closer attention to their children, putting aside their fixation on the feud, and checking in with their teens. The two adults in *Romeo and Juliet* who take an interest in helping the young people are unrelated by blood: Juliet's nurse, who has lived with the family since Juliet's infancy, presumably, and Friar Lawrence, a spiritual leader. Both are potential upstanders, though their strategies are not ideal. When the two young lovers seek guidance from these adults, the best solutions they can muster involve secrecy. The nurse helps Juliet meet Romeo for a private wedding, and the friar not only conducts the ceremony but also, to avoid an unwanted marriage to Paris, arranges for Juliet to ingest a potion to fake her own death. If a trusted adult, by today's standards, is someone who is not afraid to take action and speak up on behalf of young people, we do not see the nurse and the friar as trusted adults. Rather, they use secrecy to try to find solutions for the young people that minimize harm, but they don't seem to fully understand what is going on for Romeo and Juliet. When the friar tries to persuade Romeo that banishment is not such a bad thing, and that he will get over Juliet with time, Romeo's response, "thou canst not speak of that thou dost not feel" (*Romeo and Juliet* III.iii.67), reminds us that one of the characteristics of a trusted adult is the ability to see from the perspective of the person they are helping. Rather than minimize the pain of Romeo's devastation, a trusted adult might acknowledge and validate that banishment feels like the end of the world for Romeo and hold space for those feelings while reassuring him that this pain will pass. Had the adults been upstanders, and taken strong, caring stances to protect the children from harm, many of the play's outcomes could have been avoided.

PERFORMING THE PLAY FOR YOUTH AUDIENCES

CSF toured a forty-five-minute abridged production of *Romeo and Juliet* in the 2019–20 school year, directed by Kevin Rich. The touring company was in the midst of this three-actor tour of *Romeo and Juliet* when the COVID-19 pandemic closed all schools. We were initially hesitant to take this play to Colorado schools because it relates to the difficult topic of teen suicide. However, we found that it sparked relevant conversations with middle and high school audiences, and the responses were primarily positive to this forty-five-minute abridged version. If you wish to study *Romeo and Juliet* with your students, I recommend either taking your students to see a full performance (if available to you), using CSF's cutting (available for free download on this book's website), or creating your own cutting of the play, with an eye toward violence-prevention themes. This can be an enriching assignment for your students. Perhaps you challenge them to read the full play and then create a thirty- to forty-five-minute version of the play that focuses on the key themes of community violence, trauma, and stress. Cutting a play is one of the most exciting ways to truly engage with its complexity, as it requires students to think critically about what is most important in the story they are trying to tell and how a cut affects earlier and later events of the play.

When CSF created its abridged version of *Romeo and Juliet* through the lens of a violence-prevention curriculum, we emphasized the violence in the community and the violence that's inherited by the younger generation, as well as the goodness between the two young lovers, and the protective factors that emerged from their prosocial bond. Our abridged version was also invested in exploring the role of the trusted adult, so we paid extra attention to the interactions among Romeo, Juliet, the nurse, and the friar. I recommend, if strapped for time, omitting many of the play's minor characters, and condensing it down (if necessary for a small-size company) to the key characters: Lord Capulet, Nurse, Mercutio, Tybalt, Benvolio, Romeo, Juliet, Friar.

We used the following doubling scheme in our three-actor tour:

Juliet/Tybalt/Benvolio
Nurse/Mercutio/Friar
Romeo/Lord Capulet/Prince

All character transformations were done with a simple costume shift: a varsity jacket for Tybalt, an embroidered scarf for Juliet, a denim jacket for Romeo, an apron for the nurse. Having students watch these transformations onstage is an opportunity to highlight the nature of roleplaying and how changes are always possible. Just as one actor can change from one character to another, so can we change in our own lives.

I recommend staging the violence in a way that does not glorify or depict it realistically, but rather presents it as a heightened, abstract moment. The 2019–20 tour adopted many stylizations to avoid glorifying some of the extreme violence. The fights were staged with both actors directly facing the audience, and we watched them, side-by-side, experiencing the fight from their perspective, without staging any real physical contact. For each death, the actor removed one costume piece in a neutral manner and walked away. In the first death of the play, Mercutio had collapsed into Romeo's arms; at his death, he calmly stood up, removed his vest and put it on the floor, then left the stage. At Tybalt's death, the actor turned with their back to the audience, dropped the varsity jacket to the floor, and the actor walked offstage. In the tomb scene, Juliet pulled the dagger to her stomach, then the actor dropped the character entirely, stood, removed Juliet's scarf, and laid it down on the stage. We opted for neutral, simple, staging, rather than digging too deeply into depicting heightened emotions or overly realistic deaths.

In a more recent production of *Romeo and Juliet*, director Heidi Schmidt incorporated a device in which audience members were encouraged to raise their hands when they observed a "red flag" or a warning sign that someone in the play was struggling. This became an opportunity for the audience to participate in the performance and keep track of the opportunities for intervention.

The accompanying study guide (shared with teachers prior to the performance) included the following content warning, based on guidance from our partners at the Office of Suicide Prevention:

> *Romeo and Juliet* is a play about a community troubled with violence, and the storyline involves the deaths of young people (by homicide and suicide). This content may be triggering to some members of your school community. We encourage you to have conversations with your students prior to the performance, particularly the students who may have been personally impacted by a traumatic experience. Please work with your students to make the most appropriate decisions for them regarding the in-school performance and post-show workshops. If you are concerned about a student, please use the resources listed below.

We then added local and national resources around suicide prevention, which will vary by area. I recommend including some kind of content warning, along with local resources for your students, if you decide to approach this play with your students.

Look in the Mirror: Upstander Roleplay Exercise

Romeo and Juliet contains many inflection points in which characters face a choice to either continue the cycle of violence or take action to prevent harm. In selecting a fictional moment to roleplay with your students, I recommend identifying a scene that is upstream of the major harm in the play. In CSF's touring Shakespeare & Violence Prevention program, teaching artists roleplayed the fight between Mercutio and Tybalt in post-show workshops, a scene that happens just upstream of the first death of the play and gives students the chance to think about how they might intervene in an escalated situation.

You might also choose another moment prior to the first death: some good options are act 1 scene 1, the street fight between servants that quickly escalates to the involvement of the authorities; or act 1 scene 5, in which Capulet and Tybalt discuss Romeo's presence at the party. You may also want to write a scene that occurs before Shakespeare's play begins as a way of moving further upstream of the violence. Maybe we see a scene between Lord Capulet as a young child and his own father, in which he teaches his son to hate Montagues. The key in identifying a moment to roleplay is to find a scene in which a conflict is underway, and where harm will be caused by this encounter. With every upstander roleplay, your students are invited to step in as themselves to try to steer the outcome in a different direction. It's important to emphasize that although Shakespeare's narrative may result in violence, your students have the opportunity to alter the narrative. As we pair Shakespeare with a violence-prevention curriculum, we should be encouraging our students to repeatedly discover that things do not have to be the way they appear in the play. This refrain of "things don't have to be this way" could be a guiding mantra as we work to unpack the violence in Shakespeare. What we see in the play is not inevitable but preventable, just like the violence and harm we see in our world.

Act 3 scene 1 falls at the dead center of *Romeo and Juliet*, and it is here that the play shifts from comedy to tragedy when a street fight breaks out between Tybalt and Mercutio. A lot happens in this scene, and by its end the play's action is moving in a decidedly different direction. It can be helpful to approach this scene by thinking about what each character believes to be true at the time. Romeo has just married Juliet, so he believes he is behaving honorably by refusing to fight Tybalt (now his kinsman). Tybalt believes that Romeo is a Montague, and therefore an enemy to his family; Romeo has crashed his family party, and Tybalt believes he must get payback for Romeo overstepping his bounds. Mercutio believes that Romeo is dishonoring his loyalty to the Montagues by refusing to fight Tybalt— Mercutio is unaware that his friend is now tied to the Capulets by marriage. Romeo is the only one in the scene who is aware of his marriage to Juliet, and the lack of shared information coupled with the family's feud results in two deaths by the end of the scene, and more deaths by the play's end.

Violence is met with violence, rage is met with rage, and what starts as a hot day in Verona ends with two dead bodies (Tybalt's and Mercutio's) and one banishment (Romeo's). Tybalt is itching for a fight, and while Romeo tries to walk away, his friend Mercutio (cousin to the prince) steps into the fight on his behalf. Mercutio, neither a Montague nor a Capulet, is dead, and Tybalt has blood on his hands. Romeo can't walk away from this: his friend has been murdered. So he murders Tybalt. The violence escalates, and we seem to have passed the point of no return.

A great deal of the scene's violence stems from a lack of knowledge, truth, or openness. What would be different if these characters had made a different choice, or if everyone had a clearer understanding of the given circumstances? This moment has later ripple effects. If we could prevent the violence upstream, how would it change the death count and the outcome of the play? Often, talking things out leads to more peaceful solutions. In this situation, we have secrecy, a misunderstanding, and an inherited grudge. How are the characters acting in the present moment and how are they acting based on inherited knowledge? How can the citizens of Verona learn to see others as fully human, not as the enemies their parents made them out to be? How can we all learn to breathe before responding and pause before taking action? How can we learn healthier coping skills?

I recommend roleplaying this scene with your students, inviting them to step into the action as themselves, and to imagine this situation (perhaps a toned-down version that does not involve a secret marriage) occurring at their school. You will find the lesson plan for *Romeo and Juliet* in appendix C, along with some discussion questions and activities to support your exploration of the play with your students. As with all upstander roleplay exercises, encourage your students to practice their strategies as themselves. Remind them that there are many ways of participating. Even if they aren't joining you onstage for a roleplay, they can still participate by imagining their own strategies, and they can support their peers by watching and listening.

In our in-person tour of this production, students often responded with the following strategies:

- Pull Tybalt aside and secretly reveal the truth (that Romeo married Juliet).
- Talk to all three of them calmly to remind them of the prince's edict against fighting and to talk through the consequences of their actions.
- Give Romeo some backup to stop the fight.
- Pull Mercutio out of the situation and give him the full story (that Romeo married Juliet) and get Mercutio's help to end the fight.
- Contact the authorities.
- Distract Tybalt and Mercutio (with free popcorn, adorable puppies, kittens, etc.).

The upstander roleplay is central to the Shakespeare & Violence Prevention program we have developed at CSF, but this is only one way into the play. I encourage you to try out multiple activities, if time allows, to offer your students a range of violence-prevention approaches. See appendix C for other ideas, and, as always, make adjustments based on your student population.

Remember that no solution will stop all the violence forever and always, and that no solution is perfect. Freed of the weight of coming up with the ideal solution, encourage your students to consider what feels right for them in the moment, and recognize that one student's strategy won't necessarily feel right for another student. Practicing the solution is what matters. Try it out in your body to get a sense of how it feels to speak up, take action. When we can practice our strategies in the safety of our classroom, we may feel more prepared to take action in real life.

TAKEAWAYS FROM *ROMEO AND JULIET*

Although it's been handed down to us as a tragic love story, *Romeo and Juliet* offers young audiences the chance to grapple with challenging material about the collective impact of violence. When children are raised in a world in which violence is normalized and trusted adults don't know any better than to pass along the violence and pain of their own childhoods, communities get caught in a cycle. In *Romeo and Juliet,* things end badly for the young people and for the older generation, and although the feud has come to an end, the play concludes with deep and permanent loss. The play reminds us that "violent delights have violent ends" (*Romeo and Juliet* II.vi.9) and that we should move "wisely and slow; they stumble that run fast" (*Romeo and Juliet* II.iii.101). The play serves as a reminder to slow down, listen to the people around you, and take a moment before responding. Nothing was inevitable in the play, and much could have been prevented. It's important to emphasize that although the adults do not behave in consistently trustworthy ways in this play, in our world, there are trusted adults you can go to if you need help. When this play is approached through the lens of violence prevention, I recommend emphasizing hope, resilience, and the importance of nurturing young people, while returning to the message that we can change systems and climates in order to build a healthier future. This kind of prevention work takes time, and the hope is not only that we can build communities in which young people don't have to die violent deaths but also that we can strategize ways to build communities and climates in which people are seen, are valued, and are given opportunities to shine.

Interlude
The Comedies and Violence Prevention

In many of Shakespeare's comedies, the moments of violence and mistreatment are subtle, and while the action occasionally teeters into tragic territory, the scales tip back toward a resolution (at least, for most characters) by the play's end. While the examples in the following chapters may not feel like violence, the behaviors depicted in the comedies, including bullying, physical mistreatment, and hurtful language, can lay the foundation for an unhealthy climate. In the comedies, there is usually a partial resolution, but often someone is left out, someone doesn't have a happy ending, someone is hurt. Don John from *Much Ado About Nothing* will most likely be punished by his brother. Malvolio in *Twelfth Night* has revenge on the mind. Kate and Petruchio in *The Taming of the Shrew* may have some relationship work ahead of them. Caliban, though left on the island, may not be set up to thrive after Prospero departs. The world is always imbalanced, and hurt and harm will always happen. In the comedies we see examples of how the foundation of violence is established, yet if stopped early enough, the harm can be prevented. And, as we see in *The Tempest*, even if you are on the final day of executing your magical plan to get even with your enemies, it's never too late to make a different choice. If harm is left to fester, we end up with aggravated people who hold on to their pain. We see those people in the tragedies. They turn to larger, more overt acts of violence, which we saw in chapters 2–4.

Shakespeare's comedies provide a groundwork to grapple with some typical human behavior that often leads to violence. It might start as a simple prank, an act of deserved retaliation, or a harmless rumor. But a play provides us with a space to watch the consequences play out, and the ripples cascade through a community. Whether it's a yellow-stocking prank, a magical storm, or a plan to control a partner, these plays all demonstrate flawed, hurt humans trying to hurt other flawed, hurt humans. We see bad behavior, but it is fully human behavior. A comedy frames it perhaps in a lighthearted way, so we almost don't notice the lingering effects of hurting people by the end of the comedy. But there is Malvolio, left to plot his revenge; there is Sir Andrew, left humiliated by Sir Toby, the person he thought was a friend. There is Antonio, the brother of Prospero, who ends the play in silence. There is always pain in this world, and there are always people who don't get their peace at the end of the play. *Twelfth Night* ends with a song, "The rain it raineth every day" (*Twelfth Night*, V.i.415), the refrain of which suggests there are ups and downs in the play as well as in life. Not everyone gets a happy ending. But the comedies give us a fictional place to dissect human behavior and find some partial resolution before we return to our own lives.

In CSF's Shakespeare & Violence Prevention tour, the comedies are typically performed for grades 3–5, because these adaptations often highlight the types of mistreatment happening in elementary schools: physical mistreatment, bullying, and unkind words. The first comedy we'll explore in the next section, *Much Ado About Nothing*, is a play that works well for middle and high school students. The remaining chapters (6–9) work well with all ages, though the bulk of the lesson plan suggestions are geared toward elementary students. As always, please adjust these activities to best suit your students.

5
Much Ado About Nothing
"The Merry War": Rumors, Gossip, and School Climate

Much Ado About Nothing is a complicated comedy that threatens to tip into tragedy territory. The play centers on two contrasting romantic couples: the younger, less experienced Hero and Claudio, and the older, more seasoned (and perhaps more cynical) Beatrice and Benedick. These couples are immersed in a community that trades in words. Whether it's a well-intentioned bit of gossip or a harmful rumor, the characters inhabit a world in which words can wound, language can be destructive, and what gets said behind the backs of others wields great power in the events of the play. It's a play about the power and weight of words, inviting us to consider some important questions: What information do we believe? What stories do we choose to circulate? How do we stop a rumor once it's started? What is the difference between a merry war and a real war? When does friendly gossip go too far? How do words build this world? These questions have a direct impact on a community's climate, and exploring these questions through *Much Ado About Nothing* can provide middle and high school students with the opportunity to explore the nature of their own community's climate.

PLOT SYNOPSIS

The lively and imaginative Beatrice and her younger cousin, Hero, encounter Benedick and his comrade Claudio, both soldiers newly returned to Messina from the war. While Claudio is instantly smitten with Hero, Beatrice and Benedick, who are known frenemies, continue their merry war of witty but wounding banter.

After an initial misunderstanding that nearly derails their blossoming relationship, Claudio and Hero announce their engagement. To pass the time until the wedding, the young lovers (aided by some other acquaintances) decide to play matchmaker with Beatrice and Benedick. They gossip about the pair's mutual affection within earshot of Beatrice and Benedick, and the rumor mill is set in motion. As a result of these rumors, Beatrice believes Benedick loves her, and Benedick believes Beatrice loves him.

The disgruntled Don John attempts to destroy Claudio's happily-ever-after by spreading a false rumor that Hero is unfaithful to Claudio. When Claudio is presented with "proof" of this, courtesy of Don John, he abandons Hero at the altar, leaving her publicly disgraced and humiliated.

After the interrupted wedding, a friar (isn't Shakespeare's canon full of them?) concocts a plan to save Hero's reputation; yet another rumor is circulated, this time with news of Hero's death. After Beatrice and Benedick finally confess their mutual affection for one another, Beatrice asks Benedick to kill Claudio for ruining Hero's reputation.

Meanwhile, a well-meaning but tongue-tied constable, Dogberry, and his colleagues in law enforcement uncover Don John's plot before Benedick carries out his promise to Beatrice. The discovery of Don John's treachery makes Claudio regret his rash actions, and he publicly acknowledges his wrongful treatment of Hero. Hero emerges and reveals, via a staged wedding, that the rumor of her death was untrue. Claudio begs forgiveness, and the play concludes with the promised weddings of Claudio and Hero and Beatrice and Benedick. The ending is happy for everyone but Don John, who must face the consequences of his actions.

VIOLENCE PREVENTION CONNECTIONS TO *MUCH ADO ABOUT NOTHING*

In applying the violence-prevention lens to this play, we are interested in exploring the moments upstream of the violence or mistreatment; the risk and protective factors at play; the climate of the play, the upstander strategies or lack thereof, as well as what our own upstander strategy would be in a similar situation. There are some specific themes from violence-prevention research that may naturally arise from conversations about the play, including the importance of a healthy social climate, the harmful impact of gossip and rumors, the role of trusted adults, and the need for multitiered systems of support in which all members of a community get the resources they need.

Look Upstream: Root Causes

Although the play is a comedy, it nevertheless depicts some harm caused by rumors, gossip, and misinformation; although no one dies in the play, many characters suffer: Hero is slandered, Claudio believes he has caused Hero's death, Benedick is forced to choose between his love and his friend, and Beatrice witnesses the public shaming of her innocent cousin. If we explore some of the events upstream of those in the play, we might find some of the root causes of the suffering and harm.

First of all, the war that has ended prior to the play's first scene has presumably influenced many of the characters, especially Benedick, Claudio, Don John, and Don Pedro, who are all returning from the battlefield. Although there are no battle scenes in the play, and the main plot has little to do with war, the backdrop of war has an impact on the outcome of the play. You may explore with your students how the play might change if Benedick and friends were not returning from a war but instead from a beach vacation, a golf trip, or a camping trip. How might shifting the war setting impact the outcomes?

Additionally, the text suggests a history between Beatrice and Benedick that took place well before the play began, which may be influencing their present behavior. One of the great challenges actors get to explore is the opportunity to dig into a character's backstory, think about what past experiences have shaped the character, and uncover some of the root causes of why they act the way they act. You can explore these same questions with your students as you invite them to look upstream: What happened the day before the play begins? What happened a year before the play begins? How might these events shape the action of the play?

Encourage your students to examine other root causes at work in the play. Is Messina a community of extreme poverty or excessive wealth? Are there structural inequalities in the play that impact how characters are treated? Having a conversation about what is underneath the words, actions, and behaviors depicted in the play can lead to a more nuanced understanding of what is going on in Messina.

Look at Risk Factors: Multitiered Systems of Support

We see some risk factors on display in *Much Ado About Nothing*, especially with Don John. In the play, Don John causes a great deal of harm, and it's easy to write off that character as a villain. Don John's behavior comes from somewhere. What has happened to him in the past that is impacting his current behavior? How is he treated by others in Messina? How might the conditions of Messina be changed so Don John can fully thrive? When we recognize that Don John also needs support, and we can treat him with humanity and empathy, we can more thoroughly and carefully address the root causes of the violence.

In order to address risk factors and build positive climates, schools need multitiered systems of support and must recognize that targets are not the only ones who need support. This is partially because we know that roles can shift and that a target is not a fixed, stable identity, but also this acknowledges that a perpetrator of violence, or someone behaving as a bully, is displaying this behavior because of something happening beneath the surface. If we can scratch the surface of bullying behavior, it often reveals a world of hurt, another human in pain.

Studies continue to reveal that when carrying out attacks, plotters usually leak their plans to others (usually peers) and send signals that they are in trouble. Don John shares his plan with his comrades prior to setting up Hero to appear unfaithful. There are red flags, and we, members of a community, are in the metaphorical trenches, and need to start paying attention. In a school where bullying is an issue, students know about it. When a violent incident occurs, students are usually aware. If a child has become withdrawn and depressed, students can usually sense this. If we teach kids to take responsibility for their environment and to speak up when they witness violence or when something doesn't seem right, we could make our schools safer places to learn and thrive.

Look at the Climate

As discussed in the introduction, building a positive school climate is an important part of a comprehensive approach to violence prevention. *Much Ado About Nothing* offers a way to explore a climate that is shaped by harmful words. As you discuss the play with your students, encourage them to think about how they would describe the climate of Messina. Is this a world in which characters are seen, valued, and have a sense of belonging? Whose needs are being met in the climate? Whose needs are overlooked? Which characters are thriving, and which characters are struggling? What changes might bring about a healthier climate in Messina?

Gossip and rumors are pervasive in Messina. This play speaks to the power of language, and the harm that language can cause. Some of us may have grown up with the ill-informed adage, "Sticks and stones may break your bones, but words can never hurt you." However, we know that words can hurt, words can harm, and words can cause real damage. Gossip, rumors, and damaging words are everywhere in this play—sometimes the words appear as light, well-intentioned teasing, but at what point does the merry war turn hostile? In fact, the play opens with characters talking about people who are not present, as the messenger shares updates about Don Pedro, Claudio, and Benedick. Beatrice, who is known for her verbal sparring with Benedick, takes the opportunity to rattle off a long list of insults about Benedick in his absence, including the zinger: "In our last conflict, four of his five wits went halting off, and now is the whole man governed with one" (*Much Ado About Nothing* I.i.63–65).

This merry war between Beatrice and Benedick is common knowledge; when Benedick enters, the barbs continue to fly, this time out in the open, toward each other's faces. Later, Beatrice insults Benedick behind his back (but actually to his face, thanks to a masked ball). The gossip about other people, whether in person or in absence, is perpetual. Beatrice shares her opinions of Don John behind his back: "How tartly that gentleman looks! I never can see him but I am heartburned an hour after" (*Much Ado About Nothing* II.i.3–4). Then, with the intention of getting Beatrice and Benedick to confess their mutual affection, their friends intentionally spread rumors that they love each other, with the goal of Beatrice and Benedick overhearing. Later, for ill purposes, Don John and his henchmen spread rumors that Don Pedro is wooing for himself, with the hopes of damaging Claudio's relationship with Hero. Throughout the play, whether malicious or playful, the norm is established that gossip is everywhere.

A play is an opportunity to see a community's climate in action, and each interaction between characters can teach us about the norms of this climate, the accepted conventions of this climate, and who is excluded and included within this community. In *Much Ado About Nothing*'s Messina, we are dropped into a world in which people talk about one another when the subject of conversation isn't present. A lot is said behind closed doors. This pattern appears not just in the play's opening, but throughout, as we witness the gulling of Benedick and Beatrice. Some of it works out well, in the example of Beatrice and Benedick. Their friends spread rumors intentionally for them to overhear, in which they learn the other really loves them. In this case, the intentions of the friends are probably good, and it works out, because Beatrice and Benedick do love each other. But is the rumor-spreading necessary, helpful, and kind?

In contrast to the gossip, which is whispered privately throughout the play, some of the gossip makes its way into the public sphere. Hero's public humiliation at her wedding is a private story shared publicly. Something that should have been a private conversation between Claudio and Hero becomes the most public event in the play. These scenarios provide contemporary audiences with the opportunity to explore the role of gossip and rumors in a community.

According to the Cyberbullying Research Center, run by Dr. Sameer Hinduja and Dr. Justin Patchin, approximately one in four teens has experienced cyberbullying at some point in their life, and one in six teens has cyberbullied others. Additionally, around 60 percent of teens who experience cyberbullying report that it impacted their ability to feel safe at school (Cyberbullying Research Center n.d.a). Online mistreatment can occur at any time of day, and cyberbullying is especially pervasive. Much in the same way that Don John's rumor about Hero is easily spread, believed, and acted upon, so online rumors can circulate and turn viral in minutes. Don John's rumor about Hero is a significant area of concern, and certainly the most extreme rumor in the play, but if we consider the overall climate of Messina, we see that rumors and gossip are pervasive. As a climate, Messina is filled with words, some hurtful, some playful, and some untrue.

Look for Upstanders: Trusted Adults

Where in Messina do we see upstander behavior? One of the key components of a safe climate for young people involves the role of trusted adults; having at least one person to confide in, whether an adult or a peer, is a protective factor. The adult figures in the play do not necessarily model ideal trusted adults. Beatrice and Benedick are established as older, perhaps more jaded if not wiser, than Claudio and Hero, but they are struggling too much with their own relationship insecurities to give much advice to the young couple. Hero's father, Leonato, is quick to renounce her when Claudio publicly shames her, and his temper flares; as Leonato calls for Hero's death, he does not believe his daughter, and instead we find an adult more concerned with his own reputation than his child's well-being.

In the midst of the anger and chaos after the disrupted wedding, we have one voice of calm in the storm: the friar steps into the role of trusted adult and takes action as an upstander. "Pause awhile," says the friar. I imagine he is rapidly concocting a plan, trying to keep everyone alive, while preventing further damage. He advises Hero and her family to pretend that she is dead. It's a questionable solution, which involves more deception and emotional manipulation, but the friar is nevertheless reaching out with the best comfort he can muster in Hero's time of need. His reason is:

> For it so falls out
> That what we have we prize not to the worth
> Whiles we enjoy it, but being lacked and lost,
> Why then we rack the value, then we find
> The virtue that possession would not show us
> Whiles it was ours.
> (*Much Ado About Nothing* IV.i.228–33)

In other words, he argues, we do not appreciate what we have until we have lost it. To be familiar with loss is to gain some clarity and perspective. When we lose, we understand the thing that is lost more clearly. This resonates on many levels, particularly in the aftermath of a global pandemic. The friar hopes that hearing of Hero's death will "change slander to remorse," which, while it doesn't address all the problems, is at least "some good" (*Much Ado About Nothing*, IV.i.222). In the tradition of meddlesome friars of Shakespeare's canon, as we saw with *Romeo and Juliet*, the friar is trying to help a young person in trouble and is doing the best he can in challenging circumstances. It's not a perfect plan, but it is *some* good. Upstander solutions are rarely perfect but can often make a difference in the moment.

The play presents opportunities to talk with students about how trusted adults can support them in navigating the complexities of violence prevention or how peers can be upstanders for one another. In addition to playing a key role in preventing youth violence, research demonstrates that having a trusted adult to speak to when young people have suicidal thoughts is a protective factor against suicide. It is important to emphasize that Shakespeare's plays often show us a world gone wrong—a world in which trusted adults offer up poor solutions or are altogether absent. After viewing the play, invite students to imagine what the play would be like if one adult got Hero the help she needed.

The most active upstander in the play is the malapropistic Dogberry and his team of night watchmen. Dogberry actually does report on known harm, but he is dismissed by a busy Leonato. Even when reports are made, the people speaking up are not always believed or taken seriously. It's important to emphasize to young people that if they are aware of something that feels wrong, or they get a gut feeling that something is not okay, they have permission to speak up and to keep speaking up if things don't change. Imagine how the play could have ended if Messina had more people behaving as upstanders?

PERFORMING THE PLAY FOR YOUTH AUDIENCES

If you choose to stage this play with (or for) middle and high school audiences, and in alignment with a violence-prevention curriculum, I recommend recognizing the role of Don John as a character in need of support and focusing the production on Hero's mistreatment and the impact of rumors. CSF has staged the play as part of the violence-prevention series twice, and both productions were directed by Timothy Orr. The first production was in 2014 for a four-actor company, which would perform for audiences ranging from third to twelfth grade (ages 8–18). In our initial meetings with the CSPV staff, we debated how to address the plot point of Hero's death in our abridged play. In Shakespeare's play, Hero pretends to be dead. The CSPV wondered about the correlation between depicting rumored deaths in a play and actual suicide attempts in youth and teens. Because evidence at the time was inconclusive about establishing a connection between these things, our team opted to omit Hero's fake death. Instead, in our version she went into hiding for a while. Conveniently, the "she is dead" lines could be easily changed to "she is fled." While I am usually resistant to changing plot points in Shakespeare's plays, I could see the merit in this shift, considering that our audience would include third graders. The character of Hero still undergoes a kind of loss, but we don't offer faking death as a possible way of dealing with being the victim of a rumor.

Since that time, however, research has grown, and it is now believed that speaking about suicide to young people does not plant the idea in their mind. So when we adapted the play for sixth through twelfth graders in 2020, Hero agrees to the friar's plan to spread rumors of her death. We integrated a content warning after consultation with a suicide-prevention expert, which can be found in appendix D. If you plan to incorporate any aspect of a play that addresses suicide (or in this case is even tangentially linked to suicide through means of a death rumor), I recommend including a clear content warning for your audiences, and connecting with local resources in your area to share at your performances.

To cut this complicated comedy down to an abridged version, we eliminated Leonato entirely and reassigned his lines to Beatrice. She acts as the spokesperson for Hero, "gives her away" at the wedding, and facilitates the second marriage of the play, thus establishing Beatrice as a community leader. We cut Dogberry's team of night watchmen but left him Verges. Margaret and Ursula were combined into one character. Don Pedro, the older brother to Don John, was cut entirely. Beatrice inherits some of Don Pedro's lines, giving her more authority in the world of the play. This kind of paring down allows us to see the characters in terms of the violence-prevention roles they play (Dogberry as an upstander, Don John as a perpetrator, Hero as a target, Beatrice as a trusted adult, for example).

We stripped the villain, Don John, of his comrades, so most of his scenes become soliloquies in which he confides in the audience. This shift is especially relevant, as our culture has moved into a media-driven world of online interactions, and perpetrators are often found to be socially isolated and lacking connectedness in their social relationships. The Shakespearean soliloquy, it seems to me, has parallels to the social media status update, the Instagram story or reel, or the timeline update. It's a public pronouncement of one's inner state, simultaneously internal and external. It's a private thought shared in public. Don John's speeches are delivered directly to the audience, and they become his confidantes, his witnesses, perhaps even his cheerleaders. In this play, in which the characters delight in gossip, rumor-spreading, and secrets, the pleasure of "unpacking one's heart" in public is palpable. In rehearsals with the actors, we continually emphasized the importance of enjoying the act of speaking; Beatrice and Benedick spar with one another in public, and their verbal battle of wits is called a "merry war." Their public one-upping should be fun to watch. Hero and Claudio help spread rumors about Beatrice and Benedick to convince them to fall in love. The scenes in which the unsuspecting Beatrice and Benedick eavesdrop should likewise be delightful for the audience. The characters enjoy gossiping about one another, and we enjoy watching them gossip—especially when they fill us in on their secret plans. We, as an audience, are in on it, and included in the pleasure of rumors. It's important that the audience gets caught up in the fun of gossiping, because when Hero is publicly slandered, the audience experiences a shift in tone. The world of the play, or the climate, transforms from a light and harmless one to a serious and dangerous environment. The "merry war" turns real when Claudio shames Hero, and no one but the friar steps in.

As this is a project meant to spark dialogue about violence, we paid special attention to the moments of physical violence in the play and used them sparingly for maximum effect. The first moment occurs after Benedick has sworn to fight (and possibly kill) Claudio. Benedick challenges him, and Claudio thinks his friend is joking. In the 2014 tour, to prove his point our Benedick slapped Claudio hard across the face (as a stage slap, of course, in which no actors are harmed). In performance, this often elicited a gasp from the audience (or, in some cases, hisses, boos, or cheers). In a play dominated by language, the single slap stands alone, marked as a visceral moment of violence, and highlighting, for the audience, how the climate has undergone a shift.

In the 2014 production, to balance out the single slap, a single kiss concluded the play as Benedick tells Beatrice he will stop her mouth. A real, onstage kiss for a young audience is a risky thing—the students squeal, groan, gasp, scream, close their eyes . . . our stage manager compared it at one school to the equivalent of a reaction to the moon landing. This moment is powerful in performance because of the horrified, heightened reaction of the students to the kiss. It also gives Benedick justification for his line, "A college of wit-crackers cannot flout me out of my humor" (*Much Ado About Nothing* V.iv.104–5). In that production, our Benedick delivered that line directly to the laughing children—literally, the wit-crackers who are chuckling, guffawing, or shrieking at the kiss. It is a perfect example of how to deal with taunts. Benedick stood there and didn't let it bother him but let it roll right off him.

At the end of the play, the possibility of a new threat emerges. It seems, at first, that all will be well. Don John's villainy has been discovered, Hero's reputation has been repaired, the couples have reunited, and Beatrice and Benedick have finally revealed their love for each other, this time in public. The couples agree to head off to celebrate their newfound love, when a messenger reports that Don John, the outcast who spread the rumors about Hero, has been captured and is on his way back to Messina. In Shakespeare's original, Benedick responds, "Think not on him till tomorrow; I'll devise thee brave punishments for him" (*Much Ado About Nothing* V.iv.131–2).

We thought about the tone of the play's ending. What does it mean to end the play with Benedick's promise of future punishment? What will happen to Don John when Benedick punishes him? Will it lead to future violence? In the hopes of achieving a more ambiguous ending, we eliminated Benedick's plan to punish Don John. Instead, in that moment, Benedick looked offstage at the merriment, where Claudio and Hero had just exited. He is aware that they are waiting for Beatrice and him to join in on the festivities. He looked back at Beatrice, took a deep breath, clicked her iPhone off, and told her: "Think not on him till tomorrow. Strike up, pipers!" In this moment, Benedick seemed to say, "You know what? There's nothing we can do right now, so let's celebrate happiness when we can." There will always be violence in our world. There might always be rumors, cruelty, bullying, suicide, and shootings. The iceberg of violence isn't going anywhere soon. And yet, if we make the conscious choice to take action, either by offering up a plan to help, as the friar does, or by doing our part to keep those around us calm and present, as Benedick does, we can slowly start to change the climate.

Look in the Mirror: Upstander Roleplay Exercise

In *Much Ado About Nothing*, a powerful moment to roleplay (which is upstream of most of the play's mistreatment and harm) is act 3 scene 2, a scene between Don John and Claudio, shortly after Claudio has become engaged to Hero. Don John approaches Claudio and asks if he plans to marry Hero, then he plants a seed of doubt. He doesn't explicitly say Claudio should not marry Hero. He says he's heard things, and Claudio should see for himself. Don John manipulates Claudio's experience to frame Hero as unfaithful. In this world, when things are spoken, they are often interpreted as fact. "Sir, they are spoken, and these things are true," Don John insists to an incredulous crowd at the wedding (*Much Ado About Nothing* IV.i.70). The very act of speaking a thing is conflated, in this play, with truthfulness—sometimes this has dangerous consequences. This resonates today, when lies and misinformation can spread rapidly without fact-checking, and the truth of a statement seems to matter less than the fact that it is stated.

Let's consider Claudio's state of mind in this scene: he is newly engaged, he recently believed that Don Pedro was wooing for himself, and so the uncertainty of his relationship to Hero is already established as fragile, thanks to Don John's meddling. The prince's brother approaches him and warns him that Hero is unfaithful. What should he do? And Don John seems to have proof. What would you do?

In this moment of choice, this becomes a moment upstream of the worst of the play's mistreatments. What would happen if Claudio responded in a different way to Don John's initial rumor? What if instead of going to watch at Hero's window he communicated with his fiancée? Easier said than done, but a moment, a deep breath, might have turned this in a different direction. As you roleplay this moment with your students, invite them to step in as themselves to try out their own upstander strategies. Perhaps they choose to pull Claudio aside and encourage him to talk to Hero. Perhaps they speak directly to Don John to get more information about his motivation. Perhaps they go to a trusted adult to get advice. There is no correct solution, and no solution that will prevent all mistreatment and harm, but giving your students the chance to practice their own strategies can help prepare them for the moments they will face in real life, when they witness rumors spread about their peers.

This is an opportunity to discuss digital citizenship with your students as well. Imagine that Don John's rumors were not only circulated by word of mouth but also online. What do we do when we see unkind stories shared about our peers online? How can we be upstanders in those situations?

In appendix D, you will find CSF's lesson plan for an upstander roleplay workshop focused on *Much Ado About Nothing*, along with discussion questions and additional activities.

TAKEAWAYS ABOUT *MUCH ADO ABOUT NOTHING*

In *Much Ado About Nothing*, all it took was one person, one time, to say, "pause awhile" and to offer up a well-intentioned plan. This indicated to Hero that a trusted adult was watching out for her and that she was not alone. Research shows that 57 percent of the time when someone speaks up, bullying stops in ten seconds or less (Hawkins et al. 2001). This statistic is staggering, and I encourage you to emphasize that point with your students. That means that when you see bullying, (which includes cyberbullying) usually just saying one thing will put an end to it. Sometimes all it takes is one person, and one person can change a climate.

As we continue to adapt Shakespeare's plays for this project, I find more and more that we aren't really changing Shakespeare at all. We are just viewing the plays with fresh eyes, from our own time and place. At one point in the play, Benedick asks, "May I be so converted and see with these eyes? I cannot tell" (*Much Ado About Nothing* II.iii.22–23). Can we become what we claim we aren't? Is a transformation possible? It is easy to get stuck in a particular way of seeing. If we live in a climate where rumors, misinformation, and mistreatment are everyday occurrences, we stop seeing these acts as problematic. Once we start to reenvision a new way of being, and seeing with new eyes, a way out becomes possible . . . with or without a helpful friar.

6
Twelfth Night
Bullying and Cyberbullying

Twelfth Night, or *What You Will*, is, at first glance, a play about a resilient young woman, shipwrecked off the coast of a foreign country, who disguises herself as a boy, falls for her boss, and gets caught up in a messy love triangle. The play seems, on its surface and according to most synopses, to be about love, disguise, and desire. Its alternate title, *What You Will*, underscores the play's exploration of will, desire, and wanting. Shakespeare's plays, however, are never just about one thing. Jonathan Bate refers to Shakespeare's "myriad-mindedness," or the ability to mean many things at once (Bate 1998, 338). When considering this play through a violence-prevention lens, we might turn our attention to *Twelfth Night*'s subplot in which a silly prank gets out of hand, offering a dramatic representation of bullying, cyberbullying, and the patterns of mistreatment.

   Twelfth Night can be a powerful entry point for educators interested in aligning a study of Shakespeare with a violence-prevention curriculum; the subplot provides students, especially upper elementary students, with a story about how bullying begins, how it develops over time, and its lasting impact. The play also invites students to explore not just the moments within the play but also the ripple effects after the story ends, allowing students to grapple with violence and mistreatment in a wider context beyond the play's linear timeline. My hope in this chapter is to guide you through the play using the violence-prevention lens in order to open up the possibilities within your classroom as you approach this play.

As discussed in the introduction, the violence-prevention lens is a way to approach Shakespeare with a particular awareness of: the moments upstream of the violence or mistreatment; the risk and protective factors that impact the likelihood of violence; the climate in which the violence occurred and in which we recognize the behaviors, actions, and practices in the climate that may have contributed to the violence; and the upstander strategies or lack thereof, including the reporting tools available to upstanders. A violence-prevention lens also invites us to look at what our own upstander strategy would be in a similar situation, which requires empathy and connectedness as we bridge the gap between Shakespeare's play and our own world. An increased awareness of violence-prevention research can impact the way we watch, engage with, and connect to Shakespeare's plays.

There is always more to unpack with Shakespeare, and I trust that you will develop ideas that aren't included here. I hope that this chapter will help kick-start or continue your own work with the play through the lens of violence prevention.[1] My hope is that this gives you a framework to do some more text detective work with your students.

Please don't worry about how to pronounce the characters' names and the locations. I have footnoted the most common pronunciations in this chapter because *Twelfth Night* has some tricky names, but it's more important that your students feel comfortable pronouncing the names than you follow what some Shakespeare "expert" says. Feel free to use these recommended pronunciations if it helps you feel more comfortable in the classroom; but if your students prefer an alternate pronunciation, who am I (or you) to stop them?

PLOT SYNOPSIS

After a catastrophic shipwreck, the young, resourceful Viola[2] washes ashore in Illyria and concocts a survival plan. Believing that her twin

---

1 For example, this chapter does not address the compelling character of Antonio, because in the Colorado Shakespeare Festival's abridged touring productions, we often cut that subplot for the sake of run-time, but there is rich material to explore regarding the challenges of LGBTQ+ people in navigating issues like bullying, mistreatment, and ostracism in school.
2 VIE-uh-luh (emphasis on first syllable).

brother drowned in the wreck, she dons male attire, renames herself Cesario,[3] and finds employment with Orsino,[4] the duke of Illyria.

Orsino is currently infatuated with the countess Olivia, who, grieving the recent deaths of her brother and father, refuses Orsino's advances. Orsino sends "Cesario" (Viola in disguise) to woo Olivia on his behalf. Olivia falls in love with the messenger instead, and Viola, who secretly adores Orsino, finds herself in an inconvenient love triangle.

Meanwhile, Olivia's drunken uncle, Sir Toby Belch, encourages the wealthy but dim-witted Sir Andrew to woo Olivia. When Olivia's rule-abiding butler, Malvolio,[5] interrupts a late-night celebration, Sir Toby and other members of the household conspire to get back at Malvolio. They forge a letter from Olivia, which convinces Malvolio that Olivia loves him; the letter also instructs Malvolio to wear yellow stockings to prove his affection for Olivia. Malvolio obeys the letter's demands, dons yellow stockings, and becomes the laughingstock of the household. Malvolio's actions convince Olivia he is mentally unstable, which results in his imprisonment, as his enemies continue to torment him.

Unbeknownst to Viola, her twin, Sebastian, survived the shipwreck and has arrived in Illyria. Olivia encounters Sebastian, mistakes him for Cesario, and proposes marriage. To the Countess's surprise, Sebastian agrees. Orsino, accompanied by Cesario (Viola), arrives at Olivia's house to try to win her affection once more. When Sebastian and Cesario (Viola) appear in the same location, the confusion is sorted out, the twins are reunited, and Orsino asks for Viola's hand in marriage.

Just as happiness appears on the horizon, the wronged Malvolio is released from prison and confronts Olivia. Malvolio wants an explanation: why did Olivia write him that letter, instruct him to wear yellow stockings, only to send him to prison? When he discovers that Olivia never wrote that letter, and that he was the target of a cruel joke, Malvolio swears revenge and departs. His final words resonate: "I'll be revenged on the whole pack of you" (*Twelfth Night*, V.i.401). The happy couples make plans for their upcoming weddings, and the play

---

3 suh-ZAHR-ee-oh (emphasis on second syllable).
4 or-SEE-no (emphasis on second syllable).
5 mal-VOH-lee-oh (first syllable sounds like pal).

concludes with a song about growing up, which reminds us, in the refrain, that "the rain it raineth every day" (*Twelfth Night*, V.i.415).

VIOLENCE PREVENTION CONNECTIONS TO *TWELFTH NIGHT*

Twelfth Night aligns with much of what violence-prevention research continues to reveal about youth violence. We know that in the United States, a lot of kids are hurting. Studies repeatedly reveal that about one in five students experience bullying, and fewer than half of those students told an adult about the bullying (StopBullying.gov 2023). The research suggests that children often suffer bullying in silence, inviting more bullying. But we know that upstander behavior can stop bullying more than half the time (Hawkins et al. 2001). In the play, we see how a bullying situation escalates; we see a lack of upstander behavior, and we see how moments upstream of the mistreatment lead to more harm. We also see connections between the forged letter from "Olivia" in Shakespeare's play and contemporary examples of cyberbullying. The play depicts a climate in which characters harm others, the harm leads to misunderstanding and more harm, and the play ends with Malvolio threatening revenge. The cycle of violence, we imagine, will continue after the final scene, just as the final song promises rain. While the fictional play would be far less engaging and dramatic without the mistreatment and harm, in real life we know that we need to interrupt these cycles of mistreatment if we are to truly bring about reconciliation and healing within our communities.

Considering Malvolio's perspective can be a useful entry point for a violence-prevention focus with young audiences. The subplot in which Maria,[6] Toby, and others trick Malvolio is usually called the "gulling" of Malvolio. This comes from a term that is used throughout the play: gull can be a verb (to deceive or dupe) or a noun (a foolish person who is easily tricked). We get the word "gullible" from this term, and it's used in the play to describe Malvolio or to describe the trick they play on him. Maria promises to "gull" Malvolio "into a nayword" (*Twelfth Night* II.iii.134) and refers to "yond gull Malvolio" when he appears in yellow stockings (*Twelfth Night* III.ii.67). Fabian calls Maria "my noble gull-catcher," praising her ability to dupe Malvolio (*Twelfth Night* II.v.91). In act 5, Malvolio himself realizes he's been

---

6 Usually pronounced mu-RYE-uh (like Mariah).

made "the most notorious geck and gull that e'er invention played on" (*Twelfth Night* V.i.365–66). We could just as easily swap the word "gulling" with bullying. If we invite our students to consider the play from Malvolio's perspective, how might that impact their experience watching the play?

Look Upstream: Root Causes

If we are to unpack violence, it is helpful to go back in time, or upstream of the harm, in order to understand the root causes. Violence does not exist in a vacuum but is influenced by intersecting factors, such as mental health, poverty, home life, education, and systemic racism. Live performance gives us the opportunity to experience human behavior in real time, and to observe the ways in which one choice and action leads to another, and how these choices and actions impact the world of the play. What is the origin of the mistreatment in *Twelfth Night*? Why does the bullying occur? What is going on beneath the surface, and what occurred before the play began that might influence the events? Some things to consider are Olivia's grief at the deaths of her loved ones, Viola's grief at the presumed death of her brother, Orsino's rejections by Olivia, and Malvolio's demeaning behavior toward Feste. Discuss with your students what other events occurred before the play begins that might impact what happens in the play.

Let's explore one moment in *Twelfth Night* that directly influences the later harm: act 1 scene 5. Feste encounters Olivia and Malvolio and tries to cheer Olivia up with a joke. Feste asks Olivia for permission to "prove [her] a fool."

> FESTE: Good madonna, why mourns't thou?
> OLIVIA: Good fool, for my brother's death.
> FESTE: I think his soul is in hell, madonna.
> OLIVIA: I know his soul is in heaven, fool.
> FESTE: The more fool, madonna, to mourn for your brother's soul being in heaven.—Take away the fool, gentlemen.
> (*Twelfth Night* I.v.64–70)

Feste is doing his job by entertaining his boss, Olivia, who is mourning the recent deaths of two family members, but Feste's efforts to put her in a better mood result in a conflict with Malvolio. After Feste delivers the punchline, Olivia asks Malvolio for his opinion.

OLIVIA: What think you of this fool, Malvolio, doth he not mend?
MALVOLIO: Yes, and shall do till the pangs of death shake him. Infirmity, that decays the wise, doth ever make the better fool.
(*Twelfth Night* I.v.71–75)

This scene is an opportunity to establish a power imbalance between Malvolio and Feste. Malvolio is demeaning Feste in front of an employer. Malvolio, who perhaps considers himself the ideal employee, attempts to assert superiority over Feste, who, in Malvolio's eyes, is the inadequate employee. Have you ever seen someone throw a colleague under the bus in an effort to look better, smarter, or more prepared? After Feste comes up with a witty comeback, Malvolio escalates the situation. He tells Olivia: "I marvel your ladyship takes delight in such a barren rascal. I saw him put down the other day with an ordinary fool that has no more brain than a stone. Look you now, he's out of his guard already. Unless you laugh and minister occasion to him, he is gagged" (*Twelfth Night* I.v.81–86). Not only is Malvolio saying that Feste is stupid; he's saying Feste is worse than the worst person at his job. Not only that but Malvolio mocks Feste's inability to reply with a comeback ("he's out of his guard already"). Then Malvolio points out the real power imbalance: Olivia has the total power over Feste's livelihood. He's only able to keep telling jokes because Olivia allows it. Without her laughter and approval, Feste is voiceless and powerless ("gagged"). This scene can be a way to spark a conversation with students about how power operates between individuals and what happens when you try to make someone else look bad. Why does Malvolio treat Feste so harshly? Have they had a past encounter that is causing this behavior? Malvolio's unkindness toward Feste likely comes from a place of pain and insecurity. We can always go further upstream to prior moments, and this is an exciting part of the discovery process as you work with your students to untangle the rich landscape of a play.

Although there are many ways to play this moment in rehearsal, performance, or a classroom setting, there is an opportunity to establish a temporary rise in power of Malvolio as he demeans Feste, insults his intelligence, and points out his poor job performance. Malvolio mistreats Feste to make himself feel more powerful. This is often how mistreatment works. We seek to insult others in order to boost our own position. Olivia seeks to temper Malvolio's inappropriate response: "O, you are sick of self-love, Malvolio, and taste with a distempered appetite. To be generous, guiltless, and of free disposition is to take those things for bird-bolts that you deem cannon bullets. There is no slander in an allowed fool" (*Twelfth Night* I.v.89–93).

Here, Olivia intervenes to attempt to redirect the behavior and resolve the conflict. Malvolio tries to assert dominance over Feste and prove him incompetent, but Olivia interrupts to advocate for a more balanced approach. She instructs Malvolio to lighten up, or to be less dramatic. These "bird bolts" (or light insults) are not "cannon bullets" (huge insults), she seems to tell him; he should take these slight insults as slight insults rather than earth-shattering attacks. Work with your students to think about an appropriate metaphor. How would we phrase this idea today? Maybe we'd say, "Don't take everything personally." Everything Malvolio sees is distempered, or unbalanced, because his worldview impacts the way he interprets his surroundings.

There are also opportunities for audience interaction here. In this scene, Feste is in the role of the target, Malvolio is acting as a perpetrator, and Olivia is in the witness role. But there are other witnesses: the audience members. Might there be ways for Olivia, Malvolio, and Feste to engage the audience as witnesses—through eye rolls, direct pleas for help, or letting the audience in on the mistreatment? Direct audience interaction can help clarify the storytelling here and establish that, although they are witnessing several roles onstage, they are also playing a role—the bystander.

This encounter between Feste and Malvolio is a root cause of the later bullying; Malvolio learns he's been tricked, and Feste admits his role in the gulling. He reminds Malvolio of his earlier behavior and quotes Malvolio's language back at him: "But do you remember? Madam, why laugh you at such a barren rascal? An you smile not, he's gagged. And thus, the whirligig of time brings in his revenges" (*Twelfth Night* V.I. 397–400). Feste repurposes Malvolio's own words and warns him that what goes around comes around ("the whirligig of time brings in his revenges"). A whirligig is a spinning top, a type of child's toy, and Feste's comparison of time to a toy is a compelling metaphor, worthy of exploring with students. This scene provides opportunities to analyze the moments upstream of the mistreatment and invites students to see earlier intervention opportunities and the possibilities of making different choices.

Look at Risk Factors: Bullying

Violence prevention researchers examine the risk and protective factors that either enhance or diminish the likelihood of violence. A risk factor increases the risk of something occurring, while a protective factor reduces the risk. Bullying is one of the risk factors we see in *Twelfth Night*. Not all mistreatment is bullying, and it is important to define terms when discussing bullying with students. Conflicts are a normal part of life, but bullying is a specific type of violence, which must meet three criteria:

- Bullying is **intentional**.
- Bullying is **repetitive** (and often escalates with repetition).
- Bullying involves a **power imbalance**. (CDC 2024f)

In order for acts of mistreatment to qualify as bullying, the above criteria must be met. If I bump into you by accident, it's not bullying, because it wasn't intentional. If I bump into you on purpose once, it's not bullying, because it isn't repeated over time. If I bump into you on purpose every day for a week but we are good friends in the same grade at school, it's probably not bullying, because there's no real or perceived power imbalance. The power imbalance is a little trickier to pin down, because power can manifest in many ways. A power imbalance may emerge when someone has higher socioeconomic status, more friends, or is physically taller than another person. If all three criteria are met, it's bullying. If not all three are met, it may still be a type of mistreatment, and is probably not okay, but it is not specifically bullying. For further reading about bullying, the website stopbullying.gov has helpful resources.

Twelfth Night depicts intentionally harmful behavior, but does it meet the criteria for bullying? The text of the play suggests that the characters concoct the gulling plot in order to hurt Malvolio in retaliation for his interruption of their late-night party in act 2 scene 3. After Malvolio departs with the threat to tell Olivia about their debauchery ("She shall know of it, by this hand"), Maria hatches the plan:

> MARIA: I will drop in his way some obscure epistles of love, wherein by the color of his beard, the shape of his leg, the manner of his gait, the expressure of his eye, forehead, and complexion, he shall find himself most feelingly personated. I can

> write very like my lady your niece; on a forgotten matter, we can hardly make distinction of our hands.
> TOBY: Excellent! I smell a device.
> ANDREW: I have 't in my nose, too.
> TOBY: He shall think, by the letters that thou wilt drop, that they come from my niece, and that she's in love with him.
> MARIA: My purpose is indeed a horse of that color.
> ANDREW: And your horse now would make him an ass.
> MARIA: Ass, I doubt not.
> ANDREW: O, 'twill be admirable!
> (*Twelfth Night* II.iii.154–69)

This is an intentional plot to harm Malvolio, or at least to "make him an ass" for their own entertainment. Although the characters may not foresee all the harm it will eventually cause Malvolio, their intent is humiliation. They don't see Malvolio in the full context of his humanity, nor do they put themselves in his shoes. They do not consider that he has a job to do in the household, or how it will feel to receive love notes from his boss. Malvolio is not the only target of this prank; the pranksters do not consider Olivia's perspective, who has no knowledge she is being used as a tool to deceive Malvolio.

The teasing of Malvolio begins as a simple prank, but it quickly escalates when the pranksters expand on the joke and double down on their commitment to it. If the members of the household had written the letter and left Malvolio to find it, but then revealed to him it was a trick before it escalated, the prank might have ended there. Malvolio might have felt foolish for believing the letter, and his feelings may have been temporarily hurt, but no lasting harm would likely have come. Instead, the characters build on the prank; they bring him before Olivia, they fake their concern for him, and they oversee his imprisonment. They disguise Feste as a priest to further persuade Malvolio he has lost his mind. This scenario smacks of gaslighting, a situation in which a person is manipulated to the extent that they eventually question their sanity. The gulling of Malvolio drives him to a dark place, literally, when he is locked up, and he begs for help. It is not until the situation has escalated beyond their control that the pranksters decide to end it. In bullying situations, the behavior is repeated, and often worsens with time, sometimes becoming unbearable to the targets if the behavior isn't interrupted.

The third component of bullying, a power imbalance, is a little more nuanced and complicated (and worth exploring with your students). Power can shift over the course of a play, much like it shifts in real life. A person may hold power in one situation but not in another. Malvolio's station as an employee is lower than that of Olivia, so their relationship has a socioeconomic power imbalance. Sir Toby is related to Olivia and is therefore not an employee but a family member, suggesting a greater amount of power over Malvolio. Maria is an employee, and she's presumably below Malvolio's command; but perhaps her alliance with Toby (a relative of the boss) gives her a feeling of superiority over her fellow employee. There is a class-based imbalance between the perpetrators and Malvolio, and Malvolio is targeted for attempting to rise above his station while simultaneously being questioned for believing he is anything more than a butler.

While power can be rooted in class differences, it can also come in the form of information—who has it, who doesn't. The pranksters hold more information than the two people most directly impacted: Malvolio, the target of the joke, who lacks the information to assess the situation clearly, and Olivia, whose identity is used without her knowledge and consent. The power resides with the pranksters.

The play establishes Malvolio as an outsider; the other characters call him a Puritan and mark him as different from the rest of the Illyrians. Even Olivia offers some corrective guidance early in the play when she advises him not to take everything so seriously. The others also seem aware of Malvolio's tendency to stroll about, fantasizing about his station. Do they know he desires Olivia? There are many ways to interpret this difference in production, but if Malvolio is positioned as a social outsider, this creates another kind of power imbalance based on exclusion. Power can also simply be a question of numbers. There are several people who are in on the joke, and Malvolio is only one person.

You may want to consider how different production and casting choices may impact Malvolio's status and power. How does an actor's gender identity, race, body type, and/or accent, as well as the production's costumes and setting impact Malvolio's perceived power or lack thereof? Analyzing who has power at the beginning of the play and how that changes can help you navigate deeper conversations with your students.

In performance, act 2 scene 3, the "party scene" in which Toby, Andrew, and friends have a late-night party at Olivia's house, is rife with mistreatment and power imbalances. This is a great one to stage with an eye toward highlighting the bullying. The partiers are having a great time (and in performance, this can be a fun opportunity to get the audience involved in the party—singing along with the revelers or clapping along to a rhythm established by Toby) when Malvolio enters to interrupt the party. He doesn't want them making noise, because his job is to keep order in Olivia's house. Here's how Malvolio intervenes (in a sample of how you might cut this for an audience of students between ages eight and eleven): "My masters, are you mad, or what are you? Have you no respect for place, time, or persons in you?" (*Twelfth Night*, II.iii.87–93). This is an opportunity to lean into conflict management. How does Malvolio frame his complaint? While he critiques the revelers for their lack of respect, how is he perpetuating the disrespect in his own behavior? Toby then retaliates against Malvolio (escalating the conflict): "Art any more than a steward? Dost thou think, because thou art virtuous, there shall be no more cakes and ale? Go sir, rub your chain with crumbs" (*Twelfth Night*, II.iii.113–19). There are several images to unpack here in Toby's response.

ART ANY MORE THAN A STEWARD? A steward is like a butler. Although a high rank within a household, the steward is still a paid employee and not high-born. This is a class insult, in which Toby reminds Malvolio of his rank and reinforces that he is nothing more than his job. You may want to talk to your students about a contemporary equivalent of this moment. What happens if we replace "steward" with "custodian," "janitor," or "assistant?" How does this impact the meaning when we translate the term into contemporary language? Toby equates Malvolio with his job, thus denying his humanity, and seeing him as only his social rank.

BECAUSE THOU ART VIRTUOUS, THERE SHALL BE NO MORE CAKES AND ALE: Just because you follow the rules and live a Puritan lifestyle, Toby suggests, does that mean no one else can have fun either? Just because you are anti-fun, do you really think no one else should enjoy life's finer things, like cakes and ale? This brings to mind some contemporary phrases we could swap for virtuous: high-and-mighty, goody-two-shoes, suck-up, teacher's pet. What phrases can your students come up with that evoke the meaning of virtuous, and how does their word choice impact the scene?

RUB YOUR CHAIN WITH CRUMBS: This line refers to the chain of office, the steward's chain that indicates Malvolio is a servant (go polish your custodian's keys). Toby is demeaning Malvolio's job, again, linking his identity to his role in the household, seeing him as a mere steward. It's dehumanizing.

In this moment, you can have students look at the roles involved. Who is acting as a bully, and who is being targeted? Who is acting as a bystander? Remind your students that roles can shift; what would happen if the person acting as the bully decided to change their behavior? What if the bystander took action to help the target? What happens if the roles shift?

Look at Risk Factors: Cyberbullying

Although written centuries before the concept of cyberbullying was born, *Twelfth Night* presents young people with the opportunity to draw a connection between Maria's forged letter and contemporary examples of anonymous online mistreatment. In Shakespeare's play, a letter dropped in the garden for Malvolio to find is the Elizabethan version of cyberbullying. Defined as "willful and repeated harm inflicted through the use of computers, cell phones, and other electronic devices" by the Cyberbullying Research Center, under the direction of Dr. Sameer Hinduja and Dr. Justin W. Patchin, cyberbullying is an especially challenging phenomenon for young people to deal with because it is pervasive, it can be anonymous, and it is difficult for adults to notice when it's happening (Cyberbullying Research Center n.d.b). Although many adult readers of this text may have experienced bullying in childhood, it is likely that there was some respite from it, some safe haven away from the mistreatment. You might have been bullied on the school bus, but you could go home and be safe for a while, away from the people bullying you. When it comes to cyberbullying, technology makes the behavior pervasive and persistent. If a young person is cyberbullied today, it may seem like there is no escape from it, because it has the potential to reach the individual anytime, anyplace.

Look at Risk Factors: Substance Abuse

Involvement with drugs or alcohol is a risk factor for youth violence (meaning that it is a behavior associated with violence but not a direct cause). The play depicts ample substance abuse among Toby, Andrew, and their crew, especially when the plan is hatched to prank Malvolio. They are all consuming alcohol and continue to call for more wine as they are up late partying. In fact, the scene ends with a harbinger of more bad choices, with the closing exclamation, "'Tis too late to go to bed now" (*Twelfth Night* II.iii.188). Although the drinking may not have been the primary cause of the eventual mistreatment of Malvolio, it is one of many intersecting risk factors that led to the harm.

Look at Risk Factors: High Emotional Distress

The recent loss, grief, and trauma of the death of loved ones may impact Olivia's ability to respond to the present moment. We know that there is a connection between trauma and violence, and the ACEs study revealed that early childhood trauma can be a risk factor for later violence (CDC 2024a). Viola and Sebastian lost their father at age fourteen, and then they each suffered the presumed loss of their twin in a shipwreck. Olivia, likewise, lost her father and brother recently. This kind of sudden loss and early exposure to trauma can have a negative impact on mental health and is a risk factor for violence. Yet how many of these characters behave in violent ways? The presence of a risk factor does not determine an outcome, a subtlety worth exploring with your students.

Look at Risk Factors: Disconnection and Secrets

A lack of connectedness within a community can be a risk factor for violence. The play features secrecy and disconnectedness in Viola's storyline. She is alone in a strange world, puts on a disguise, and pretends to be someone she isn't. When viewed through the lens of connectedness, Viola's secret also makes her less connected to her community. She reveals that "I am not what I am" (*Twelfth Night* III.i.148). This kind of separation from the self, while dramatically engaging, can have a negative impact on one's mental health and well-being. Viola is resilient, yes, but she is also isolated by her disguise and not able to feel safe, secure, and valued in her true identity.

Look at Risk Factors: Antisocial Relationships

We see plenty of antisocial relationships within the play. Toby's friendship with Andrew is primarily formed because of Andrew's wealth, and the text suggests that Toby uses Andrew for his money; the bond between them proves weak when Toby denies Andrew by the end of the play. Antisocial relationships or weak prosocial bonds can be risk factors for violence, and, in fact, by the end of the play, violence has occurred, when Toby is injured in a fight with Sebastian, getting a "bloody coxcomb" (*Twelfth Night* V.i.186). Ask your students to consider which other relationships in the play are antisocial (vs. prosocial) and why? Perhaps the terms "healthy bonds" and "unhealthy bonds" could be useful as you discuss antisocial versus prosocial relationships with your students.

Protective Factors

On the flip side of risk factors, we see protective factors that reduce the risk of violence. In the play, there are moments of connectedness in which characters are seen and valued in positive ways. We see characters putting themselves in the shoes of others; in Viola's aside to the audience after Olivia sends her the ring, she asks, "What will become of this? . . . What thriftless sighs shall poor Olivia breathe?" (*Twelfth Night* II.ii.36–39). Here, Viola is stepping out of her own perspective to consider the perspective of Olivia, and how it will feel to be in her shoes. This kind of empathy is a form of connectedness, and these prosocial attachments can support feelings of belonging, safety, and being valued within a community. Likewise, Viola and Sebastian seem to have a deep, prosocial bond—although they only share one brief scene toward the end of the play, their reunion suggests that the twins know each other, care for each other, and are invested in one another's happiness and thriving. The twins demonstrate a sense of resilience and inner strength; Viola navigates the unfamiliar land of Illyria with optimism and creativity, and we learn that Sebastian is "most provident in peril" (*Twelfth Night* I.ii.13). It seems the twins have been through hardships and they reveal their strength of character in difficult circumstances. A growing awareness of where risk and protective factors show up in the play can support a student's deeper understanding of these same factors in their own lives.

Look at the Climate

In staging a play, designers, directors, and actors can depict and embody a climate through costumes, scenery, blocking, and acting choices. Likewise, educators can encourage students to analyze a play's climate, which can prime students for deepening their awareness of their own community's climate. What is the climate of Olivia's household, in which late-night parties are quickly shut down, the mourning lady of the house sets a tone of grief and melancholy, and pranks are hatched behind the backs of others? Do people make eye contact and greet one another in a supportive and friendly manner? Is there violence and mistreatment? When harm occurs, who intervenes? What does Orsino's household feel like, in which Viola keeps her identity and gender a secret, the master of the house sends others to deliver his sentiments of love, and clowns are brought in for entertainment? Do these two households have different climates of culture and support? Which individuals are thriving in their climate, and which individuals are struggling? Who is being mistreated? Just as violence-prevention researchers ask questions like this in school climate surveys, we can ask these questions of a play to spark an unpacking of how climate is built, reinforced, and changed.

The climate of *Twelfth Night* depends largely on the artistic choices made in production, but the text gives us some clues about what kind of world we are entering in the play. Illyria is a world of excess, in which the leader of the land (Orsino) is consumed by love ("give me excess of it" he says in act 1 scene 1), while a prestigious citizen (Olivia) is consumed by grief. It is a culture of extremes, in which the leaders demonstrate unbalanced emotions. Orsino is struggling with his affections for Olivia, while Olivia is struggling with grief for the loss of her loved ones. These struggling leaders, perhaps, have no outlets to grapple with their complex emotions, so they cloak themselves in "disguises"—Olivia wears all black and refuses to see any men, while Orsino surrounds himself with flowers and music. However, they are alone in their challenging emotions, and they lack a network of support to work through their hardships.

Although secrecy and disconnection are identified above as risk factors, Illyria's culture of secrecy also shapes the climate. Viola keeps a big secret in disguising herself as a man, and then conceals her affection for Orsino, while also concealing her identity to Olivia and

Orsino. Toby and Maria keep a secret from Malvolio about the truth in the letter. Feste keeps a secret about where he has been (he's been absent from the court for a while). It's not until the truth comes out (starting with the confession of Fabian, one of Olivia's servants) that we learn of Viola's true identity, Malvolio's gulling, and the plotters' guilt. In a culture of secrecy, people can get hurt.

Music is a key part of *Twelfth Night*'s climate. This is a world in which music heals and gets us through hardship. The play begins with Orsino's "if music be the food of love, play on" (*Twelfth Night* I.i.1), and throughout the play the characters continue to call upon music in times of need. The drunkards integrate singing and dancing into their joyful celebration. Near the play's end, Feste leads a song about the cycle of life, in which we are reminded that throughout life "the rain it raineth every day" (*Twelfth Night* V.i.415). Music taps into something the characters can't quite articulate, and it addresses an ache, a need, a foundational wound that needs healing.

These clues about the climate can help students hone their skills in climate analysis. What else do your students notice about the world of the play? Try reading one scene from the play and ask your students to make a list of all the things (big and small) they notice about the world of Illyria.

Look for Upstanders

Where do we see upstander behavior, or opportunities for upstander behavior in *Twelfth Night*? When Malvolio appears before Olivia in yellow stockings, kissing his hand and smiling in a way that is out of character, Olivia is confused by his change in behavior. She interprets Malvolio's erratic conduct to mean that he has gone mad, so she instructs Sir Toby (one of the key perpetrators of the mistreatment) to look after her transformed servant. Malvolio is, at Toby's command, thrown in a dark prison. In some productions, this is a heartbreaking part of the play, when we see Malvolio alone in a prison, often blindfolded, and degraded. It's often a moment in the play in which a character who was the butt of the joke becomes instead an object of pity, due to the dehumanizing treatment of him.

After Malvolio is thrown in jail, Toby orchestrates further torment. He arranges for Feste to visit Malvolio, disguised as a priest, and further convince Malvolio that he is mad. After this encounter, Toby begins to regret the whole thing: "I would we were well rid of this knavery" (*Twelfth Night* IV.ii.70–71). The joke has gone too far. Malvolio is pitiful; the grimness of the situation becomes clear, and Toby wants it over. This is a good example of the way mistreatment can escalate. What began as a silly prank, a way to get even with someone he didn't like, turned into a dehumanizing affair, and it feels like it's too late to end things. In performance, this is an opportunity to connect with the audience through direct address and eye contact, to bring the audience along on the journey of mistreatment. A bully is not born a bully; someone who behaves as a bully can make a different choice and decide to change behavior. Maybe this starts with regret, and with seeing another as human. This moment could be staged as Toby's decision to become an upstander.

It is important to look at how the moments upstream of Malvolio's gulling have a later impact on the events of the play. Examining this ripple effect subtly reinforces the idea of connectedness, as the actions of one person impact another person. In the final scene of the play, Malvolio swears retribution: "I'll be revenged on the whole pack of you," he says (*Twelfth Night* V.i.401). His final line may be directed not only at the conspirators who pranked him but also at everyone onstage, the population of Illyria, and possibly, if staged to support this interpretation, the audience too. Who is the "you" in this moment? The "pack of you" suggests it is more than one person, much like a pack of dogs or a pack of wolves. Is it Toby and Feste? Is Olivia included? Is Orsino, who has possibly never met Malvolio, included? How far does the pack stretch? This raises the question of who is responsible for mistreatment in a community. If the climate is built and reinforced in every interaction, what role do we, as community members, play? What about the audience, who has witnessed the action unfolding? Does Malvolio include them too? In performance, we might let this moment sink in, and turn out to the audience, as if to say, "What do we do?" What will Malvolio do next? He never speaks another word in the play, and we are left to wonder about his future. In a 2019 Secret Service study about planned school attacks, most plotters cited the cause as a personal grievance with a peer (National Threat Assessment Center 2019). This can be an opportunity for a class discussion about what Malvolio might do next. Has he been harmed enough to want to hurt others and possibly follow through on the plan?

Orsino, in Shakespeare's full text, commands others to run after him and "entreat him to a peace" (*Twelfth Night* V.i.403). In the original, this is because they need Malvolio's information about the captain, so they can get Viola's clothes back. Shakespeare intentionally places this conversation in the future, offstage, after the events of the play have concluded, but this could also be an opportunity to think about healing and repairing relationships. What would this peace-making conversation look like?

PERFORMING THE PLAY FOR YOUTH AUDIENCES

In performance, *Twelfth Night* can give students a firsthand experience of witnessing mistreatment, bullying, and power imbalances. This play was the first title the Colorado Shakespeare Festival developed as part of the Violence Prevention work in 2011, and my team continually returns to it because it aligns so well with the curriculum. CSF has toured several three-to-four-actor versions of the play to schools across Colorado; directors have included Timothy Orr, Crystal Eisele, Lynn Nichols, Kevin Rich, Rodney Lizcano, and Anastasia Davidson. When performing the play for young audiences, CSF touring shows emphasize simplicity in scenic and costume elements so everything can easily fit in a van. We also have actors play multiple roles, which reinforces the notion that change is possible; just as we shift from one character to another, so we can choose to change our own behavior. CSF's scripts are available on this book's website. These three-to-four-actor versions designed for professional actors to perform in school settings can easily be adapted for classes to perform. As a guideline, remember that a play is not a sole-author essay, a public service announcement, or a PowerPoint presentation; a play contains a multitude of perspectives, competing ideas, and contradictions. A play does not offer up clear answers but can be a site of witnessing human behavior, and, with thoughtful follow-up, a way to spark discussion and action around how violence operates within a community.

The best way to encounter Shakespeare is through live performance, and if you can engage your students with *Twelfth Night* in this way, I highly encourage it (whether the students are performing the play or watching the play). I recommend abridging the script for performance if planning to stage a performance for young audiences. One of the best ways to connect with a script is to create the cutting yourself or have the students work on the cutting with you. If you are creating your own cutting, the Folger Shakespeare Library's website is an excellent place to start. A run time of thirty minutes is generally good length for an audience of eight-to-eleven-year-olds to sit and watch a play, while twelve-to-eighteen-year-olds may have more success with forty-five-to-sixty-minute performances. A thirty-to-forty-five-minute performance also fits nicely into an assembly period. However, educators need not feel obligated to abridge the play to any specific length. Engaging with the play, whether working on a single scene or a full-length version, will provide you and your students with plenty of opportunities to grapple with violence-prevention connections. You may consider the following cuts to get to your desired length and content:

- Focus on Malvolio's gulling and mistreatment as much as possible.
- Downplay the love interest storyline between Orsino/Olivia, Viola/Orsino—not for any reason other than it's more relevant to focus on the mistreatment than the unrequited love for a group of eight-to-eleven-year-olds. (With middle and high school groups, you may retain more of this plotline).
- Cut Antonio's storyline (for time and number of actors you have).
- Cut the planned fight between Cesario/Andrew—again, for time in a full performance. But this could be a great scene to focus on in a class session because it deals with a planned fight. I have found that to get to a thirty-minute assembly period, losing this fight, although it has great comic value, helps push the show along.

Look in the Mirror: Upstander Roleplay Exercise

CSF's touring Shakespeare & Violence Prevention curriculum uses roleplay activities to strategize and rehearse upstander behavior. After viewing the performance, students are guided through an activity in which they are invited to witness problematic behavior, which is usually upstream of the violence, and then they have the chance to step into the action as themselves and change the narrative, while steering toward a healthier, more peaceful outcome.

One of the key findings our partners at the CSPV continually emphasize is that upstander behavior is extremely effective in preventing violence, but translating that research into practice poses challenges. How do we get this research into the hands of people who need it? We know that upstander behavior works to reduce violence; 57 percent of the time, bullying stops in ten seconds or less when a bystander becomes an upstander (Hawkins et al. 2001). Just as we practice important skills like CPR, tying our shoes, or multiplication tables, upstander behavior is a skill that requires practice.

There are many ways of being an upstander. It could be as simple as saying, "Hey, that is not cool" or "Why are you doing that?" It could mean reporting anonymously or getting a trusted adult. The key thing to focus on when guiding students through a rehearsal of their strategies is to emphasize that there is no correct way to be an upstander, and no solution will stop all the violence all the time. After the students view the performance we recommend giving them the chance to practice their own strategies to prevent the mistreatment.

In these roleplays, try to keep the students solution-focused and upstander-focused. We occasionally see students who are eager to step in as Toby, Malvolio, or other characters in the play. I recommend a best practice of guiding the students to step in as themselves in the role of the upstander—with limited time, that is the behavior we should spend our time rehearsing rather than having students practice the role of the perpetrator or the target.

Let's look at one of the key moments of choice, which is a useful starting point for a roleplaying exercise: the scene in which Maria gets the idea to prank Malvolio, perhaps motivated by a desire to impress Sir Toby (the play concludes, after all, with their reported marriage). When the prank is executed, however, she will notably not be there. She'll write the letter, leave it in the garden, and she'll plant Toby and friends to observe.

What are the choices made in this moment? Maria makes the choice to concoct the plan and speak it aloud. Toby listens, assists, and agrees. Sir Andrew chooses to go along with it. What do these choices mean later? What if, when Maria concocted the idea, Toby or Andrew laughed it off but didn't encourage her? What if they took their concerns directly to Malvolio the next day and had a rational conversation with him? What if Maria paused to consider the ethical issues at stake in forging her boss's handwriting? This moment is upstream of the more consequential mistreatment, but it provides students with an opportunity to wrestle with the complicated web of the plot—if this happened, how would it change the later outcome? A play is a complex tapestry in which you pull one thread, and the entire thing unravels. These healthier choices would make for boring theatre, but ultimately, healthier life choices.

In appendix E, you will find a sample lesson plan for an upstander roleplay activity about *Twelfth Night* in which the teacher roleplays a character sharing the idea to trick Malvolio and students are invited to step into the scene as themselves. Ask them to consider what they could do to prevent harm? Who would they talk to? What would they do? With each scenario, discuss what the students appreciated about the scene. Did it prevent harm? Did it help keep people safe? Emphasize the importance of keeping themselves safe.

It's also important to think through the later impacts of this moment of choice. By the play's end, Malvolio pledges to get revenge on everyone, and that is the last thing we hear from him. Shakespeare includes this not-so-happy ending and leaves the audience with an unresolved plot line. What will Malvolio do next? We know that hurt people hurt people, and he has just publicly threatened his peers. Will he escalate the situation and attempt to retaliate with violence? Does Malvolio's threat rise to the level of a warning sign or a red flag? Will he resort to self-harm? The play's end is a direct result of subtle choices along the way to engage in further mistreatment. This play reveals how one choice to prank can quickly escalate and lead to real harm. It generates rich conversations about the cycle of violence and how one act of mistreatment can turn into a cycle of bullying, which escalates and gets out of hand fast.

In appendix E, you will also find some post-show discussion questions and additional suggested activities to accompany your work with *Twelfth Night*.

TAKEAWAYS ABOUT *TWELFTH NIGHT*

Twelfth Night can spark conversations about the cycle of violence, how silly pranks can escalate, how hurt people hurt people, and how harm ripples throughout a community. Although this is not the only interpretation of the play, if educators wish to use the play to explore a violence-prevention curriculum, *Twelfth Night* is an enriching starting point. As with all Shakespeare plays, *Twelfth Night* offers upper-elementary students some critical distance from their own time; through the safety of metaphor, they can creatively explore these ideas without hitting too close to home. While encountering the play, the discoveries they make can provide them with tools to practice how they might speak up when they're aware of planned mistreatment, pranks, or other harmful behavior. When students can practice this kind of upstander behavior when the stakes are low in the classroom, they may be more prepared to step into situations like this in real life, and they may have the language and the experience to intervene before bullying escalates.

7
The Comedy of Errors
Presence, Breath, and Mindfulness

"I to the world am like a drop of water
That in the ocean seeks another drop.
So I to find a mother and a brother,
In quest of them, unhappy, lose myself."
—*Comedy of Errors* I.ii.35–40

"Imagine two trains running at different speeds on parallel tracks. Passengers on both trains are at the windows, trying desperately to communicate, but one train is speeding up or slowing down. . . . Only briefly are the trains traveling at the same pace, and while the passengers at opposite windows can see and hear one another, they capture only snippets of what the other is saying. While this may seem like a comedy of errors, it rather accurately describes the inadequate nature of communication and connection in a world where trauma and disrelation is allowed to remain unprocessed and unintegrated. . . . For understanding, connection, and accurate communication to occur, there must exist attunement and presence—within and across trains, self, and other."
—Hübl 2020, 45

One of Shakespeare's earliest comedies, and the shortest play of the canon, *The Comedy of Errors* provides ample opportunities for students, particularly upper-elementary-age students, to grapple with issues relevant to their own direct experiences around mistreatment in a

https://doi.org/10.5876/9781646427246.c007

school setting. The play is rife with physical abuse, power imbalances, poor communication, and impulsive behavior. It is a terrifically confusing play, centering on the adventures of not one but *two* sets of identical twins, and both sets of twins have identical names. One can easily get swept up in the confusion, miscommunication, and chaos at the root of this dizzying play.

If approached thoughtfully, this play offers more than a dizzying plot and can lead to important classroom conversations. *The Comedy of Errors* depicts many characters who choose violence or unkind words when faced with conflict or confusion, inviting the questions: How would things change if the characters stopped, took a breath, and thought before they reacted? What if we took in the world around us with more awareness and became curious about our surroundings? Might that provide the time, space, and breath to respond in more informed ways, rather than reacting based on impulse? We have a choice in how we respond when the going gets tough, and this play highlights plenty of those moments of choice. Many studies indicate the benefits of mindfulness on youth development, and the ways in which a mindfulness practice can hone curiosity, non-judgment, and more awareness of one's surroundings (Morley, Jantz, and Fulton 2019; Gillions, Cheang, and Duarte 2019). Mindfulness training can support emotional regulation, which reduces reactivity and, as part of a chain reaction, can minimize the behaviors that often lead to violence. If we can learn to open up space, build awareness, and take a breath, we can get more skilled at preventing violence. The play gives us a chance to examine reactivity, impulsivity, and lack of presence.

The Comedy of Errors features two pairs of long-lost identical twins, and the whole play hinges on the one laughable fact that the two characters who are searching for their long-lost twins don't take one moment to breathe and think when they find themselves in unfamiliar waters. If they paused to connect the dots, they might realize that the reason they're being treated strangely is because they're being mistaken for the very twins they've traveled the world to find. This impulsive behavior is not limited to the searching twins; characters in the play respond quickly and rashly when they don't have the time, space, or breath to think before acting. When we don't have the training to pause, breathe, think, and communicate clearly in challenging situations, we might resort to impulse and violence. Where words prevail not, violence prevails. This play offers an opportunity for students to practice pausing in moments of conflict. In addition to the focus on physical mistreatment, the play can also be harnessed to think about the pain of early childhood trauma and its impact on behavior later in life.

PLOT SYNOPSIS

Many years ago, the Syracusan merchant Egeon married Emilia, and they had twin sons, the Antipholus twins. They also raised another pair of twin boys, the Dromio twins, as servants to their sons. When Emilia and Egeon crossed the ocean by ship with their infant twins, a storm split their vessel in half and severed the family: one half of the ship held Egeon, one Antipholus twin, and one Dromio twin. The other half of the ship held Emilia and the other Antipholus and Dromio twins. Egeon raised "his" Antipholus and Dromio in Syracuse, but Emilia was separated from the boys left in her care, and those children grew up in Ephesus; throughout the play, they are called Antipholus of Ephesus and Dromio of Ephesus. When Antipholus of Syracuse turned eighteen, he was filled with a longing to find his missing mother and brother, so the Syracusan duo went searching for their twins. Egeon followed them later, and ended up in Ephesus, not realizing that his Syracusan twins were also there . . . as well as the long-lost twins. When the play begins, Egeon has been captured for being a Syracusan in Ephesus (they aren't welcome), and he's given a day to find money or he'll die. Throughout the play, the two sets of twins wreak havoc on Ephesus when they are mistaken for one another. Their impulse is to hit, yell, or get defensive when they don't understand what's happening. At the end of the play, their identities are revealed, their father is freed, the local abbess in Ephesus turns out to be Emilia, the mother of the Antipholus twins, and the family is restored. The whole play boils down to miscommunication and misunderstanding as a divided family seeks connection. We do get that connection at the end of the play, as the Dromio twins agree to "go hand in hand, not one before another" (*Comedy of Errors* V.i.440–41).

VIOLENCE PREVENTION CONNECTIONS TO *THE COMEDY OF ERRORS*

The Comedy of Errors contains several patterns of violence that are relevant to youth audiences, including physical violence, power imbalances, miscommunication, and information silos. The following chapter explores the play through the violence-prevention lens, which means, as covered in chapter 1, that we will consider the root causes, risk and protective factors, the climate, the upstanders, and our own strategies.

Look Upstream: Root Causes

At its heart, the play starts with deep pain. The quotation that begins this chapter is spoken by Antipholus of Syracuse, who, after a childhood spent without his twin and mother, decides to seek his missing family, making this also a play about childhood trauma and its impact on long-term well-being. As Antipholus of Syracuse points out, the quest to find his missing family members feels as hopeless as searching for a single drop of water in the ocean. This ongoing search leaves him feeling that he has lost himself. This quotation is also about connectedness; Antipholus thinks of himself as a single drop of water rather than as part of a whole ocean. He is in pain, and his suffering leads him to think individually and not about his connectedness to others or, to pursue the metaphor, his part of the ocean. Thomas Hübl, author of *Healing Collective Trauma*, observes that "trauma breaks relation; it damages human capacities for trust, connection, and mutuality" (Hübl 2020, 27). Stuck in the past story of trauma, likely sparked by the early loss of his mother and twin, Antipholus cannot see himself as part of an interconnected community. This isolation could be a root cause of some of the later mistreatment and harm that occur in the play.

Look at Risk Factors: Physical Mistreatment

So much of the mistreatment in *The Comedy of Errors* is physical; when faced with a moment of conflict, characters often resort to physical abuse. After a mix-up about a rope, Dromio of Ephesus details his master's abusive behavior: "When I am cold, he heats me with beating. When I am warm, he cools me with beating. I am waked with it when I sleep, raised with it when I sit, driven out of doors with it when I go from home, welcomed home with it when I return" (*Comedy of Errors* IV.iv.36–40). According to Dromio of Ephesus, this abuse is perpetual and intentional. This depiction stems from the dramatic trope of the dissatisfied servant who is always hungry, always messing up, and always being punished by his master, so this moment is worth discussing with students. Where do we see this stereotype about disgruntled employees in popular culture today? What does this say about the world of the play if this kind of physical beating is the norm? The household of the Ephesian Antipholus and Dromio seems to be accustomed to beatings, and Dromio of Ephesus has come to expect the behavior from his master. However, in the Ancient Roman comedy by Plautus, *The Menaechmi*, from which Shakespeare adapted *The Comedy of Errors*, the enslaved character in that comedy is not physically beaten and is notably freed by the play's end. Shakespeare inserts the physical abuse and removes the liberation of the enslaved character (Hunt 1997). Invite your students to consider why Shakespeare might have made that change from his source material.

During Shakespeare's time, it's likely that many household servants, though not technically enslaved, were regularly abused, mistreated, and denied basic human rights. While this depiction of the mistreatment of a servant has its roots in earlier dramatic forms, Shakespeare's inclusion of the abuse of the Dromios, particularly in its divergence from the source, cannot be ignored. When viewed through the lens of violence prevention, it becomes clear that Antipholus of Ephesus reacts to moments of conflict with an immediate and violent response. The attitudes around violence within a community have a direct impact on the occurrence of violence. In the world of the play, physical mistreatment is normalized, and even used as a source of comedy. Dromio complains to the audience about it, but no one in the play intervenes on his behalf. Perhaps the collision with an additional set of twins presents an alternative reality, which introduces the citizens of an unhealthy climate (Ephesus) to a healthier version of what an employer/employee relationship might look like (although the Syracusan dynamic is not perfect).

Physical fights are still a reality in schools today. According to the 2021 Youth Risk Behavior Survey, 18 percent of high school students report being in a physical fight within the prior twelve months, more than 6 percent were threatened or injured with a weapon on school property in the prior twelve months, and nearly 20 percent reported ever seeing someone get physically attacked, beaten, stabbed, or shot in their neighborhood. Nearly 9 percent of high school students said they had stayed home from school at least one day in the prior thirty days due to safety concerns (Youth Risk Behavior Survey System n.d.). Fearing for physical safety can negatively impact a young person's overall well-being, as well as their ability to learn and thrive in school.

Look at Risk Factors: Miscommunication and Impulsivity

The play features a series of snap decisions and impulsive reactions. Antipholus of Ephesus has more extreme reactions than his twin, notably his volatile responses to a mistakenly delivered rope, an arrest due to a jewelry mix-up, and other confusing moments. Throughout the play, with each miscommunication that occurs, we rarely see characters stopping to breathe and think. Words fail, and therefore violence prevails. The signs are misinterpreted. We know that clear communication and strong SEL skills are critical to violence prevention in schools; when people know how to report dangerous behavior and are aware of the systems in place to prevent harm, we have swifter responses to address harm and violence. Because of the foundational miscommunication at the heart of the play—stemming from the identical long-lost twins—the play is rife with poor communication, exaggerated to extreme, comical measures. But it is also a good opportunity to talk through what it means to listen, to take a breath, and to communicate clearly. These SEL skills can serve as protective factors to reduce the likelihood of violence.

Look at the Climate

The climate of *The Comedy of Errors* showcases a world of power imbalances. In Shakespeare's text, the Dromio twins were enslaved from birth, and this history of dehumanizing practices and unearned privilege manifests itself onstage, as, throughout the play, a Dromio twin is mistreated by his enslaver. The enslaver/enslaved dynamic presents a clear (albeit troubling and inhumane) imbalance of power and shapes the climate. How might the play's depiction of a power imbalance resonate with young audiences? In school settings, there are often specific groups of students made to feel inferior. There may be groups systematically, and over a long period of time, treated differently than others. While the type of hierarchy varies, children and teenagers are keenly aware of the shifting power dynamics between peers. One student might have more popularity, more wealth, superior grades, more athletic skill, and these differences can affect a young person's status within the school. What appears to be a power imbalance based on birth, class, wealth, and privilege in *The Comedy of Errors* could easily resonate with a young person's understanding of power in contemporary terms.

To build a positive school climate, violence-prevention experts emphasize the importance of a strong information-gathering system, a platform that enables people to speak up when they are concerned, and to piece together the various silos of information in a school community. In *The Comedy of Errors*, the lack of collective information has negative consequences. Each individual holds knowledge, but the characters do not have the tools in place to pool their knowledge. Antipholus of Syracuse knows he is searching for his twin, but he does not clarify his purpose to anyone in Ephesus because Ephesus does not welcome Syracusans. Words fail, and violence prevails. This situation gets pushed to comic extremes, but each moment of misunderstanding is an opportunity to examine the ways all the characters are responding to what they believe to be true, and how those beliefs come into conflict with the beliefs of others. As you work through the play, unpack each scene and ask these questions with your students: What does this character believe to be true right now? How could we connect the dots to assemble a larger picture of what is true? What does this tell us about the climate? Let's imagine how the outcome would have changed if Ephesus were more welcoming to Syracusans or if citizens had healthy outlets for managing their frustrations? It makes for less exciting drama when characters communicate clearly, and when pushed to these extremes, the miscommunication and misunderstanding are comical. Yet in real life we value clear communication, unlike the poor communication depicted in the play.

Look for Upstanders

Where in the play do we see upstander behavior or opportunities for upstanders to step in? Who could have prevented the physical mistreatment and cleared up the misunderstandings? When Dromio of Ephesus reports his abuse to the audience in act 4 scene 4, no one intervenes to protect him. Adriana brings in Dr. Pinch to attempt to stop her husband's behavior, but Dr. Pinch's efforts to "heal" Antipholus of Ephesus only anger him further. The interventions that occur in the play only escalate matters. Where else do you see characters stepping in as upstanders? How is the Abbess an upstander when she offers the Syracusan twins sanctuary in the priory? In what ways do the upstander strategies work and in what ways do they fall short? Discuss with your students which characters could have taken action as upstanders and how they might have changed the outcome.

PERFORMING THE PLAY FOR YOUTH AUDIENCES

This is a challenging play to adapt for a small, touring production, particularly the three-actor, thirty-minute cuttings we strive for at the Colorado Shakespeare Festival. The biggest difficulty is the unavoidable fact that this play has two sets of twins. You may choose to cast one actor to play both Dromio twins and another actor to play both Antipholus twins. In adapting this play for elementary-age audiences, I recommend emphasizing the physical mistreatment in the play, because this is such a big part of the kinds of mistreatment children will be exposed to in elementary school. CSF has toured this title several times, directed by Wendy Franz (twice) and by Kevin Rich. These productions fully embraced theatricality by placing the character transformations onstage and in full view of the audience. The recognition that change is possible is a critical part of preventing violence, and this theatrical embodiment of change and transformation makes that idea palpable, as audience members watch one actor play a scene in which he is reunited with a long-lost twin (played by the same actor).

To trim the play down to thirty minutes, you may eliminate the storyline about Egeon and his capture (or if the storyline is retained, at least remove the character from the play, and allow the story to exist as exposition), remove the storyline about the jeweler and the courtesan, and keep the focus on the twins and their servants. One actor may play both sets of twins to highlight theatrical transformations. I recommend omitting the enslaver/enslaved dynamic, making Dromio an employee in the world of the play. As the boss, Antipholus is still in a position of power, enabling audiences to explore the power differential. You may experiment with gender as it serves your cast and your audience; in recent tours, we have swapped genders, making the Antipholus twins women, and renamed Antiphola, while Adriana became Adriano, and spoke primarily in Spanish. Dr. Pinch can be played handily by a puppet, or can double with Adriana (in one version, Pinch was a punching Shakespeare puppet; in another, Dr. Pinch wore a hat that said "Trust me, I'm a doctor"). There are lots of opportunities to adjust the script to serve your students.

Look in the Mirror: Upstander Roleplay Exercise

In *The Comedy of Errors*, we see a series of choices unfolding; in each moment of choice, many outcomes are possible. Part of the fun of live theatre is exploring these discoveries in the present moment. Let's look at a moment of choice in the play from act 4 scene 4, in which Antipholus of Ephesus is arrested by an officer due to a misunderstanding. He sends Dromio of Syracuse (thinking it's his real servant, Dromio of Ephesus) to fetch bail money from his house. Earlier in the day, Antipholus had sent his real servant Dromio to buy a rope, and this Dromio returns with the rope. However, now that his circumstances have changed, Antipholus doesn't want the rope, he wants the bail money, but he doesn't realize he had requested the money of Dromio's twin, the Syracusan. When they meet, the pressure is mounting. Antipholus has been arrested, and his liberty depends on his servant obeying commands. The stakes are high.

> ANTIPHOLUS OF EPHESUS: Here comes my man. I think he brings the money.
> How now, sir? Have you that I sent you for?
> DROMIO OF EPHESUS (*handing over the rope's end*): Here's that, I warrant you, will pay them all.
> ANTIPHOLUS OF EPHESUS: But where's the money?
> DROMIO OF EPHESUS: Why, sir, I gave the money for the rope.
> ANTIPHOLUS OF EPHESUS: Five hundred ducats, villain, for a rope?
> DROMIO OF EPHESUS: I'll serve you, sir, five hundred at the rate.
> ANTIPHOLUS OF EPHESUS: To what end did I bid thee hie thee home?
> DROMIO OF EPHESUS: To a rope's end, sir, and to that end am I returned.
> ANTIPHOLUS OF EPHESUS (*beating Dromio*): And to that end, sir, I will welcome you.
> (*Comedy of Errors* IV.iv 8–19)

While the language in this scene is straightforward, I recommend talking through the text to clarify the misunderstanding. At the heart of this scene is the fact that Antipholus is talking to the wrong Dromio twin; he is talking to the Dromio he's known all his life, but not to the Dromio he commanded to collect his bail. This moment can be used as a starting point for a roleplay in which you invite your students to strategize their own solutions. To do this, we have found success in "translating" the scene into contemporary language. Here is an example of how one might bring this into contemporary language (though you may want to have your students write their own versions):

> DROMIO: Hey boss! Here's the rope you asked me to buy!
> ANTIPHOLUS: Dromio, where is my money?
> DROMIO: Uh... I gave the money to the store, and the store gave me the rope.
> ANTIPHOLUS: Five hundred dollars for a ROPE??? You idiot!
> *(Begins smacking Dromio.)*
> DROMIO: Ow, boss! Stop it! *(Turns to the audience.)* You see what I have to put up with?

We staged this incident of violence with a baguette, inspired by a 2016 CSF mainstage production of a Parisian *Comedy of Errors*, directed by Geoffrey Kent. When we toured this play to schools, the students overwhelmingly remembered the moment of violence because of the baguette. Something visible (and not too realistic) served to get the audience's attention and ensure this mistreatment would stick in their memory. When CSF actors went into classrooms after the performance and asked the students if they remembered the moment with the mix-up about the rope and the baguette, they often responded in the affirmative (and in their roleplays, they often used the baguette as a way of strategizing a peaceful outcome: e.g., "we could share the bread instead of hitting with it"). Every scene is an opportunity to understand a character's choices and their impact on the outcome of the play. What would this scene, for example, look like if Antipholus listened? Or if Dromio communicated his confusion more specifically? Or if Antipholus asked more questions of the arresting officer? Or the officer confirmed identification before making the arrest? As with real-life instances of violence, the play reveals many moments of missed communication.

Thomas Hübl notes that "seeing through the filter of the past is a recipe for conflict" (Hübl 2020, 58). In this moment, Dromio is operating on the assumption that the past events can be trusted—his boss asked him to purchase a rope. Antipholus, however, is influenced by a more recent past event, and is seeing the events through that filter—he's just been arrested and sent his servant to get him bail money. Neither of the characters sees the situation through the present moment. Instead, they see through the filter of their most recent past encounter. What would it look like for both characters to be more present with what is happening? The comedy of errors, the confusion, the chaos might settle down, their nervous systems might co-regulate, they might take a few deep breaths and feel the presence of the other person. Maybe they'd each ask some questions. "Hold on, I hear you talking about bail money, but I don't understand why. Can you explain?" This is an extreme situation, yes. But might many of the high-anxiety, high-urgency moments we encounter in our lives be better managed with some skills in being present, more mindful, more able to stop and take a deep breath?

When you introduce this roleplaying exercise with your students, encourage them to try to step into the scene as themselves, not as some fictional character in a Shakespeare play. If they witnessed something like this happening at their school, how could they respond as an upstander? Encourage them to think through direct and indirect approaches. No solution will feel comfortable to everyone. One student might be comfortable directly intervening and addressing Antipholus, encouraging him to stop. Remember that 57 percent of the time, when someone directly intervenes, the bullying stops in ten seconds or less (Hawkins, Pepler, and Craig 2001). But that strategy will not feel safe and comfortable for everyone. One student might be more comfortable telling an adult nearby or reporting anonymously online. You may want to explore anonymous reporting tools available in your community, such as Colorado's Safe2Tell platform. One student might be tempted to distract Antipholus with humor ("accidentally" spilling their water bottle right in front of Antipholus and Dromio, which temporarily distracts them). The key thing to emphasize is that not every solution will feel comfortable to everyone, so it's important to think through what will be safe and comfortable for each person, in their bodies. Safety is key. You do not want to encourage your students to insert themselves in a dangerous situation.

The other important thing to emphasize is that no solution will stop all the violence right away and forever. No solution is perfect; so free yourself up to think through various options that might prevent the immediate harm (Dromio's injuries) in the moment. Rehearsing upstander behavior in these moments of choice in *The Comedy of Errors* can help students practice how they might respond when they witness these moments in real life. If we can rehearse our strategies in advance, we may be more prepared to act when it matters most.

In appendix F, you will find post-show discussion questions, an upstander roleplay lesson plan, and suggested activities to support your work on *The Comedy of Errors*.

TAKEAWAYS ABOUT *THE COMEDY OF ERRORS*

On my more cynical days, I think it's overly idealistic to say that if we all breathed more, we could prevent violence. However, on a fundamental level, violence often occurs in a moment of extreme rage or fear. Violence, as Thomas Hübl posits, is a disconnection with the present moment. When actors are not connected to the present moment, they are trained to breathe. To breathe is to connect with the present moment, to connect with your thoughts, to connect with your feelings, and to respond to the given circumstances truthfully. If we could refine our abilities to pause, breathe, and think before we act, we could avoid a lot of harm. Time, as is often the case in instances of violence and mistreatment, has the potential to be a healing force. Responding with words is more productive than responding with blows. Treating the people we encounter as people we care about, rather than as strangers, can help build connectedness. With breath and presence, we might see that we are not separate drops of water in the ocean; we are the ocean.

8
The Taming of the Shrew
Gender and Relationship Violence

In her book *This is Shakespeare*, scholar Emma Smith describes the range of interpretative possibilities within *The Taming of the Shrew*. Kate is "a woman who, depending on how you look at it, is feisty and independent, lonely and misunderstood, or strident and antisocial," while Petruchio is someone "who, depending on how you look at it, is a quirky and unorthodox guy who knows his own mind and wants a woman who knows hers, or a psychopathic bounty hunter with sadistic and misogynistic tendencies." Of the play's ending, Smith says: "Katherine is, depending on how you look at it, broken-spirited, parroting patriarchal ideology and utterly submissive, offering to put her hand under her husband's foot, or ironically and unabashedly vocal, preaching the interdependence of husband and wife to earn herself half of a fat wager placed by her husband" (Smith 2020, 7–8). This refrain, "depending on how you look at it," could be applied to many of Shakespeare's plays. The act of staging a play is a way of interpreting the play through the lens of a specific production concept, and shaping how your audience experiences it. When approaching *The Taming of the Shrew* through the lens of violence prevention, as with previous chapters, I encourage educators to be aware of the root causes of the mistreatment and violence in the play, the risk and protective factors depicted onstage, the climate in which the action occurs, the upstander opportunities within the play, and our own upstander strategies in similar situations. This play can be taught in elementary school as a way to discuss appropriate and inappropriate behavior; it can also be taught in middle and high schools if teachers wish to explore topics such as gender violence and relationship violence.

Shrew is one of Shakespeare's tricky plays, often considered sexist and misogynistic, and many artists and educators avoid it altogether out of fear of reinforcing harmful ideas. However, sexism and misogyny continue to impact twenty-first-century communities, and this play can be a way to explore unhealthy behaviors and beliefs with our students. In doing so, it is important to stay curious about the play, while not holding anything within as precious or immutable; as we engage with this play as educators, we are learning to walk the line between wrestling with a story and endorsing a story. I encourage educators to ask questions while engaging with a play like *The Taming of the Shrew*. What does this play reveal about our own world? Our own nature? Our own communities?

On its surface, the play is about a bet between suitors of a young woman, a controlling father, an independent daughter who defies gender expectations, and multiple examples of abusive relationships (between parents and children, between siblings, between employees and employers, and between spouses). However, most conversations about *The Taming of the Shrew* overlook its opening, known as the Induction, and thus miss out on an important aspect of the play. While the Induction is often cut from performances, it can serve as an important frame for educators looking to situate this play in a conversation about control, manipulation, and inequality. Below are two plot synopses: one summarizes the Induction, while the other describes the play within the play (the story people typically think of when they think of *The Taming of the Shrew*).

INDUCTION SYNOPSIS

Christopher Sly, a poor tinker, is tossed out of a tavern by its hostess. Sly is intoxicated, has broken some of the tavern's glasses, and cannot pay his bill. Sly passes out on the street. A nobleman (who remains nameless throughout the play), returning from a hunting trip with friends, stumbles upon the drunk and unconscious Sly. The nobleman is repulsed by the sight, "O monstrous beast, how like a swine he lies?" (*Shrew* Induction.i.35), and he decides to trick "this drunken man." He concocts an elaborate plan: he will take the beggar (Sly) to his fancy home, dress him in nice clothes and jewelry, prepare a delicious feast, surround him with servants, hire musicians to entertain him, and convince him that he is not himself but a wealthy lord. After Sly is carried to the nobleman's house, a troupe of actors arrives, seeking employment. The nobleman sees their presence as a welcome addition to his ploy and hires them to perform a play for his new houseguest. Finally, he instructs a young boy in his household to dress as a woman and pretend to be Sly's wife. When Sly awakens, he is perplexed by his surroundings and initially insists that he, Christopher Sly, doesn't belong in this house. However, when the servants continue to convince Sly he is a mighty lord who has been having delusions of being a beggar, Sly questions his sanity and accepts the new identity:

> Am I a lord, and have I such a lady?
> Or do I dream? Or have I dreamed till now?
> I do not sleep: I see, I hear, I speak,
> I smell sweet savors, and I feel soft things.
> Upon my life, I am a lord indeed
> And not a tinker, nor Christopher Sly.
>   (*Shrew* Induction.ii.68–73)

Sly relinquishes his identity and accepts a new one because the people around him tell him it is so. A messenger announces that a play will be performed to celebrate their "lord's" recovery:

> They thought it good you hear a play
> And frame your mind to mirth and merriment,
> Which bars a thousand harms and lengthens life.
>   (*Shrew* Induction.ii.130–38)

As we, the audience members, prepare to watch Sly watch this play, we are in on the joke hatched by the nameless nobleman. Sly has been persuaded he is not who he believes himself to be, and as he prepares to see a performance, he is unwittingly part of a manipulated drama himself. The players perform a play about an outspoken woman (the shrew) and the man who "tames" her. Except for one interruption when Sly is growing bored with the play, this is the last we hear of the Induction plot. We never return to Sly's storyline, and when the play within the play concludes, we may have forgotten the frame entirely.

But the play introduces an important theme by opening with a story about a man tricked into believing he is someone else, about a wealthy man pranking a beggar, about manipulating reality and controlling an experience (a little like staging a play). The induction invites us to think about control, manipulation, inequality, and identity. Framed as a play within a play, *The Taming of the Shrew* has us questioning our own reality, and our own role as "watchers" as we become audience members to Sly's story, with Sly being an audience member for Kate and Petruchio.

Let's learn about the play Sly is watching . . .

PLOT SYNOPSIS

The two Minola sisters are polar opposites. The younger, Bianca, is popular and agreeable while the older, Kate, is outspoken, strong-willed, and argumentative. Although Bianca has many suitors hoping to marry her, their father, Baptista, forbids Bianca from marrying until Kate has found a spouse. Bianca's suitors convince a newcomer to the city, Petruchio, to pursue Kate. Petruchio is motivated by Kate's wealth, and Bianca's suitors offer to cover the cost of the courtship if he successfully marries her. After Kate's enforced marriage to Petruchio, Petruchio "breaks" her the way one might train a stubborn mule or a wild bird. He starves her, keeps her awake all night, and gaslights her until she bends to his will. Throughout the "taming" Kate continues to speak out against Petruchio's manic behavior. Finally, on a journey to Baptista's house, in broad daylight, Petruchio insists that it is in fact nighttime. At this turning point, when Petruchio refuses to budge until Kate agrees with him, she relents. "Forward, I pray, since we have come so far, / And be it moon, or sun, or what you please. / And if you please to call it a rush candle, / Henceforth I vow it shall be so for me" (*Shrew* IV.v.14–17). By the play's end, Petruchio places a bet that Kate will obey him—she does, and then advises other wives to make peace in their marriages (depending, of course, on how you look at it).

Plot Synopsis for Younger Audiences

While middle and high school students can have enriching and thoughtful conversations about the abusive relationships depicted in this play, educators of elementary students may wish to tone down the severity of the abuse and introduce a broader discussion about appropriate versus inappropriate behaviors. Below is a plot synopsis CSF used for an abridged version for third-to-fifth-graders:

> Kate is fed up. Everyone talks about her behind her back, calling her a "shrew" (a nasty name for a sharp-tongued woman). She has a reputation for being headstrong, and people don't exactly like her for it. Her little sister, Bianca, gets away with everything and gets *all* the attention too. Baptista, Kate and Bianca's dad, just wants to see both his daughters happy, but everyone prefers Bianca, his younger daughter. No one wants to spend time with Kate. To secure happiness for both daughters, he decides no one can spend time with Bianca until Kate finds someone who wants to be around her. Lucentio really likes Bianca; he disguises himself as a tutor, so he can spend time with Bianca right under her father's nose. Petruchio swoops into Padua in search of money. He learns about Kate—she's rich, but also mean, outspoken, and difficult. Petruchio decides to spend time with Kate and try to calm her down, whether she likes it or not. After all, Petruchio is always up for a challenge. Petruchio shows up late to meet Kate, wearing all the wrong things, humiliating Kate. They continue to fight like cats and dogs. Neither Kate nor Petruchio have ever had to compromise, and if they just keep pushing and refuse to back down, they'll win . . . right? In the end, the shrews (Kate and Petruchio) learn to find the middle ground, and to look out for each other to make this "mad match" into a match made in heaven.

The Taming of the Shrew does not depict the world as we'd like it to be, but it can invite us to observe human behavior and strategize how we can do better. It's a layered exercise in manipulation and bad behavior, featuring ample mistreatment, inequality, and unhealthy relationships. Much ink has been spilled over this play. Should it even be staged? Is it so misogynistic that it doesn't speak to us any longer? Regardless of where you fall on the "should we stage *Shrew*" spectrum, the play depicts harmful behavior that results in (or is caused by) an unhealthy climate and provides a rich topic for engaging young people with conversations about twenty-first-century issues.

VIOLENCE PREVENTION CONNECTIONS TO *THE TAMING OF THE SHREW*

When interpreted through a violence-prevention lens, *The Taming of the Shrew* can provide opportunities to engage young people in conversations about many aspects that are pertinent to a violence-prevention curriculum, particularly related to gender and relationship violence. Over half of women and almost one in three men have experienced sexual violence involving physical contact in their lives (CDC 2024d). Many of the prevention strategies related to sexual violence overlap with youth violence-prevention science, including training bystanders, creating protective environments, and addressing the root causes of sexual violence. Intimate partner violence is another public health issue that has a negative impact on health and well-being and can include physical violence, sexual violence, stalking, and psychological aggression. People who experience intimate partner violence are at a higher risk for other risky behaviors (CDC 2024c). In *The Taming of the Shrew*, Petruchio doesn't lay a hand on his wife, though he abuses her through psychological manipulation and aggression. He controls her reality, confines her in isolation, restricts her food, prevents her from sleeping, and establishes dominance in every way but physical violence (Detmer 1997). The play can be an opportunity to consider boundaries and consent, topics that young people can be taught from a young age. As students are learning that their bodies are their own, we can analyze where consent does and does not show up in the play and discuss how the play would be different with a culture of consent, and with boundaries that are defined and respected.

Look Upstream: Root Causes

It is helpful to explore the underlying concepts about gender that are represented in the play, because these ideas lay the groundwork for much of what occurs in the play. A classroom exploration of *The Taming of the Shrew* might start with the early modern attitudes about women. In late-sixteenth-century England, women who defied gender norms were feared, punished, accused of witchcraft, and sometimes all of the above. Although a woman ruled England for much of Shakespeare's lifetime, women were the property of men in the eyes of the law. While the early modern period saw shifting attitudes around the acceptability of wife-beating, the patriarchal culture nevertheless approved of violence as a means of disciplining wives when they were noncompliant. The treatment of women was not so different from the training of a hawk, a horse, or a dog: discipline was key. Women who were accused of rudeness, scolding, or quarreling would wear a "scold's bridle" as a public punishment: an iron headpiece with a metal part to literally hold a woman's tongue (Detmer 1997). Beliefs around the inferiority of women are baked into the text of the play. Classroom conversations about *The Taming of the Shrew* might start with addressing these underlying beliefs as root causes of the harm that is enacted in the play. What are the unspoken attitudes that might have been held about women during Shakespeare's time? How do those beliefs and attitudes differ today? Where do we see traces of these ideas now?

Aside from their genders, Kate and Petruchio are very similar. Kate is critiqued for being *too rough* while Petruchio proudly asserts that he is *rough* and woos not like a babe. A positive trait in Petruchio is a negative trait in Kate. She is described as "froward" (or disobedient), loud, a wildcat, obstinate, and stark mad—traits one might use to describe an animal or a toddler. By contrast, Bianca is painted as mild, sober, and silent. Grumio, servant to Petruchio, observes that his boss's behavior matches Kate's supposed shrewishness: "An she knew him as well as I do, she would think scolding would do little good upon him" (*Shrew* I.ii.109–11). Why are different expectations upheld for men and women within Padua? Compare Bianca to Kate, compare Petruchio to Kate, and it becomes clear that there are molds at play, but Kate doesn't fit the mold. Often targets of bullying and violence are different from their peers and don't conform to societal expectations. Targets may be singled out for their body type, their skin color, their intelligence, their socioeconomic status, their actual or perceived gender identity, their actual or perceived sexuality, or their religion. Though we learn, as we age, to celebrate our differences, K–12 students are often singled out and targeted for their differences. A 2023 multi-country study found that some of the ways to reduce violence against women involve engaging men to challenge unequal gender norms through trainings and education. Promoting positive masculinity can be a way to improve gender equity and reduce violence against women (Daoud et al. 2022). The inequality that appears in *Shrew* suggests that tinkers are less worthy than lords, fathers have more power than children, masters have more autonomy than servants, and women are not equal to men. Beliefs such as these can reinforce a hierarchy that increases the likelihood of violence within a community.

Look at Risk Factors

Some of the risk factors for intimate partner violence include belief in strict gender roles, belief in male dominance, and hostile attitudes toward women (CDC 2024j). Among teens, girls suffer disproportionately from severe violence in relationships and are more likely than boys to be seriously injured or suffer sexual abuse because of dating violence (Youth.gov n.d.). Teen dating violence affects millions of US teens each year, and youth from groups that have been marginalized, such as sexual and gender minority youth, are at greater risk of experiencing sexual and physical dating violence. The consequences of teen dating violence are long-lasting and can have a significant impact on health and well-being. Teens who experience dating violence are more likely to abuse substances, feel suicidal, and exhibit antisocial behaviors (CDC 2025). Social emotional training programs can help young people navigate challenging relationships and create strong, healthy, and positive bonds. This play can highlight what unhealthy relationships look like and reveal opportunities for interventions. When could someone have taken action to prevent some of the abuse in the play? Where do we see upstanders stepping in?

Another risk factor in *The Taming of the Shrew* is that many characters lack the skills to handle conflict and stress in healthy ways. When pressed, the characters erupt. There is very little stopping to think or to apply reason. As with *The Comedy of Errors*, we have a level of reactivity and explosiveness in the play that isn't sustainable. Tempers flare, characters move quickly, and much harm occurs. Inability to handle stressful situations and conflicts can lead to changes in appetite, difficulty sleeping, and chronic health issues. The volatility and reactivity in the play can serve as reminders to young audiences of the importance of good sleep hygiene, healthy diet, and prosocial bonds.

Although Petruchio does not lay a hand on Kate, he is physically abusive to others: he wrings his servant Grumio by the ears, smacks the priest at his wedding, and beats Grumio on the trip home from Padua. This kind of repeated violence is a risk factor for more violence—and it's pervasive in the play. Kate ties Bianca up, smashes Hortensio over the head with an instrument, slaps Petruchio at their first encounter, beats Grumio when he denies her food and, we might presume, engages in other violent behavior before the play begins. Invite your students to make a list of all the physical violence they observe in the play. These acts of violence increase the likelihood of more violence occurring in the community. Physical violence is not the only type we see in the play. Petruchio's treatment of Kate is psychological violence, or gaslighting, a type of manipulation that makes the target question their sanity. What starts off as a bellicose courtship to which Kate does not consent quickly turns into a cycle that escalates as Petruchio abuses Kate through starvation, sleep deprivation, and mind games, all while claiming he loves her ("he does it out of perfect name of love," *Shrew* IV.iii.12).

Economic factors may contribute to behaviors in *Shrew*; Petruchio is blunt about his financial motivation: "I come to wive it wealthily in Padua; if wealthily, then happily in Padua" (*Shrew* I.ii.76–77). Baptista likewise promises to select a husband for Bianca based on the suitor's wealth. Economic stress and money concerns, such as unemployment, are risk factors for intimate partner violence; communities with high rates of poverty and unemployment can see higher rates of intimate partner violence (CDC 2024j).

Look at the Climate

The climate in *The Taming of the Shrew* contains power imbalances, which, when depicted in a play, can help us unpack inequalities and imbalances in our own cultures. Baptista legislates his daughters' relationships, thus stripping Kate and Bianca of decision-making agency. In a twenty-first-century context, we might equate Baptista with a helicopter parent, or a parent concerned with how to monitor their children's online life. There are power imbalances and structural inequities in the world of the play that can help students see where the violence comes from. Who holds power in the play? What would it look like if the power were shared rather than hoarded? What would a healthier climate look like, and how would that impact the play's outcome?

Padua lacks a clear concept of consent; some voices matter more than others, and while boundaries are established, they are not respected or upheld. Consent is a topic of focus in professional theatre, as theatre practitioners realize the importance of integrating consent in the workplace, not only when staging onstage intimacy but also throughout the collaborative process of theatre-making. When plays get put together quickly, sometimes people can feel unsafe and pressured to put themselves in dangerous situations because "the show must go on." This toxic attitude that prioritizes the play (a product) over the people making the play has been called into question by many—of note is the "Chicago Theatre Standards" (Not in Our House Theatre Community 2017), a handbook aimed at establishing safe practices for theatre professionals.

When Kate rejects Petruchio's proposal, her refusal is not heard, believed, or honored. She is forced to marry a man without her consent. After the wedding, Petruchio defends his right to control Kate, announcing, "I will be master of what is my own" (*Shrew* III.ii.235), and he is legally correct. What cultural shifts would need to happen for Petruchio's statement to be untrue? Bianca's plight, in which she cannot pursue a relationship that interests her because of rules set by her father, exemplifies her lack of agency and autonomy. Twice in the play, a wager is placed, and Kate, without her consent, is the subject of the wager; first, Petruchio bets he can marry her; second, Petruchio bets on her obedience. As others gamble on her behavior, as one might bet on a racehorse, the absence of consent in Padua is palpable.

When thinking about consent, let's not forget Christopher Sly, the tinker tricked into believing he has dreamed his identity and now he learns that he is a wealthy man with a beautiful wife. This scenario feels like a prequel of Bottom in *A Midsummer Night's Dream*, who suddenly becomes the object of Titania's affection, or like Malvolio in *Twelfth Night*, learning Olivia loves him; in these examples, the duped characters find themselves playing roles in fictions they believe to be real.

The Padua of *Shrew* (as well as the Elizabethan London of the Induction) depicts a climate of non-consent, inequality of women, and relationship violence. As a result, some people are not seen in terms of their whole selves. Kate gets reduced to a shrew, while Bianca is a perfect woman. The rules about gender, the cultural norms about patriarchy, and the pervasive inequality all get in the way of individuals being seen as themselves.

Look for Upstanders

We don't see many characters speaking up on behalf of others or taking action to prevent harm in *Shrew*. One of the only upstanders is Kate herself, who confronts Petruchio:

> Why, sir, I trust I may have leave to speak,
> And speak I will. I am no child, no babe.
> Your betters have endured me say my mind,
> And if you cannot, best you stop your ears.
> My tongue will tell the anger of my heart,
> Or else my heart, concealing it, will break,
> And, rather than it shall, I will be free
> Even to the uttermost, as I please, in words.
> (*Shrew* IV.iii.78–85)

In the absence of upstanders, Kate speaks up to her abuser. In the play, who else could have supported her? Could Baptista have advocated for his daughter? Could Bianca have attempted to make life easier on Kate? Could Petruchio have been an ally to Kate rather than an adversary?

How would the play look different if it were situated in a healthier climate that normalized and celebrated upstander behavior? If the nobleman stumbled upon a person unconscious in the street, might he call him a cab, get him to safety, or wake him up? How would the play within the play look different if Baptista didn't make rules about his daughters' marriages?

Kate is repeatedly described as a shrew, disobedient, and headstrong. These labels prevent others from looking any deeper or attempting to see Kate's true self and her potential. What would this look like if someone paid attention to Kate as a full, complete, complicated person? What if the other characters, from Bianca to Grumio, were seen not in limiting terms (ingenue, servant) but in terms of their whole humanity? Padua is a culture in which women should be seen and not heard. Kate recognizes that she must speak up for herself, and continues to speak up when facing injustice, but her self-advocacy earns her the label of a shrew. She is not seen as herself, as a whole person with potential, but as a loud-mouthed woman. This is what Otto Scharmer refers to as "attentional violence." What if Kate didn't have to fight so hard to use her voice but her voice was heard, valued, and respected?

This idea of letting people be who they are is a pattern in Shakespeare. In *The Two Gentlemen of Verona*, Julia insists: "Let me go, and hinder not my course" when her servant tries to stop her from following her heart (*Two Gentlemen of Verona* II.vii.33). Don John tells his comrades to "let me be that I am, and seek not to alter me" (*Much Ado About Nothing* I.iii.34–35). In *Henry V*, the Dauphin insists that "self-love, my liege, is not so vile a sin / As self-neglecting" (*Henry V* II.iv.80–81). If we can all learn to get out of each other's way, let people become who they will become, feel safe in their identities, and feel a sense of belonging because of who they are, we can build the conditions for healthier communities. Sometimes being an upstander is not about interrupting harm but about cultivating spaces where we honor others by taking the time to truly see them while also seeing and honoring ourselves.

PERFORMING THE PLAY FOR YOUTH AUDIENCES

CSF toured *The Taming of the Shrew* in 2016, directed by Laurie Keith. This production toured to elementary, middle, and high schools; since that time, CSF has started targeting titles to particular age groups; however, educators can approach this play with students of any age, though I recommend making age-appropriate adjustments. In adapting this play for the school tour, we thought carefully about gender and casting. Considering the historic violence against women's bodies to be found in a production history of *The Taming of the Shrew* our creative team decided to explore an all-female, three-actor production of the play. By reversing the Elizabethan convention of all-male companies, we hoped to get young audiences thinking about gender roles. In staging the play, it's important to remind students that they will see a lot of unkind behavior throughout the play; how can watching unkind behavior in a play help us be kinder in our real lives? By watching for the behavior, and discussing it afterward, can we draw more attention to it? This production took place before the #MeToo movement took the world by storm in 2017. Post-#MeToo productions of this play can confront concepts of sexual violence, domestic abuse, and violence against women.

When CSF toured *The Taming of the Shrew* to schools, our team was conscious of the use of direct address, and we employed it as much as possible. This became especially effective when Petruchio shares his plan with the audience to mistreat Kate and announces: "He that knows better how to tame a shrew, now let him speak" (*Shrew* IV.i.210–11). In this moment of direct address, the actor playing Petruchio often paused, in case a student wanted to respond. In one school performance, a student tentatively said to Petruchio: "You like Kate, don't you? Why don't you try being nice to her?"

The 2016 tour of *The Taming of the Shrew* marked the first time CSF began incorporating Spanish-speaking characters into the school-touring program, and we have retained this convention for all tours since then. Incorporating characters who speak Spanish or code-switch between languages can normalize Spanish speaking, which is common for many Colorado families. It also encourages audience members, regardless of Spanish fluency, to lean forward and listen a little more carefully . . . which is similar to the way we watch a Shakespeare play.

When staging a play as part of the Shakespeare & Violence Prevention series, we can call into question aspects of the play, and *The Taming of the Shrew* strikes me as one of those titles. Just as we invite students in a roleplay exercise to interrupt a scene, you might consider building in disruptions or "time outs" to the play itself. Consider Christopher Sly, the character watching the play within the play. You could incorporate this as a frame to question the action of the play. Perhaps your Sly remains onstage throughout the play as an onstage audience member, and occasionally comments on the action, thus voicing some of the contemporary concerns one might have with the play. You might ask your students to help craft these interruptions. (For example: Has anyone ever heard of consent? Someone please tell Petruchio you can't force someone to marry you. Ever heard of the #MeToo movement?)

When CSF staged *The Merchant of Venice* in a 2022–23 school tour, directed by Anne Penner, our team introduced a convention in which the actors interrupted the performance to try an especially problematic scene another way (see the epilogue for more on this). I recommend trying this approach in education-focused productions of *Shrew*. What if the first wooing scene between Kate and Petruchio unfolded two different ways? Perhaps the first version as Shakespeare wrote it, and another version with consent, clear boundaries, and honest and direct language in which people say what they need, and their needs are heard and respected? How might things turn out differently?

The movement to incorporate boundaries and consent in the theatre has led to some revolutionary work in the field; the Intimacy

Directors and Choreographers (IDC) is an organization focused on training intimacy professionals in the theatre; these are professionals who help actors stage moments of intimacy with safety, boundaries, and respect. Prior to this professional shift toward boundaries and consent, actors who voiced safety concerns might have been viewed as difficult. In the aftermath of the #MeToo movement, theatre professionals have begun to normalize consent and boundaries as key parts of the theatre-making process. These lessons could likewise be incorporated in discussions of *The Taming of the Shrew*.

UPSTANDER ROLEPLAY EXERCISE

After Petruchio's wedding to Kate and the couple has returned to his home together, he delivers a soliloquy that can provide a roleplaying opportunity for young people to step into the narrative. In a sort of confessional, Petruchio shares his plan to tame Kate as he would tame a hawk, which includes starvation, sleep deprivation, and gaslighting:

> PETRUCHIO: Thus have I politicly begun my reign,
> And 'tis my hope to end successfully.
> My falcon now is sharp and passing empty,
> And, till she stoop, she must not be full-gorged,
> For then she never looks upon her lure.
> Another way I have to man my haggard,
> To make her come and know her keeper's call.
> That is, to watch her, as we watch these kites
> That bate and beat and will not be obedient.
> She ate no meat today, nor none shall eat.
> Last night she slept not, nor tonight she shall not.
> As with the meat, some undeservèd fault
> I'll find about the making of the bed,
> And here I'll fling the pillow, there the bolster,
> This way the coverlet, another way the sheets.
> Ay, and amid this hurly I intend
> That all is done in reverend care of her.
> And, in conclusion, she shall watch all night,
> And, if she chance to nod, I'll rail and brawl,
> And with the clamor keep her still awake.
> This is a way to kill a wife with kindness.
> And thus I'll curb her mad and headstrong humor.

> He that knows better how to tame a shrew,
> Now let him speak; *'tis charity to show.*
> (*Shrew* IV.i.188–211)

This speech is disturbing, to say the least, as Petruchio compares his treatment of his wife to the training of a bird. The final couplet (my emphasis) is an opportunity for the audience to step into the narrative. In sharing the plan to tame Kate, Petruchio does what happens a lot in Shakespeare. He turns to the audience and asks them for advice. What would you do? Will you help me? Shakespeare was fond of direct address, and I imagine that in performances in Elizabethan England, which were performed in broad daylight in the open air, the audience members might answer back. This opportunity to reflect on Petruchio's position, to take a "time out" and to seek advice is something that rarely happens in moments of real-life violence. Here, in the playhouse, we might take a moment to pause . . . and to invite empathy. Imagine that the audience gave Petruchio advice. Imagine that Petruchio listened to their advice. This is one of those fine moments of openness in a Shakespeare play, which holds room for ambiguity. In Petruchio's asking for advice, there is an opportunity to reflect on how we might behave in this situation. Is this not empathy in practice, as Petruchio, a fictional character, asks a very real audience in a very real theatre, what they would do if they were in his shoes? I suggest using this scene as a roleplaying opportunity and giving students a chance to strategize how they might take action as themselves if they witnessed this. In appendix G you will find a lesson plan that uses this moment in the play, along with discussion questions and suggested activities.

Some questions to consider as you plan your upstander roleplay activities: What could have turned out differently in this scene if we listened to Petruchio, knowing that the person he is talking about is experiencing abuse? How could we frame the conversation in a way that encouraged positive masculinity rather than a patriarchal concept of masculinity? How might we introduce the ideas of respect, consent, and boundaries? How might we support Kate as a whole person, not as a subordinate of Petruchio? What kind of advice could we give Petruchio here? What changes could we implement in Padua to prevent this kind of situation in the future? Petruchio's father has recently died; how might this impact his behavior? Are there expectations his father may have placed on him that influence his approach to winning Kate over?

There is no correct upstander solution—there are only the solutions that feel comfortable and possible for your students. Give them the chance to practice how they might take action. Who would they go to? What words would they use? Would they confront Petruchio directly? Would they tell Kate of Petruchio's plan? Would they go to a trusted adult? Your job, in leading this roleplay, is not to suggest solutions but to hear from students about their own upstander strategies and let them practice those solutions in the safety of a classroom roleplay.

Some students may feel more comfortable than others participating in a roleplay; remind them that there are many ways of participating and they can find ways that are most appropriate for them. This might mean getting up in front of the class to participate in a roleplay, or it might mean watching and listening to support our peers. Theatre activities often valorize extroverts and ignore introverts, but it is important to recognize the value of everyone in the class, whether or not they get up in front of peers to participate in a roleplay.

When we consider upstander strategies, we often think about individual actions; what could I do in this moment? However, in the context of *Shrew*, there are also systemic factors at play that make individual actions seem ineffectual and inadequate in fictional Padua, where women don't have legal rights and violence is normalized. How can one upstander possibly make a difference? As you roleplay individual strategies with your students, I encourage you to simultaneously have conversations about the systemic, underlying forces at play. Encourage your students to consider how one upstander action might eventually impact the systems and structures that hold up a culture.

TAKEAWAYS FROM *THE TAMING OF THE SHREW*

The Taming of the Shrew offers an opportunity to interrogate healthy and unhealthy relationships, prosocial and antisocial bonds, and relationship dynamics. An upstander who can interrupt the action and redirect the play's outcome could lead to a more peaceful, less violent world of the play. Although *Shrew* presents us with a world we don't want to inhabit, and depicts unhealthy behavior, if paired with appropriate pre-show and post-show activities and "nestled in thought," it can become a tool to help young audiences grapple with some challenging questions in a healthy, solution-oriented way, and change the narrative Shakespeare gave us.

In a post-#MeToo world, *The Taming of the Shrew* speaks to questions about control, manipulation, and inequality. Framed as a play within a play, we have the opportunity to question many things depicted in the play. Remember that a play can be a tool. A play provides an experience, a temporary community process that may bring up feelings, memories, and thoughts. We can use a play as a starting point, notice the thoughts we have about it, and think about how the play and our reactions to it connect to our lives, our communities, and our time. By the end of this chapter, you might still worry that working on *The Taming of the Shrew* could reinforce harmful ideas. This is a challenging and legitimate concern, and I invite you to talk those concerns over with colleagues and even your students (if you feel it's age-appropriate). I have learned, in my years of working in theatre and education, that we cannot control audience response. We see many examples of Shakespeare's characters trying to control others. In *The Taming of the Shrew*, the nobleman thinks he can manipulate Sly, surround him with fancy things and he will imagine he is a lord. Baptista believes he can manage his daughters' behaviors, make rules to govern their experiences, and that will lead to a good outcome for all. Petruchio believes that he can put Kate through a taming process and by the end of it she will behave in an obedient way. But these scenarios leave out the inner experience, the hidden workings of a human consciousness. We may set up the conditions whereby an audience will laugh at a pratfall, stay silent in a poignant death scene, and clap at the end of the play, but your individual experience is your own. Just as Elizabeth I knew that she could govern a country but she could not "open windows into men's souls," the job of an educator or an artist is not to control the inner thoughts of our students and audience members. We cannot. We can cultivate experiences, facilitate conversations, get curious about discoveries in the room, and not be in control of the takeaways. When we invest too much in dictating the inner workings of others, we fail to trust them. We must trust our students, trust our audiences, that they are themselves. We can believe in them. The "what if" moments are scary. What if I am reinforcing stereotypes? What if they are not getting it? Engaging with

Shakespeare is a process. We don't always get it right, but we can keep talking about it, and stay curious, right alongside our students, trusting that we are getting somewhere.

9

The Tempest

Prospero's "Rarer Action": Forgiveness and Breaking the Cycle of Violence

The Tempest, one of Shakespeare's last plays, is commonly categorized as a comedy, though it feels like a decidedly different kind of comedy than the earlier works. Scholars label the late plays (*The Tempest*, *Pericles*, *Cymbeline*, and *The Winter's Tale*) as romances, plays that integrate fairy tale elements, magic, epic journeys, and the passage of many years. Unlike Shakespeare's earlier comedies, *The Tempest* focuses on reconciliation, forgiveness, and righting past wrongs. Marjorie Garber describes the play as "one of Shakespeare's most compelling 'revenge tragedies,' turned, at the last moment, toward forgiveness" (Garber 2004, 853). It is in *The Tempest*'s movement from revenge to forgiveness that educators may find opportunities to reflect with their students on the cycle of violence, the long-term impact of holding a grudge, and the transformative power (but complicated challenges) of forgiveness. The play works well with elementary school students, but this approach could be appropriate for middle and high school students as well. This is a play that depicts the ripple effect of mistreatment, including oppression and colonization, and depicts the interruption of mistreatment. When the play's main character chooses to abandon plans to harm others and makes a different choice, shifting the tone from violence to reconciliation, it can help students see the alternatives present in any seemingly harmful situation.

https://doi.org/10.5876/9781646427246.c009

PLOT SYNOPSIS

Twelve years ago, Prospero, the duke of Milan, was supplanted by his brother, Antonio, cast out of Milan with his toddler, Miranda, and sent out to sea on a ramshackle boat. Prospero now lives on a deserted island with the fifteen-year-old Miranda, along with two servants: the magical sprite Ariel and the island-born "monster" Caliban. During his twelve years on the island, Prospero has sharpened his magical abilities, and on the day the play begins, Prospero's usurping brother will be sailing near the island, along with a royal party from Naples. Among them are King Alonso (who aided in Antonio's overthrow of Prospero), Alonso's brother Sebastian, and Alonso's son, Prince Ferdinand. With Ariel's help, Prospero plans to create a tempest, which, he hopes, will wreck the ship on his island and bring his enemies to his turf, where he can exact his revenge.

The storm is a success, and Ariel strategically places the survivors in different parts of the island. Miranda meets the shipwrecked Ferdinand, the heir of Naples, and they fall in love. Antonio, Sebastian, and Alonso are stranded in a different part of the island and tormented by Prospero's spirits. Caliban meets up with two drunken servants of the king, Trinculo and Stephano, and forms an alliance with them.

Left to their own devices, some characters continue the cycle of violence, while others choose the "rarer action" of virtuous behavior. In the royal party, Antonio encourages Sebastian to murder Alonso and become the new king (a plot that is thwarted by Ariel). Elsewhere on the island, Caliban encourages Stephano to kill Prospero and become the king of the island (also thwarted by Ariel). Miranda and Ferdinand, however, do not engage in harmful cycles but find themselves in love, which Prospero calls "a fair encounter of two most rare affections" (*Tempest* III.i.89–90).

Just as Prospero is ready to complete his final act of revenge, with some prompting from Ariel, he chooses to forgive his enemies instead. He reveals himself as the wronged duke of Milan, and King Alonso restores Prospero's rightful dukedom to him. Prospero forgives his brother Antonio for past wrongs. Miranda will marry Ferdinand, thus securing her legacy not only as leader of Milan but also of Naples, and Prospero will return home to Milan, but not before freeing Ariel and Caliban, assuming that the audience releases him from the island with applause.

VIOLENCE PREVENTION CONNECTIONS TO *THE TEMPEST*

The Tempest provides young audiences with the opportunity to witness the aftermath of bullying, the cycle of violence and trauma, and power imbalance in action while also opening a discussion about the role of forgiveness. While the play deals with harmful mistreatment and violence, it also invites audiences to consider what healing looks like, and it shows us a path out of violence and toward peace. With the violence-prevention lens, we will explore the root causes, risk and protective factors, climate, upstander behaviors, and our own upstander strategies.

Look Upstream: Root Causes

Although it takes a stretch of the imagination to view a seventeenth-century story about a ducal overthrow in a twenty-first-century setting, there are many parallels between Antonio's mistreatment of Prospero and contemporary examples of bullying. Antonio's actions toward Prospero, which include a violent ousting from his position of power and a potentially deadly trip across the ocean, certainly qualify as unwanted aggressive behavior and can be viewed as root causes for some of the harm depicted in the play. The behavior was repeated over time and escalated; what began as small attempts to steal control gradually became an overthrow. Antonio was intentional in the plan and openly acknowledges his involvement to Sebastian (*Tempest* II.i.310–19). The situation also involves a power imbalance regarding Prospero's lack of information and knowledge. Prospero didn't know of the planned overthrow as it was happening, and so he lacked power to act in response. Even though Prospero held the political power on paper, Antonio was operating things behind the scenes, turning friends against him. To stage this play with an eye toward violence prevention is to recognize that Prospero has been deeply harmed by a loved one and still carries those wounds today. Just as targets of bullying are not required to forgive the people who bully them, so should we recognize that Prospero carries deep and legitimate pain, and his forgiveness of his brother is not required. We can instead shift the conversation to focusing on how Prospero might find ways to disrupt the cycle of harm rather than passing it on to characters like Caliban and Ariel.

Contemporary research around bullying can help students contextualize Prospero's experience, particularly when we consider the events he experienced in the years before the play began. The research around bullying consistently reveals that between 20 percent and 25 percent of students report that they have either been bullied or bullied others in the past year. Bullying negatively impacts everyone involved, not just the target. Students who experience bullying are also at an increased risk for depression, anxiety, sleep difficulties, low academic performance, and dropping out of school (CDC 2024f). Although Prospero's story is not set in a school context, we do see that he is forced into social isolation, and he does appear to have mental health challenges because of his experience.

Shakespeare's plays are steeped in history, steeped in the past, and filled with references to what has come before. *The Tempest* gives audiences the opportunity to see not just one act of harm but a history and a cycle of harm. In many tales of revenge, we hear the phrase "getting even," a term that is both pervasive and not possible. There is no such thing as "even" when it comes to the cycle of violence; instead, the scale is always tipping when one uses violence to right a wrong.

Upstream of the events of the play, much of Prospero's pain originates with Antonio's usurpation and Prospero's stolen dukedom. Prospero has been wronged, and he desires to get even. In the act of doing so, as he fixates on his past harm, he ends up hurting more people, including Caliban, Ariel, Antonio, Sebastian, Alonso, and Ferdinand. Violence leads to more violence and suffering. If we go backward in time, we even see that the offstage characters in the play have, for years, been caught in similar cycles. Caliban's mother, Sycorax, was banished from her home long before the play begins, rejected from society, much like Prospero was, for witchcraft. She was sent off to parent her child on her own in unknown territory; she was wronged by her society, isolated from her support network, and she continued the cycle by inflicting harm on others; she enslaved Ariel in a tree for disobeying her, and this enslavement continued until Prospero arrived after Sycorax's death and freed Ariel.

This cyclical nature of violence is not confined to the 24-hour period of the play. It is ancestral, and repeated, we presume, over the centuries. Unlike most Shakespeare plays, which unfold over a matter of days, weeks, or years, *The Tempest* takes place over the course of a single day. Despite its tight focus on the present moment, the long history of violence and trauma endured by these families is clear. The pattern, we presume, will continue, unless someone takes action to interrupt it. Ariel is the one to jam a pebble in the cycle of violence by suggesting Prospero might feel compassion toward his enemies. Ariel's small upstander action gives Prospero enough distance and space from his fixation on revenge to allow him to take a breath and reconsider.

Look at Risk Factors

Prospero's past influences the risk factors we see in *The Tempest*. Though Antonio's usurpation of Prospero's dukedom took place before the action of the play begins, these wrongs have etched themselves into Prospero's brain and impel the play's forward momentum. Students who experience bullying are twice as likely as non-bullied students to experience negative health conditions, including headaches and stomachaches (Gini and Pozzoli 2013). Prospero experiences something akin to a panic attack and explains to his daughter and future son-in law that he needs to take a breather: "A turn or two I'll walk to still my beating mind" (*Tempest* IV.i.179–80).

Prospero was bullied by his brother, and he then proceeds to bully Caliban (and also, in different ways, Ariel) when he seizes power on the island. This dual role of bully and bullied is yet another risk factor. The risk for mental health and behavioral problems is greater among young people who bully others and are targeted by bullying, compared to students who only experience bullying but do not go on to bully others (CDC 2024f). Prospero betrays a fixation on revenge, he is impatient with his daughter ("dost thou attend me?" *Tempest* I.ii.96), he threatens physical harm to Ariel and Caliban when they are disobedient, and he confesses he has a troubled mind, all of which can be connected to his experience of being bullied, abused, and harmed by a close family member. None of this justifies Prospero's mistreatment of Caliban and Ariel, but rather it contextualizes his mistreatment as part of a larger cycle.

Prospero's trauma is tangible in the play, and we should not dismiss the harm he experienced and the ways in which hurt people hurt people. *The Tempest* has a late point of attack, which means that if the story is told in a linear timeline, the moment in the story in which the play begins is very close to the end. The *story* of *The Tempest* would likely begin twelve years ago, when Prospero was overthrown by his brother. However, the *plot* begins wherever the first scene begins (the shipwreck, in this case), which is very late in the story. This requires a lot of exposition in the first few scenes to get the audience up to speed. As a result, we don't see Prospero experience the overthrow; we aren't experiencing it in real time alongside him. This is a notable divergence from plays like *Pericles* or *The Winter's Tale*, in which we witness the main characters experience some of the most challenging and traumatic moments of their lives, and we move through time with them. In *Pericles*, the eponymous character begins the play as a young man, and we see him meet his wife, become a father, and grow old over the course of the play. *The Winter's Tale*, likewise, begins in Sicilia when Leontes erupts in jealousy and loses his family, all of which we watch unfold in real time. Then sixteen years pass, through the help of the allegorical character of Time, and we end the play with Leontes as an older man—but we got to watch the events of Leontes's *année terrible* unfold. *The Tempest,* by contrast, begins late in the story, and we meet Prospero after he's experienced the worst of his trauma. We don't meet Prospero when he is being evicted from his dukedom; we meet him years later, when the experience has hardened into history. As a result, one might overlook the story Prospero tells as just that—a story, something in the past, something that has already concluded. However, if we put ourselves into Prospero's shoes, it is highly likely that he continues to relive these moments. He may be stuck in the past trauma more than in his present moment, and perhaps the revealing of his story to his daughter for the first time sparks a trauma response. He suffered great loss, great betrayal, great fear, all while caring for his young child, trying to protect both of them from a violent death at sea. The events of the first scene, in which Alonso's ship is wrecked by the storm, are similar to moments that Prospero and Miranda have likely *experienced* twelve years ago.

Taking the time with your students to look at the way Prospero describes the encounters with his brother can be a helpful exercise in perspective-taking. Encourage them to consider how Prospero feels about these memories. Encourage them to write about a moment from that time, and imagine how Prospero responded, which moments continue to haunt him. It can be useful to draw parallels to their own lives. Twelve years can feel like a long time to a child, but to an adult, it may not feel like the distant past. Encourage them to think about a past wrong, perhaps something that happened in their more recent memories. How does it feel to look back on that moment? Although some time has passed, what details do you remember? Prospero's pain can serve as an important reminder that all behavior comes from somewhere, and violence rarely occurs in a vacuum. Focusing on the legitimacy of Prospero's pain, and especially looking at his behavior to determine the risk factors, can add nuance and complexity to the play.

Look at Protective Factors

In a study conducted in the aftermath of the Rwandan genocide (Staub et al. 2005), researchers designed an approach to support healing and reconciliation, which reduced trauma symptoms and brought about more positive feelings about the "other" group, paving the way for reconciliation. This method included naming and understanding trauma symptoms, learning about the causes and process of genocide, sharing painful experiences with an empathetic group, and answering a series of questions about attitudes toward forgiveness and reconciliation. The findings suggest that carving out a path to reconciliation and forgiveness can have a wide variety of positive outcomes. The study concludes that "participants began to integrate their own experiences of the genocide with the information they received about the origins of genocide in general, and in specific instances at other places (Staub 1989, 2003). This seemed to bring about an *experiential understanding* that had emotional meaning, rather than simply the acquisition of information. . . . They came to see the genocide as the outcome, although a horrible one, of human processes, rather than of incomprehensible evil. The discussion suggested that this made them feel more human, that they felt rehumanized by it" (Staub et al. 2005).

Perhaps a great deal of the work around preventing violence is related to the concept of rehumanization, as we remind ourselves of our own humanity while acknowledging the humanity of others. Just as Ariel reminds Prospero what a human might do in this situation, Prospero is reminded of his own humanity, of the humanity of his "enemies," and of his connectedness to his fellow humans.

Forgiveness has been identified as a key variable in the reduction of bullying: "An absence of forgiveness and reconciliation destroys the chance to build the emotional scaffolding that is needed to boost self-regulation" (Ahmed and Braithwaite 2006). When punishment, expulsion, and suspension are the primary ways bullying is addressed in schools, there is little room for reconciliation. When we see forgiveness in action in *The Tempest*, perhaps an alternate path for our schools comes into focus. Forgiveness, however, is not required to prevent violence, and in many cases, forgiveness is not appropriate. When analyzing the play with students, it is important to understand that some of your students may have direct experience with being physically or emotionally harmed by family members. Forgiving the person who harmed you is not a requirement; instead, we might focus on ways to avoid perpetuating the cycle of mistreatment and harm. Prospero was hurt by a family member; even though his pain is real, it is not okay for him to hurt others because he is hurting. Holding that complexity in your classroom space can be a powerful way to unpack the complexity of violence within families; Prospero is hurt and wants to hurt his brother, but instead he forgives him. Remember that a play does not always show us the world as it should be, but it can kick-start conversations about our own communities. Discuss the role of forgiveness with your students: When is forgiveness appropriate? How can we disrupt harm without forgiving those who have done us wrong? These are complicated, nuanced conversations, and we can use Shakespeare to help us begin those conversations. Please be sure that you have trained professionals (school counselors and mental health professionals) if your work with *The Tempest* brings up challenging personal experiences for your students.

Look at the Climate

The Tempest takes place entirely on Prospero's island but depicts two different climates: the climate of Milan, which is reported to us by Prospero; and the climate of the island we witness throughout the play. In many ways, the climate of Milan, in which one leader overthrows another, has been replicated on Prospero's island. Just as Antonio overthrew Prospero, so Prospero established himself as the leader of the island when he arrived, even though it meant making Caliban and Ariel serve him. In this climate, might makes right, and we see a pattern of conquering and ruling over others. What else do you notice about the climate? What kinds of behaviors are acceptable in this climate? What kinds of alternatives to the climate are introduced? Encourage your students to think about the climate of the play and what a healthier climate might look like.

Look for Upstanders

In *The Tempest*, there are several moments that exemplify upstander behavior. Below are a few that we have found to be especially meaningful in the context of a violence-prevention lens. As you dig more into the play with your students, I encourage you to pay close attention to these moments.

Shakespeare's play starts with a storm, in which we see the mariners and the nobles aboard the ship, experiencing the tempest that eventually wrecks the ship on Prospero's island. We don't know it yet, but the storm was an act, a mirage, a bit of theatrical magic assembled by Prospero and Ariel. However, in the second scene of the play, the first voice we hear is Miranda's, the fifteen-year-old daughter of Prospero, who says,

> If by your art, my dearest father, you have
> Put the wild waters in this roar, allay them.
> The sky, it seems, would pour down stinking pitch,
> But that the sea, mounting to th' welkin's cheek,
> Dashes the fire out. O, I have suffered
> With those that I saw suffer! A brave vessel,
> Who had, no doubt, some noble creature in her,
> Dashed all to pieces. O, the cry did knock
> Against my very heart! Poor souls, they perished.
> Had I been any god of power, I would
> Have sunk the sea within the earth or ere
> It should the good ship so have swallowed, and
> The fraughting souls within her.
>   (*Tempest* I.ii.1–13)

This speech, delivered by a young person who has grown up outside of the trappings of society, demonstrates empathy and upstander behavior in action. Miranda begs her father to stop the storm, which seems to still be happening, based on her present-tense statement: "The sky, it seems, would pour down stinking pitch, but that the sea... dashes the fire out." She then reflects on what she has already seen. Miranda's "O I have suffered with those that I saw suffer" could be paraphrased to mean "I was suffering right alongside the people on that ship." Here, Miranda is demonstrating a clear sense of empathy and compassion, as she expresses concern for the people she saw suffering at her father's hands.

Empathy, as discussed in chapter 2, could be defined as feeling with someone, putting oneself in someone else's shoes, and seeing the world from another person's perspective. It comes from the Greek, "em" (in) and "pathos" (feeling). There are different types of empathy, but cognitive empathy, which involves not necessarily taking on a person's emotions but thinking about how they might be feeling, can be a helpful tool. In this way, we are not encouraging students to feel exactly what someone else is feeling, or to suffer alongside them, but to *think about* how another person might feel; it is more about tuning in to someone else and deepening awareness than asking students to change how they are feeling in order to align with the emotions of another person.

Compassion comes from the Latin "com" (with) and "pati" (suffer) and means to suffer with someone. Here, Miranda is feeling alongside the people on the ship ("O I have suffered," "O the cry did knock against my very heart"), but she is also taking action. She is speaking to the person she assumes to be in charge (her father). Then she imagines what action she might take if she were in charge ("Had I been any god of power"). This is the act of imagination, in which someone who is not in charge envisions an alternative and reminds us that it does not have to be this way—the violence she witnesses is not inevitable but preventable.

The Tempest includes several hypothetical moments in the play in which a character imagines a scenario, or practices imaginative and cognitive empathy. Gonzalo does this when he imagines what he would do if he were the leader of the island. We will also see Ariel use cognitive empathy when imagining how a human might respond to Prospero's revenge plot. This key moment in which Miranda imagines the suffering of others sets us up to see a parade of people (and sometimes spirits) imagining what they'd do if given the chance, if they were in someone else's shoes. Some plan harm (Antonio and Sebastian, Caliban and Stephano), and some plan compassion (Miranda, Ariel, Gonzalo). This refrain of "what if" can spark our imaginations as we contemplate being in the shoes of others.

In the instance of Miranda's opening speech, you might have your students paraphrase her words, then imagine a contemporary scenario. Have you ever spoken up to someone in a position of power when you thought they were planning to hurt someone? What did it feel like? What words might you use to convince Prospero to ease up on the storm? What tactics would you try? How do you think Miranda feels when she is speaking these words to her father? This moment can help tease out how this scene explores empathy, compassionate action, and upstander behavior.

Training our students in empathy and compassion can have positive results. There is a noted connection between empathy and prosocial behavior, between empathy and lower rates of aggressive behavior, and between empathy and a reduction in implicit racial bias (Klimecki 2019). We can help our students unpack empathy as they watch the plays unfold and discuss what it means to consider the world from someone else's perspective. Having this kind of emotional literacy can support children as a foundational part of a safe school climate. According to the Center on the Social and Emotional Foundations for Early Learning, "Emotional literacy is the ability to identify, understand, and respond to emotions in oneself and others in a healthy manner. Children who have a strong foundation in emotional literacy tolerate frustration better, get into fewer fights, and engage in less self-destructive behavior than children who do not have a strong foundation" (Center on the Social and Emotional Foundations for Early Learning n.d.). Miranda's demonstrated willingness to connect with fellow humans, understand the world from their perspective, and her desire to help alleviate the suffering of others, can serve as an opportunity for students to witness this behavior in performance, and follow up with discussions about empathy and compassion for others, all of which can support a positive foundation in which students are more emotionally regulated.

Throughout the play, Ariel frequently steps in to prevent harm and takes action to interrupt planned violence. Ariel is also, in the context of the play, a magical creature with magical abilities, so what does this suggest about upstanders? In conversations about the play, we can link upstander behavior to a magical superpower—but instead of a fictional superpower, it is a superpower that we all possess, and that we all have the potential to use in our daily lives.

Early in the play, Ariel describes the storm, and Prospero asks if everyone remained safe; he doesn't want anyone actually hurt by his magical storm. Ariel assures Prospero that not only are his enemies safe, but that their clothing actually looks better than it did before their journey. Ariel also intervenes (invisibly) to prevent Antonio and Sebastian from murdering king Alonso in his sleep. Ariel toys with Stephano and Caliban when they plan to hurt Prospero. Ariel tries many strategies to prevent harm. Perhaps the most effective strategy, however, is Ariel's quiet confrontation of Prospero. As the play draws near its end, Ariel has assembled the Italian nobles, and Prospero asks for an update about how they're faring under his spell. Ariel informs Prospero that Alonso, Antonio, and Sebastian are all "distracted" (spellbound), and the rest of the Italians are mourning the catatonic states of their leaders.

> ARIEL: Your charm so strongly works 'em
> That, if you now beheld 'em, your affections
> would become tender.
> PROSPERO: Dost thou think so, spirit?
> ARIEL: Mine would, sir, were I human.
> PROSPERO: And mine shall.
> Hast thou, which art but air, a touch, a feeling
> Of their afflictions, and shall not myself,
> One of their kind, that relish all as sharply
> Passion as they, be kindlier moved than thou art?
> Though with their high wrongs I am struck to th' quick,
> Yet with my nobler reason 'gainst my fury
> Do I take part. The rarer action is
> In virtue than in vengeance. They being penitent,
> The sole drift of my purpose doth extend
> Not a frown further. Go, release them, Ariel.
> My charms I'll break, their senses I'll restore,
> And they shall be themselves.
> (*Tempest* V.i.21–40)

This scene contains some powerful moments related to forgiveness, connectedness, and empathy. In this moment, Ariel practices cognitive empathy through imagining what it might be like to be a human ("Mine would, sir, were I human"). I can imagine using that line as a starting point for a freewrite exercise, in which students explore what makes someone a human; I might start with the opening question: What does humanity mean? Ariel's empathy sparks empathy in Prospero as well: He wonders that a spirit ("which art but air") can feel the pain of another ("a touch, a feeling of their afflictions"); and if so, shouldn't he, a human himself, in kinship with the people suffering, feel compelled to take action ("one of their kind . . . be kindlier moved than thou art?").

Something might shift with Prospero in that moment, when he witnesses his spirit-servant (not a human) reflecting on how a human might respond to this situation, and then he decides that he will become "tender" to his enemies. Ariel, though inhuman, imagines the possibility of feeling forgiveness, compassion, and tenderness. Sometimes all it takes is another person to reflect back to us what they see; this can help us gain more clarity about our present actions.

Prospero makes a choice and acknowledges the complexity of the situation. He has been deeply hurt by his brother and his confederates, and he knows that his pain is authentic ("though with their high wrongs I am struck to th' quick"). "Quick" means alive (as in the phrase "the quick and the dead"), so when something is struck to the quick, it means that one is affected at the very center of one's being, at the most alive and tender part of oneself. Although struck to the quick, Prospero can also choose to separate himself from his deep pain with some breath, time, and space ("yet with my nobler reason 'gainst my fury"). He has reason and he has fury. Humans are complicated. We are capable of rage and of rational thought. Here, he consciously chooses to act on his rational thought, from a calm, centered space, and with the quiet encouragement of Ariel's empathetic upstander behavior.

Finally, the decision to break the magic spell allows Prospero to accept that his "enemies" are who they are ("and they shall be themselves"). Learning to accept others for who they are, flaws and all, and letting people be who they are, is another throughline in many of Shakespeare's plays. This is tied into not only violence prevention, but also cultivating spaces in which individuals can flourish, thrive, and live up to their full potential, or achieve their "spark."[1] This

---

1 For more on this research of sparks and thriving, visit Search Institute: https://www.search-institute.org/our-research/youth-development-research/sparks-and-thriving/.

moment reveals some emotional maturity on Prospero's part as he recognizes the importance of letting people be who they are. He cannot change his brother, but he can stop himself from perpetuating the cycle of harm.

Despite the great pain Antonio and the others have caused for Prospero, Prospero steps out of the cycle of repeated violence. He chooses to be rational instead of emotional. He chooses to "take part" with reason rather than vengeance; he joins in as a rational creature instead of a furious creature. To "take part" may mean to participate or join in, but this could also be an acting metaphor. A "part" in a play is the character you're assigned to play. In Shakespeare's day, actors didn't receive the full script, only their "part" or their cue script: a scroll (or "roll," from which we get the term for an actor's "role" in a play), just their lines and their one-to-two-word cue. Paper was expensive, and handwritten "parts" were cheaper than copying out a full script for actors. There were no laws protecting copyright, so you didn't want too many full copies of a script out there; that would risk the play being stolen and performed by another company or printed and sold. Theatre companies were protective of their scripts. Just as an actor might pick up another actor's part and play that role in a performance, so Prospero decides that today, he'll play the role of one who forgives.

Let's look again at Prospero's decision: "Though with their high wrongs I am struck to th' quick, / Yet with my nobler reason 'gainst my fury / Do I take part. The rarer action is /In virtue than in vengeance." Prospero draws a distinction between virtue and vengeance. It is more common to act on vengeance, to want an eye for an eye, to act from a place of self, ego, and pain. But the rarer action, the more sacred action, and perhaps the more difficult action, is choosing virtue, choosing connectedness, choosing to act from a place of connection rather than separation. It's a more vulnerable choice to act that way, because it opens us up to pain.

"Rarer" is an interesting word choice to describe Prospero's choice to forgive. Elsewhere in the play, the word "rare" is used to describe the love between Ferdinand and Miranda ("a fair encounter of two most rare affections"). It means uncommon, but also scarce, and therefore valuable, like a rare gemstone. It conjures up the image of something made more valuable by its uncommonness, something that is one in a million.

Shakespeare's use of the word, however, is not rare; it appears eighty-seven times across the canon in the plays and sonnets (and four of those times are in *The Tempest*). In fact, the word rare (and its variations: rarer, rarely, rarest) appears thirty-four times in the four romance plays, which means that almost 40 percent of Shakespeare's "rares" appear in only four plays: *The Tempest* (4), *Cymbeline* (14), *The Winter's Tale* (10), and *Pericles* (6). In *A Midsummer Night's Dream*, Bottom describes his "most rare vision" (*A Midsummer Night's Dream* IV.i.14–15). In *The Winter's Tale*, Dion is comforted by the fact that when the message from the oracle is delivered, "Something rare / Even then will rush to knowledge" (*Winter's Tale* III.i.25–26). In addition to denoting something scarce, rare is often associated with sacredness, holiness, divinity, spirituality, and transcendence.

How might we translate the concept of "rare" today? Precious? Endangered, like a species? How might your students connect to the idea of rareness? A rare Pokémon card? A rare type of bird? This can be a great way to dig more into this moment, to unfold the meaning of Prospero's transformation, as he realizes he has a chance to be the rare human who chooses connectedness over division.

Before facing his enemies, Prospero has the opportunity to look at the people of his past without them knowing him; they are awakening from his spell and don't recognize him. One by one, he looks at them and remembers their role in his traumatic past: "O good Gonzalo, / My true preserver and a loyal sir / To him thou follow'st, I will pay thy graces / Home, both in word and deed" (*Tempest* V.i.77–80). Prospero remembers the kindness shown to him by Gonzalo, the one person who reached out to help him in his time of need. This speaks to the power of an upstander. Perhaps this act of kindness kept Prospero going during these challenging twelve years. Then he turns to King Alonso of Naples and Alonso's brother Sebastian, both of whom aided in his overthrow: "Most cruelly / Didst thou, Alonso, use me and my daughter. / Thy brother was a furtherer in the act.— / Thou art pinched for 't now, Sebastian" (*Tempest* V.i.80–83). Then he faces his brother, Antonio:

> Flesh and blood,
> You, brother mine, that entertained ambition,
> Expelled remorse and nature, whom, with Sebastian,
> Whose inward pinches therefore are most strong,

> Would here have killed your king, I do forgive thee,
> Unnatural though thou art.
> (*Tempest* V.1.84–89)

Prospero sees his brother clearly as someone who is driven by power and has lost his natural tendencies of remorse (the "milk of human kindness" as described in *Macbeth*). And not only does he reflect on the harm done to himself but also that this is his brother's pattern. Prospero realizes Antonio is flawed and unnatural, and he still forgives him. Perhaps this moment is linked to Prospero's acceptance that "they shall be themselves" as he learns that we cannot control the actions of others. This raises a question: Who does forgiveness help? Is Prospero doing this for the sake of his brother or for his own sake? Does forgiveness somehow help the climate and the community, rather than solely helping individuals?

Once the enemies awaken fully, and recognize Prospero, he confronts his brother: "For you, most wicked sir, whom to call brother / Would even infect my mouth, I do forgive / Thy rankest fault, all of them, and require / My dukedom of thee, which perforce I know / Thou must restore." (*Tempest* V.i.149–54). It is forgiveness, though not necessarily a reconciliation or an invitation to continue a relationship. He is simply letting go, acknowledging that his brother has many faults, and finally sees him as he is.

By the end of the play, the story we thought might end with revenge instead unravels and quickly becomes a tale of forgiveness. Prospero relinquishes his magic and plans for the return trip to Milan. But first, he asks the audience to free him, thus allowing him to return home. Review the epilogue with your students and encourage them to imagine being in Prospero's position. He closes with the final lines: "As you from crimes would pardoned be, / Let your indulgence set me free" (*Tempest* Epilogue 19–20). This final couplet continues the new cycle: Prospero pleads with us to do what he just learned to do, to free others, to forgive others, and to let others be themselves. He has broken the cycle, and he challenges us to do the same. The play ends with the promises of freedom and peace.

Throughout the play, there is an undercurrent of empathy, compassion, and perspective-taking. Theatre can be a powerful tool to build awareness in our students about what it means to consider the world from someone else's perspective. This play, and many of

Shakespeare's plays, can be used as empathy-strengthening opportunities. We can use the plays to practice analyzing the perspective of others; this kind of work can deepen our students' emotional literacy and deepen connectedness between humans—these are critical parts of a healthy, vibrant community in which individuals recognize their mutual connectedness and can be celebrated for who they are.

PERFORMING THE PLAY FOR YOUTH AUDIENCES

CSF has toured productions of *The Tempest* several times as part of the Shakespeare & Violence Prevention program. Our directors have included Rand Harmon, Kevin Rich, and Laurie Keith. We have learned some valuable insights about staging it with young audiences. If possible, I highly recommend involving live performance as you encounter the play, whether from a local theatre company, the school drama department, or within your own classroom. Shakespeare's plays work best on the stage, and meaning can be conveyed in live performance in ways that aren't always evident on the page. If you decide to stage the play for your students, or if you are a theatre company looking to perform the play for local schools, I hope you find this section helpful. None of these suggestions should be interpreted as prescriptive or formulaic; they are simply suggestions. Please make the best decisions to support your performers, your creative team, your staff, and your audiences.

The Tempest is neatly composed of three distinct groups: the shipwrecked nobles (Alonso, Sebastian, Antonio, Gonzalo), the "drunkards" (Caliban, Trinculo, Stephano), and the islanders (Prospero, Miranda, Ariel). Some characters cross into multiple categories. Caliban, for example, is both a drunkard and an islander, but in general, these broad categories work nicely with small-size casts.

The script cuttings CSF developed require actors to play multiple roles, and this can invite students to engage in meaning-making as they reflect on the show. When they see the same actors enacting those three distinct groups, students might subconsciously become aware of the patterns of mistreatment within all three circles; just as Prospero is plotting against his enemies, so we see Caliban and the drunkards plotting to overthrow Prospero, and we see the nobles plotting to overthrow Alonso. Doubling invites deep thinking about similarities and differences between characters, and how one person can play many roles. In our touring productions, we frequently use the following doublings:

ACTOR 1: Ariel/Miranda/Stephano
ACTOR 2: Prospero/Alonso/Trinculo
ACTOR 3: Caliban/Ferdinand/Antonio

In the suggested doubling/tripling above, we can see some resonances in terms of character similarity, or character distinction in the roles assigned to the actors. For example, the same actor may play Prospero and Alonso, both of whom are leaders. One of them (Prospero) has been usurped, while another (Alonso) has a brother who plots a similar overthrow. This embodiment of both roles by the same actor can be meaning-laden for audiences as they draw parallels between the roles an actor plays. Doubling can also be an opportunity to showcase an actor's versatility, and an opportunity for students to delight in the power of transformation. The same actor playing Miranda, Ariel, and Stephano gets to be an empathetic witness (Miranda), a nonhuman entity who ruminates on what humans might do when faced with emotion (Ariel), and a drunkard tempted by power (Stephano). When one actor embodies Ferdinand, Caliban, and Antonio, audiences often enjoy seeing one actor transform from a shipwrecked prince to an island creature to a usurping sibling. The onstage transformation can reinforce that none of the roles we play in violent situations are fixed but are instead malleable and can be changed, just as an actor tries on a role and transforms into someone else with the change of a hat. If a small cast size requires you to double or triple some roles, I encourage you to use it as an opportunity to explore what resonances emerge in a variety of casting choices. An introduction at the start of the show, in which your actors quickly review which characters they'll play and demonstrate which costume pieces indicate the different characters, can serve to support clarity in storytelling.

CSF's touring *Tempest* productions often engage the audience with the creation of a group storm. The actors direct members of the audience to play a different part of the storm when Prospero cues them: a section of the audience creates the wind sounds with their voices, another section creates thunder sounds with feet-stomping, and another section is responsible for making rain sounds by clapping their hands. Whenever Prospero references a storm and gives the audience its cue, they are invited in as co-performers, with a specific role to play. We have also experimented with having Ariel or Prospero "conduct" the audience to help with magical moments.

When our three-actor troupe did not have enough bodies onstage to enact all the characters required for one scene, we resorted to a solution that involved the audience stepping in as performers. In act 3 scene 2, Trinculo, Stephano, and Caliban are plotting Prospero's overthrow when Ariel interrupts their scene in an effort to halt their plot. Ariel speaks (in a voice that Stephano hears as Trinculo's voice), while Caliban is sharing the plot, and says, "Thou liest." This storytelling is difficult with only three bodies, so we solved it in the following way. Prospero (who doubles as Trinculo in our cutting) came onstage before the scene began and addressed the audience:

> Hi everyone. I need your help, some people are planning a really mean trick, and we need you to be upstanders. When you hear this cue (*rings a bell, shakes a thunder tube, etc.*), you say, "Thou liest." It means "you're lying." I think that will help stop their plan. Can you help me with that? Let's practice!

Before the scene begins, the audience members are primed to step in as upstanders, and they are watching intently, ready for their cue to step in. Then the actor playing Prospero transitions into Trinculo, and the scene begins. This kind of direct involvement, if achieved in a consensual way between actors and audience, can be a way to embody upstander behavior before moving into a classroom setting to practice.

The Tempest, one of the most musical of Shakespeare's plays, can benefit from the integration of music throughout the play (whether using Shakespeare's lyrics, contemporary lyrics, Elizabethan music, or contemporary tunes). The opportunities for incorporating music include (but are not limited to) Ariel's "Full Fathom Five" as Ferdinand enters, Caliban's "Freedom Hey Day," and Ariel's "Where the bee sucks." We also often have a stage manager who plays simple Foley cues (a thunder tube, a small portable harp to give a flourish to Ariel's magical entrances, a rain stick, etc.). All of these aural elements can give students accompanying sounds to underscore their experience of the play.

As with the other touring CSF shows, I recommend using easily recognizable hats, vests, or other noticeable pieces to visibly mark which character an actor is playing. When the same actor plays Prospero and Alonso, we typically have a cloak for Prospero and a crown for Alonso. The actor only needs to remove the cloak and pop the crown on to suggest the shift. The actors often wear neutral clothing as a base layer, to allow them to easily transition between characters. The bases are often jeans and a black T-shirt or black pants and a white T-shirt; ideally, the base layer can metaphorically disappear under the costume piece and students learn to recognize the character shifts—a hat equals one character, a cape equals another. Sometimes another actor can help with the transformation (i.e., an actor can hold out the crown as Prospero transitions into Alonso). I recommend using the costumes as an opportunity to differentiate the characters and work with the actors to highlight the differences between each character they play in terms of their vocal and physical work.

In the Shakespeare & Violence Prevention program, the touring troupe often performs in gyms, under fluorescent lights. While these are not the most dramatic venues, and because these scenarios usually feature universal lighting, the emphasis is best not placed on spectacle or illusion but on imagination. A scarf, a puppet, or a billowing sheet to represent the ocean are all elements we have incorporated. We have learned to leave room for imagination, keep it simple, and avoid the need to awe while instead embracing theatrical magic and imagination. In the opening of *Henry V*, the chorus laments that we don't have all the fancy trappings we need to tell this story: "O for a muse of fire that would ascend the brightest heaven of invention!" (*Henry V* Prologue 1–2). Likewise, the CSF touring company cannot carry fancy scenery and props in our trusty minivan (lovingly nicknamed "Calivan"). Instead, as the chorus instructs us, we must use our imaginations: "Piece out our imperfections with your thoughts . . . think, when we talk of horses that you see them" (*Henry V* Prologue 24–27). When students are given the opportunity and the responsibility to fill in the blanks, they become the meaning makers. "For 'tis your thoughts that now must deck our kings" (*Henry V* Prologue 29–30).

LOOK IN THE MIRROR: UPSTANDER ROLEPLAY EXERCISE

When facilitating activities to explore violence prevention in *The Tempest*, it can be effective to explore the moments upstream of the mistreatment and violence in the play. These are often the ideal moments to focus on as we engage students in a roleplay, because they allow us to consider the root causes of the violence depicted in the play. Because *The Tempest*'s point of attack comes so late in the story, most of the violence has already occurred and most of the harm has already happened. However, finding a violent or harmful moment within the events of the play can also remind students that no matter how far down the cycle we've gone, no matter how much harm has occurred, there is always the opportunity to prevent further harm. You cannot forget what has occurred, and harm doesn't always merit forgiveness, but the play highlights the opportunity to choose, late in the story, a different path.

Appendix H includes a lesson plan focused on *The Tempest*, which suggests roleplaying a moment that occurs before the play begins: a moment when Prospero tells Ariel about his plan to create a storm to wreck his brother on the island. What if you witnessed that conversation between Ariel and Prospero? How might you take action to prevent harm? Would you speak directly to Prospero? Would you pull Ariel aside? Would you report the plan to a trusted adult? You may swap in any moment in the play (or before the play begins) in which your students rehearse their own upstander strategies.

The key is to invite students to try out their own strategies rather than come in with a prescriptive way to respond. The other key idea is that they should step into the scene as themselves, not as a character from the play. When you have limited time to work with students on this, we recommend focusing on the work that makes the biggest difference (upstander behavior) rather than having students roleplay as perpetrators or targets of mistreatment. We know that practice makes better, and just like we practice any skill we want to refine, we need to practice our own upstander strategies before we need to use them in real life. We practice so these tools are easier to access when we need them.

The suggested upstander roleplay activity in appendix H includes the opportunity to take action, the practicing of a skill, and the recognition of the work. These are all key ingredients in how social bonds are formed, according to social development theory, and this kind of connectedness can also have benefits beyond the goal of practicing upstander behavior.

NOTE ABOUT REAL APPLICATIONS: It can be hard to measure the impact of this kind of work, but even when it's not visible to you, the work may be affecting students in unseen ways. I recall a moment in a workshop when we staged this scene and invited students to step in. A fourth-grade student volunteered, and I recall a look of surprise exchanged between the teachers in the room. The student walked into the scene and pulled Ariel aside. "You don't have to do what Prospero says," the student told the actor playing Ariel. Ariel responded with: "But Prospero is my friend, and I'm worried if I don't do what he says, he won't be my friend anymore." The student thought for a moment, and responded, "I'll be your friend," taking a tentative step toward the actor, arms outstretched and ready for a hug. Ariel thanked the student and accepted the hug. It was a simple solution, and a kind act of alliance. The student didn't solve all the problems. The student didn't stop Prospero from causing the storm. But the student took a step toward human connection, and let Ariel know someone was watching out for them. Later, in the hallway outside the classroom, the teacher pulled me aside and said this moment was surprising because the student who participated in the scene had sensory challenges and rarely engaged in physical or eye contact with others. Stepping into a fictional scene seemed to have opened something up in the student that was typically dormant in a classroom setting.

Roleplaying the *Tempest* scenario with your students can be a fun way to explore how they might act when someone is planning harm. If you are playing the roles of Prospero and Ariel, when your students come up with their upstander strategies, you may need to adapt the scene to suit the strategy. For example, a strategy may involve telling someone else about Prospero's plan. In that scenario, you may need to adapt to play the role of King Alonso, as your student rehearses the strategy with you. You may need to play Prospero, if the student wants to try out a direct strategy to interrupt the harm. In these scenarios, you may want to give the students a bit of resistance, to encourage them to keep at their strategy. In other words, as Prospero, you may not want to give up on the storm plan so easily; what if you resist the student's upstander attempts first? "But my brother really hurt my feelings and I need to get back at him," for example. The important thing is that you are playing the role(s) of the perpetrator or target, and your students should be in the role(s) of the upstander. The more you can reinforce positive upstander behavior when you see it, the better. Remind your students that there is no one-size-fits-all approach. This is a chance to practice a strategy, not to perfect a strategy. There is no such thing as a perfect strategy that will stop the harm once and for all. But we can use our time together to practice strategies so we feel a little more comfortable using the strategies when we need them.

THE TEMPEST TAKEAWAYS

The Tempest can provide elementary school students with some opportunities to think not only about how to prevent harm in communities but how to move past harm and toward healing. As Prospero makes the choice to shift from a revenge tale to a tale of forgiveness, so we can make choices to deepen our connections to the people around us and practice empathy; in every moment of our lives, we are dealing with other humans, all of whom behave the way they do because of what has happened to them. While the action of the play is tightly packed into the events of a single day, the lead character is haunted by events from the past; this play can emphasize how it feels to be in the present moment. Prospero's plea to the audience is essentially a plea for empathy: "As you from crimes would pardoned be, let your indulgence set me free" (*Tempest* Epilogue 19–20). Treat me the way you would want to be treated, he seems to tell us, if you were in my position. Although forgiveness is not required, it might help us become free.

10

Conclusion

Hope and Peace through Shakespeare

At the heart of this handbook are a few key beliefs: that Shakespeare's plays can be harnessed to provide school-age children with violence-prevention skills; that practicing behaviors through roleplays can improve those skills; and that Shakespeare's plays offer some critical distance through metaphor to analyze human behavior. These beliefs are rooted in practical experience, after more than thirteen years of watching young people, ages eight to eighteen, connect Shakespeare's plays to their own lives through performances and post-show role-playing activities. Throughout this book, I demonstrate how live, performance-based approaches to Shakespeare's plays reinforce violence-prevention skills in school-age children. Shakespeare's plays provide opportunities for students to witness problematic behavior in performance and to strategize their own peaceful solutions through roleplaying, imagination, and creativity. While teaching the twenty-first-century skills of creativity, collaboration and communication, a performance-based approach to Shakespeare in the classroom also lays the groundwork for the goals of violence prevention: empathy, teamwork, and the possibility of change. I have seen first-hand Shakespeare's potential as a tool to address violence prevention in schools. My hope is that this handbook provides readers with the skills to put this kind of work into practice in their own learning communities.

When I tell people about the Shakespeare & Violence Prevention project at the Colorado Shakespeare Festival I am often asked, why Shakespeare? Why not write a new play for youth audiences that addresses contemporary situations of violence in schools? My answer to that is rooted, at least partially, in the complexity, openness and heightened language of the plays. When students encounter Shakespeare's elevated language, they are introduced to something larger than life and from a time beyond their own. In the twenty-first century, when a young person's encounter with another is often confined to small spaces, tiny screens, hashtags, and abbreviations, the openness that comes from hearing Shakespeare's words can serve as a vital kind of expansion. Shakespeare's plays, even when abridged to thirty to forty minutes, don't moralize, don't provide simple answers, and are not straightforward. They require work and imagination on the audience's part; they encourage us to listen, to lean in, and to be present. As students watch a complicated story unfold in real time, they are subtly learning about cause and effect, about power dynamics, and about human relationships. This unraveling of a complicated story, or "grappling with a complex text" (Thompson and Turchi 2016) is a healthy exercise for a young person's mind. Shakespeare's plays don't provide many answers but leave us with questions. What will Malvolio do next? Has Prospero truly forgiven his brother? What will happen to Don John? Storytelling is an engaging form of instruction, and Shakespeare's plays are compelling stories with big, bold language. They do not provide singular, stable meanings; rather, they encourage meaning-making on the part of the creative team and the audience members.

My colleague Dr. Beverly Kingston, the director of the Center for the Study and Prevention of Violence, talks a lot about healing. The science, she says, is not enough to get us through the healing that needs to happen in our world. We also need stories and creativity and connectedness. We need the arts and sciences to come together, so that we can not only reduce violence but also increase peace, wellness, and presence.

Shakespeare's plays are not perfect, and neither are the characters within them. Yet if we, as educators and artists, can use them as tools to dig deeper into our own culture's problems surrounding violence, perhaps they can help equip young people with some critical skills to support their own journeys with violence prevention. Shakespeare's plays are deeply integrated into the curricula of many school systems, and their reach is far and wide. What if we used these plays, not as works of art we hang on a wall, but more like Play-Doh, which we don't consider precious? What if we treated Shakespeare like something we can wrestle with, change, adapt, and wonder about? What if Shakespeare could be treated like a tool we use to develop the critically important skills of connectedness and empathy?

After many years of producing the Shakespeare & Violence Prevention program at the Colorado Shakespeare Festival, witnessing its impact on young people, and thinking about how Shakespeare and violence prevention are connected, I am left with some guiding principles that emerge from this work, and which apply equally to the practice of engaging with Shakespeare and the work of building healthier, safer communities:

1. Slow down
2. Practice empathy
3. Notice our connectedness
4. Speak up
5. Have hope

Slowing down teaches us to be present, to be in the moment we are in. When we slow down, we can breathe and put some space between ourselves and the situation, in order to approach our circumstances with more clarity. **Practicing empathy** reminds us that the person we are dealing with may have a different perspective than ours. **Noticing our connectedness** reveals the ways in which we are all part of the same climate; we all breathe the same air, and our actions impact those around us. **Speaking up** reminds us that we have voices, and we have the power to change an outcome by using our voice (through words or actions). **Having hope** keeps us going and reminds us that change is possible. This is slow work, and violence will not stop all at once. But we can maintain hope that small actions will make a difference. These are all lessons that emerge from the practice of staging, studying, and witnessing Shakespeare's plays, and all of these lessons naturally reinforce violence-prevention goals.

1. SLOWING DOWN IN SHAKESPEARE; SLOWING DOWN IN VIOLENCE PREVENTION

> "Wisely and slow: they stumble that run fast."
> —*Romeo and Juliet* II.iii.101

At the first rehearsal of a Shakespeare play, longtime Colorado Shakespeare Festival director Carolyn Howarth often says, "We have very little time, so we must work very slowly." In CSF rehearsals, we devote time to dissecting Shakespeare's text, analyzing the actions of each character, and carefully staging scenes. Taking care with each of our actions is a key part of theatre-making, encouraging all to be present at each step of the play-making process. When the process of theatre-making is rushed, we often lose the complexity, the nuance, and the truth of the scenes. When delivering the text, young actors often want to plow through the most difficult sections; seasoned actors know that slowing it down and chewing on the words can help clarify meaning.

In *Freeing Shakespeare's Voice*, Kristin Linklater writes, "Becoming aware of images in language is a process of slowing down.... In the case of reading, you almost certainly have a linear habit—you read quickly along the lines of print to find out what information is in them. This is not wrong, but in the search for Shakespeare's meaning it is not enough." She urges actors to "slow down, be patient, and swear off all interest in results for the time being" (Linklater 1992, 33–34). Slowing down with our approach to Shakespeare yields deeper connection to the meanings embedded in the text and in our own minds.

Many characters in Shakespeare's canon speak to the power of slowing down. Friar Lawrence urges the impulsive young couple in *Romeo and Juliet* to go "wisely and slow. They stumble that run fast" (*Romeo and Juliet* II.iii.101). In *A Midsummer Night's Dream*, Theseus is called in to settle a domestic dispute between Hermia and her father, and he urges them to "take time to pause" (*Midsummer* I.i.85). Portia encourages Bassanio in *The Merchant of Venice* to "pause a day or two before you hazard" (*Merchant* III.ii.1–2) in the hopes that he will avoid making a rash (and wrong) decision. The wisdom courses throughout the plays, although often it is ignored by the rest of the characters, that if we slow down and get some space between our circumstances and ourselves, we can often see more clearly.

While slowing down can lead to deeper connections to Shakespeare's plays, it also connects with violence prevention; time is a powerful tool as we work to reduce violence and deepen peace. When violent incidents occur, the involved parties are often acting on impulse, rather than using the rational part of the brain. We can learn to settle our bodies, calm our nervous systems, take deep breaths, and connect with the present moment in order to deepen the space between impulse and action. If we are witnessing violence, our nervous systems may be rattled, and we may not think clearly about how to take action. Theatre training, in which we work to reduce tension and deepen focus on the breath, can help individuals connect to the present moment. As educators, we can use theatre as a way to slow students down, get them into their bodies and breath, and create space for them to act from the most conscious versions of themselves.

The act of being in a present moment with another human being, sharing a space, can invite a fundamental shift. When you pick up a character and put it on, you are entering the mind and experience of someone different from you. When you watch an actor transform onstage and become someone else, maybe part of you is vicariously experiencing the world from someone else's perspective—a key ingredient in building safer worlds. Breath is vital to being present, and to seeing what is happening in the moment. Taking a breath in our most difficult moments can bring some clarity, space, time, and openness to the situation. What if we all practiced taking a breath whenever witnessing mistreatment, and we slowed down enough to respond *after* taking that breath? This habit of slowing down with breath can be a skill we build with students to develop mindfulness, presence, and clarity.

2. EMPATHY IN SHAKESPEARE; EMPATHY IN VIOLENCE PREVENTION

> "I have suffered / With those that I saw suffer."
> —*Tempest* I.ii.5–6

Empathy, or stepping into someone else's shoes, is a superpower. We see it in many of Shakespeare's plays. In *The Tempest*, Miranda thinks about the people suffering on the ship as they experience her father's storm. In *Twelfth Night*, Viola considers Olivia's experience of being in love with the wrong person. "What thriftless sighs shall poor Olivia breathe!" (*Twelfth Night* II.ii.39) she exclaims, expressing empathy for her crush's crush. In the collaborative, incomplete play partially attributed to Shakespeare, *Sir Thomas More*, the eponymous character encourages the citizens of London, who are demanding the removal of "strangers" (noncitizens, immigrants) to imagine what it would be like to be expelled from England. He implores the Londoners to "imagine that you see the wretched strangers/ Their babies at their backs, with their poor luggage / Plodding to th'ports and coasts for transportation" (*Sir Thomas More* II.iv). Throughout Shakespeare's plays, a pattern repeats of characters who pause and take a moment to consider the perspective of another person or group of people.

Putting yourself into someone else's shoes can help you see the world from a different vantage point. Empathy requires slowing down (see step 1). Just as we practice CPR to save lives, we can practice cognitive empathy with our students by asking, What do you think this character feels right now? Why? If you were this character, how would you show it in your body/voice? This constant practice of "perspective-hopping" as we explore the world from a different character's point of view can help students recognize that other people (just like Shakespeare's characters) are complex, multifaceted, and motivated by their past and present experiences. When actors play a character, they use empathy to imagine what it is like to be this person and to consider this person from the inside. When watching an actor play a character onstage, we might use empathy to consider what the character is thinking and feeling. Just like an actor approaching a role, we can think about the people in our own lives as worthy of curiosity, worthy of attention, and worthy of time. If we can harness these moments of possible empathy and integrate them into our approaches to Shakespeare, we raise awareness about what it means to consider the world from the perspective of another.

3. CONNECTEDNESS IN SHAKESPEARE; CONNECTEDNESS IN VIOLENCE PREVENTION

> "I to the world am like a drop of water / That in the ocean seeks another drop."
> —*Comedy of Errors* I.ii.35–36

When encountering Shakespeare in the classroom, we have the opportunity to build our students' awareness of connectedness. How do one character's actions connect to another character's actions?

How does one word affect the overall tone of a line of text? How can our class, as we work together to stage one scene, deepen our own connectedness? When we sit in a theatre to watch a play, how are we connected to the people onstage? How are we connected to the other people in the audience? How are we connected to our own thoughts and feelings? Realizing our connectedness with those around us takes time (see step 1), and when we consider the world from the perspective of someone who is not us (see step 2), we can begin to notice our connectedness.

Since the first humans gathered around campfires to tell stories, we humans have needed connection. Building connections within a community is not only a very human impulse, which makes us feel like we are part of something larger than ourselves, but it's also a protective factor in preventing youth violence. If we can use Shakespeare as a tool to see connectedness (among the characters, between the past and present, between peers), we are truly making the plays our own. When we engage with Shakespeare's plays, we learn that another person's experience can directly shape our own. My pain is your pain, my joy is your joy. Violence is about dividing people, seeing them as less human. Connecting is about peace-making, bridge-building, uniting people, and seeing the humanity in every life we encounter.

We shape the world by our actions, and our actions have a deep impact on those around us. Imagine a world in which the friar in *Much Ado About Nothing* had not stepped in to concoct a plan. Would Beatrice have taken her own revenge against Claudio? Imagine a world in which someone intervened to prevent Sir Toby and Maria from pranking Malvolio. How would that impact Malvolio's experience and his well-being? Imagine a world in which the Montagues and Capulets settled their feud without violence. What would Romeo and Juliet's relationship look like in a community that centered connection over feuds and that fostered empathy instead of enmity? Imagine a world in which Ariel did not speak up to confront Prospero at the end of *The Tempest*. Would Prospero have exacted revenge on his brother? When we ask these questions about a fictional play, perhaps the concepts they evoke are easier to grasp than trying to find the same lessons by taking a hard look at our own communities. These plays reveal connectedness in practice and the way one person's actions circulate within a community. A play reveals the ripple effect of violence on a culture, and that cycle of violence, if uninterrupted, does not end. Likewise, we see how one small action can bring about a peaceful resolution. Our actions have consequences; one small upstander action will affect one's community, and one small violent action will affect one's community.

4. SPEAKING UP IN SHAKESPEARE; SPEAKING UP IN VIOLENCE PREVENTION

> "Give sorrow words."
> —Macbeth IV.iii.246

Throughout Shakespeare's plays, characters use words to power through challenging circumstances as they work to clarify their thoughts. When words are stopped, things get even harder. Hamlet tells us, "But break, my heart, for I must hold my tongue" (*Hamlet* I.ii.164). Language can help us navigate difficult circumstances. When Macduff learns he has lost his family, he is counseled to "give sorrow words. The grief that does not speak / Whispers the o'erfraught heart and bids it break" (*Macbeth* IV.iii. 246–47). The characters in Shakespeare's plays risk heartbreak if they cannot express themselves. When students encounter Shakespeare's plays, they can gain a sense of ownership of these words and can learn to put thoughts into language. They can make the language, written four hundred years ago, alive and present in their own bodies and voices.

Language and communication are also powerful tools not only to cope with but also to prevent violence. Putting our thoughts into words is something we can learn through exposure and familiarity with Shakespeare's plays, and it can then expand into our communities in positive ways. As educators, we can bridge the gap between the plays and our world by addressing the value of speaking up about what we know to be true. As one character concludes in the final scene of *King Lear*: "Speak what we feel, not what we ought to say" (*King Lear* V.iii.393). Learning to name what we observe is a powerful tool in the face of violence.

Speaking up really can make a difference. Research continues to demonstrate that upstander intervention is effective, that plotters consistently show signs of concern prior to planned attacks, and that the people most aware of planned school attacks are peers. Although many young people are aware of unsafe behavior, they are often reluctant to speak up. For schools and communities to become safer, we must work to improve the school climate and create a culture of speaking up, reporting mistreatment, and responding fairly and consistently to it. We must listen to students, because they know what's going on. Engaging the voices of young people and reminding them of the power of speaking up is a key part of making safer, healthier communities.

This is where the gap between research and application comes in. We can't rely on the research alone. We need to lift the research off the journal page and into our school buildings, our bus routes, our playgrounds, and the spaces in which our young humans live and interact with others. We need to practice what it feels like to put the research into our bodies. This research belongs not only to social scientists and public health experts but to all of us.

So many people would probably like to imagine that, when faced with a situation in which someone is being mistreated, we would take action to protect that person and prevent harm. But how? What would that look like in action? How would it take shape in my body, my voice? Who would I approach? What words would I use to ask for help? Rehearsing such interventions will tell us. Upstander behavior is something we must practice, get better at, and then practice again. We cannot rely on instinct alone, because there are too many factors that make it challenging in the moment. But if we train, if we practice, we get better.

I took a refresher CPR class recently, and the instructor gave a clear explanation and set of tools. Thirty compressions. Two rescue breaths. Check for signs of life. Repeat until paramedics arrive. After talking us through the instructions, however, all the students practiced this technique with a mannequin. The stakes were low; no one was dying. We could practice safely, mess up, try again, and it would make us more prepared for a real-life encounter. While the issues of violence prevention are often messier and more complicated than physical injuries warranting CPR, and the processes might not be as physical or literal as thirty chest compressions and two rescue breaths, I do think we could establish some guiding principles and practice those skills with our students in ways that leave room for imagination, creativity, and their unique selves. If we are not formalizing upstander trainings, perhaps we could at least normalize upstander behavior. Giving young people the chance to get creative and experimental with their solutions is key, because helping others can be fun and joyful. It can engage one's creativity and imagination while bringing about a deeper awareness of our interconnectedness.

The fun of upstander behavior is that there is no one-size-fits-all approach, so I encourage you to use the classroom as a creative space to try out what works for your students as they find their own solutions and voices and then practice using them. What feels comfortable for one student may not feel comfortable for another. They can practice their individual strategies. The practice is the key part—they'll be more prepared in real life and will have already thought through what works. Regardless of whether you introduce a formal strategy with your students, or simply normalize upstander behavior as part of daily life, we should practice these actions, over and over, until they are automatic, until we get to the point of acknowledging that, of course, when I witness mistreatment, I speak up or take action to prevent the harm.

5. HOPE IN SHAKESPEARE; HOPE IN VIOLENCE PREVENTION

> We,
> Great in our hope, lay our best love and credence
> Upon thy promising fortune.
> —*All's Well That Ends Well* III.iii.1–3

Just as each Shakespeare play ends with a forward movement, with characters moving offstage to continue conversations, and perhaps with a new world order sweeping in, so we can continue to learn, grow, and change our communities for the better. Shakespeare is full of hope (which is different from uncomplicated happy endings). The families reconcile at the end of *Romeo and Juliet*. After Malvolio swears revenge, we hear a command: "Pursue him and entreat him to a peace" (*Twelfth Night* V.i.403). A rightful king takes over after Macbeth's death. Petruchio and Kate (depending on how you look at it?) learn to work as a team. Change is ever present in these plays—and the conversations will continue offstage after the play is over. The story doesn't end where the play ends. It is a call to action for us to do better. *The Merchant of Venice* concludes with "I am sure you are not satisfied / Of these events at full; let us go in / ... / And we will answer all things faithfully" (*Merchant* V.i.318–21). As *Cymbeline*'s Posthumus Leonatus says, "Live / and deal with others better" (*Cymbeline* V.v.511–12). We can always do better. Although these endings, in which the conversations continue offstage, are likely due to the theatrical conventions of the time (how do we get actors offstage plausibly in a theatre with no curtains or blackouts?), this subtle forward-leaning motion of the plays reminds us that the world keeps moving.

These same lessons about hope that we find in Shakespeare's plays also appear in violence-prevention research. We know that violence is preventable. If we apply what works, we can reduce it. We can make a difference by taking small actions: slowing down, practicing empathy, noticing connectedness, speaking up, and maintaining hope. These small steps can add up, allowing us to do the harder, longer work of changing the systems and foundations that incubate conditions for violence to occur. Our small actions can slowly transform the foundation into one in which all people can thrive as their truest selves.

NEED FOR FUTURE RESEARCH

While the Shakespeare & Violence Prevention program at the Colorado Shakespeare Festival has made significant strides in reaching young people with translating violence-prevention research into practice, I see several key areas in which more work is needed to deepen the impact of this kind of interdisciplinary endeavor.

With further time, funding, and effort, the Shakespeare & Violence Prevention program would benefit from an evidence-based impact study. Future researchers could measure whether and how roleplaying strategies in a classroom setting influences upstander behavior outside of the classroom, for both the student engaging in roleplay and the observer. Studies like this could lead to a clearer understanding of how the arts can be harnessed in translating research into practice. Initial evaluation measures suggest that the Shakespeare & Violence Prevention program increases upstander behavior among school-age children. The positive response rate to the program is high, but more research and testing would provide an objective basis for replicating the work more widely. In the meantime, our observations and the anecdotal response from educators who have experienced the program suggest there is reasonably strong evidence for continuing the rollout of these methods.

I hope that this book leads readers to recognize the need for broader support for arts in education and increases awareness about theatre's natural reinforcement of mindfulness, connectedness, and empathy. As we find ourselves facing greater mental health challenges across the spectrum of the population, we could turn to some theatre-based practices to deepen our abilities to be present. Many theatre professionals and amateurs know that practicing theatre has positive benefits to one's overall well-being, but this notion could be more broadly shared. We need more theatres doing this work, testing it out, learning and stretching Shakespeare's plays to explore how they can truly be tools to improve our world.

After many years of watching this program play out in schools, I have observed qualitatively that many students respond to the model of watching a Shakespeare play and stepping into moments upstream of the violence to try out their own solutions to prevent harm. They open up when the stage is theirs, when they are seen, heard, and valued, and they have the freedom and space to practice their own strategies. CSF's Shakespeare & Violence Prevention program uses simple surveys to measure the effects, but I am confident that social scientists, neuroscientists, and other researchers could find ways to more precisely and thoroughly measure the impact on young people over time. Can we measure how students gain upstander skills when they practice through roleplaying? How does roleplaying a fictional scene from a Shakespeare play provide skills that translate into the real world? How does watching a play impact a student's empathy? How is empathy impacted when a student watches a peer roleplay upstander behavior? How is empathy impacted when a student stands in front of peers to roleplay upstander behavior? How do these exercises impact the trajectory of a student's behavior?

The Shakespeare & Violence Prevention program takes a broad view of violence overall, and there are intersecting factors that contribute to violence, such as race, class, gender, body type, disability. I believe educators could adapt the model of performance and post-show roleplaying activities to explore any number of those more targeted issues.

CALL TO ACTION

After spending more than thirteen years grappling with Shakespeare and violence, the wisdom I continue to find through this interdisciplinary work is that *words can help, time can help, and empathy can help*. If we find ways to practice speaking up, taking time to pause, and thinking about how others might be experiencing things, we will move toward a more peaceful state.

I close with a call to action; we have the ability to change the iceberg's foundation, one individual action at a time. Let's do it. A climate is made up of many small interactions, and all of them contribute to the environment. Everyone is part of the climate, and each action within the system reinforces the system. Although one person cannot change the climate alone, small, repetitive actions add up to big change. What are some actions you can take to deepen your empathy, to connect with others, and to open up to the possibility of change? These plays are not the only way to engage with building a more peaceful world, but these plays are everywhere in contemporary culture, so they can be a helpful starting point as we seek ways to translate research into action.

The plays of Shakespeare can serve as a canvas, an endless playground of explorative potential. Rather than staging and studying these plays because they have been appreciated and performed for hundreds of years, I invite you to look to them to address our present world and its challenges. Be curious and present as you explore these plays, because I believe they hold lessons for us today that might help us navigate our way out of a culture of violence and toward a culture of peace.

> "As you from crimes would pardoned be,
> Let your indulgence set me free."
> —*Tempest* V.Epilogue 19–20

Epilogue

THE PROCESS OF WRITING THIS BOOK AND BUILDING THIS PROJECT IN A CHANGING WORLD

I started working on this book in the middle of 2018. It is now the middle of 2024, as I work through final edits. During the six years I spent writing the book, my colleagues and I have continued running the Shakespeare & Violence Prevention school tour while also running many other Shakespeare education programs, and we have weathered a challenging pandemic that included living in isolation, homeschooling children, transitioning to virtual programming, working with film crews, and developing COVID-19 protocols for a safe return to live performances. Our community experienced a mass shooting in March 2021 at a grocery store down the street from the CSF office, when ten members of our community were senselessly murdered. Later that year, a wildfire destroyed over one thousand homes in a nearby suburban town. There is pain and suffering in our community, and sometimes it seems relentless. In the midst of trying times, in a nation that seems to be growing increasingly divided, I find solace and inspiration in continuing to run the Shakespeare & Violence Prevention program in Colorado. Each year, our team gathers a group of actors, violence-prevention experts, and community leaders. With each new rehearsal and tour process, we adjust our curriculum, refine our training, ask hard questions, and craft our lesson plans to adapt to the changing needs of our world. The work, it seems, does not end. It is never complete and likely never will be. The learning and growing always continue.

I have noticed a pattern in my years doing this work, as the outside world influences the program. Each time another mass shooting, planned attack in a school, or act of high-profile violence occurs in our country, I lose hope. You would think that the repeated news of mass shootings would have a numbing effect, but for me it is the opposite. I absorb the information as new, shocking pain. My heart breaks for the innocent lives lost, for the heartbroken families, for the suffering of so many people. I feel hopeless. I feel stuck. I feel like the violence will never end. I want to give up.

In this vulnerable state, I am full of questions. Judgmental questions such as: How can people be so intentional about hurting their fellow human beings? Don't we know better? How can someone purchase a weapon with the intent of killing another human? How did we get to the point in which another human sees a fellow human as a threat, rather than a full, complete human being, utterly irreplaceable and precious? How can we *not* see, given what we know from violence-prevention findings, that violence is preventable? How can these acts keep happening? And personal questions: Why am I wasting my time putting on plays when our world is so very broken? Is this work making a difference?

In the face of these internal questions, I occasionally want to give up and stop wasting my time with theatre, because it all seems so frivolous, so disconnected from reality. But that is my inner critic. You have yours, too, I am sure. Mine is judgmental and thrives on comparison and division.

But then I slow down, and I can begin to interrupt this cycle. If I pause to take a breath, a deeper truth emerges. It comes from the part of myself that runs on connection and presence, rather than on division and absence. I know, deep in my bones and fibers, that the foundational practice of thinking about our fellow humans as fully human and deserving of respect makes a difference. The foundational practice of giving space and time and openness to a moment makes a difference. The foundational practice of putting our thoughts into words and using language to connect with others makes a difference. I know it because I have witnessed this process in action, whether in a classroom roleplaying workshop or in my own lived experience. I know this is why plays matter—they teach us, in their roundabout, experiential, metaphorical way, to see the connectedness between all living beings.

In the hardest of circumstances, I find comfort in sharing tears with colleagues, hugs with loved ones, and in spending time with my own children. When the pain is so big and awful, connectedness helps. Digging into my community helps. Countless times over the years, when I have grown tired and jaded about theatre's potential in the face of mass violence, colleagues, actors, and experts in violence prevention have reminded me, often through their words and actions, that the work of Shakespeare & Violence Prevention does matter, and that I am not alone. One of my favorite moments of comfort came from a former colleague, Mark Lanning, with Safe2Tell, who told our team to remember that we can't solve all the problems, all by ourselves, all at once. We are in this together. My colleagues repeatedly pull me out of my rut and encourage me to continue.

We need practices to make our world safer, yes. We need appropriate tools to report dangerous behavior, we need emergency lifesaving resources. In fact, we have many of these tools already. But we also need empathy, connectedness, and the ability to be present. When we are present, truly present, we can take in our surroundings and see the real humans in our midst. Theatre can serve as one way of putting empathy, connectedness, and presence into practice. Theatre is not a better way to prevent violence than a public health approach. Theatre is another way to complement the existing tools. Theatre, a time-based art form in which humans enact stories with bodies and voices, is deeply intertwined with the human experience and is interlaced with stories of humanity.

Books such as *Post Traumatic Slave Syndrome*, *My Grandmother's Hands*, and *Healing Collective Trauma* focus on the importance of working through our own trauma, settling our nervous systems so we can tackle some of the hardest challenges of our time, from systemic racism to collective trauma. So much of the necessary work comes down to the breath and presence, as we learn to deal with our unhealed pain, so we don't pass along unmetabolized anger, pain, and fear to the next generation. I have passed along many things to my children: an appreciation of Shakespeare, the joy of language, a love of music. I don't want to pass along the pain I received from earlier generations. We owe it to subsequent generations to work on our hard things. We owe it to them to have the hard conversations, acknowledge and name the harm and violence that shape our world, and process it in a healing-centered way. As we take a difficult look at the hard and divisive feelings of the present moment, we are healing pain for future generations.

THE MERCHANT OF VENICE: TACKLING ANTISEMITISM

After transitioning the Shakespeare & Violence Prevention program to a virtual format for two years, our team gathered in the fall of 2022 for a return to in-person performances in schools. We had planned to produce a three-actor tour of *The Merchant of Venice* for middle and high schools—a new title in the series. With *Merchant*, we had the opportunity to put a tale of bias, discrimination, and antisemitism on the stage and to examine the ways in which this four-hundred-year-old play invites us to question some of the biases and discriminatory practices that still hold power in the twenty-first century. We hired a consultant from CU Boulder's Program in Jewish Studies to provide trainings for the actors and to create study guide content for teachers.

In rehearsals, our director, Anne Penner, established a convention that helped our audiences encounter the play: in a pre-show introduction, the actors asked audience members to raise their hands when they noticed moments of mistreatment, or of one character treating another character as less than human. By the time the courtroom scene rolled around, the audience had witnessed and raised hands to many moments of mistreatment, the bulk of them towards Shylock: Antonio knocked off Shylock's kippa early in the play, Portia gossiped about how much she disliked her suitors, and once Shylock appeared in court, the Duke of Venice demonstrated clear biases against him.

In Shakespeare's original courtroom scene, Shylock is stripped of his money, property, and religion, and is forced to convert to Christianity. The actors agreed that this felt like the most violent moment in the play. As a way to more deeply integrate the practice of interrupting moments of harm, the team decided that the actors themselves would raise their hands to flag this moment. After Shylock is told to convert, the actor playing Shylock walked upstage, as if exiting the courtroom, then raised her hand. She explained to the audience that this is what Shakespeare wrote. Then she turned to her castmates and asked if they could try the scene again. The actors then played out the scene a different way, this time with Shylock saying no to the request to convert to Christianity. The actors then tried it again; this time, Shylock said no, and then the Duke of Venice agreed, saying, "You're right, that's too much. Antonio, be content. Shylock, you are free to go." Then the actors tried a third redo in which Antonio intervened and requested that the case be thrown out altogether. These redo scenarios ended with a group breath, and the actors returned to the action of the play as written.

In performance, these four versions of the scene existed alongside one another. At first, the actors craved clarity: which version really happened? But something complicated and poignant emerged in the layered accumulation of the different versions: the possibility of change. It became clear that none of these outcomes was inevitable, but that in every moment, there were other possibilities.

As we toured *Merchant* to schools in 2022–23, we saw students tentatively raising their hands at the mistreatment that appeared in the play, and we often noted that their "upstander" hand-raises were infectious. It gave young audiences an outlet to act on their desire to help. One teacher who approached us after viewing the play was awed that we could incorporate interruptions to these classic texts in ways that shine light on problematic moments for a contemporary audience.

During the tour of *Merchant*, we saw a rise in antisemitism in popular media outlets from some high-profile celebrities and politicians; this raised questions about the ethical impact of staging this play. Were we reinforcing Jewish stereotypes by staging this play? Or were students walking out with a deeper awareness of biases and antisemitism?

In this production of *The Merchant of Venice*, we hoped to identify some of its depicted harm, antisemitism, and misogyny through the convention of audience members flagging those instances in the performance, in the post-show conversation with actors and in the post-show upstander roleplays. We hoped to use the production as an opportunity to invite questions about why the events of the play occurred. Why was Antonio so full of hatred for Shylock? How has the systemic treatment of Jews in the world of the play led to Shylock's behavior? How does justice operate in this world? Who is set up to thrive in this play, and who is set up to fail? Choosing not to stage *Merchant* is a choice some individuals have made. However, that does nothing to make the antisemitism in our world go away.

Our production of *Merchant* revealed to me how much pressure we place on a play these days. We want to do it right, to think through how we are telling this story in a careful way. Despite ample preparation, we cannot control how audiences receive a play. In the Shakespeare & Violence Prevention project, however, we can stage plays in a thoughtful and present way, and then introduce framing devices and post-show activities to examine and analyze the play. By choosing to stage moments of harm, we do risk audiences interpreting the harm onstage as acceptable. But if we don't put these moments onstage, we miss the opportunity to interrogate them. When we carry the burden of trying to prevent all violence and harm, the pressure is too great, and we risk inaction. As you set out to use live performance to introduce concepts of violence prevention, and if Shakespeare is the tool you use to implement these lessons, be very clear with your students that a play does not teach a lesson, moralize, or provide clear answers. A play puts a fictional world onstage. We get to be the meaning-makers, the interpreters, and the ones who find the connections between the world of the play and our own time.

Shakespeare's plays were new to his time. They are old to our time. But even in Shakespeare's theatre of new works, he was always plunging back into the past to dig up characters, plots, and wars, shine them up with his words, and make them present. I often think about the last line of *The Great Gatsby*: "So we beat on, boats against the current, borne back ceaselessly into the past" (Fitzgerald 1995 [1925]: 189). We are always going backward while moving forward in time. Fitzgerald's image of being borne back ceaselessly into the past reminds me of the work of violence-prevention researchers. They analyze school violence, they look closely at what has happened, they measure school climates, they decipher what unfolded and why. But why do they do it? It is not to honor the past but to improve the present and the future.

Does Shakespeare hold too much baggage from white supremacy, Eurocentering of literature, and the exclusion of BIPOC voices? The baggage abounds, undoubtedly. Does Shakespeare speak to everyone? Definitely not. However, if we reframe our approach to Shakespeare, encourage using Shakespeare as a tool rather than something to revere without interrogation, and build intentional on-ramps to help people see that Shakespeare belongs to them, then we can start getting somewhere.

When we get precious about the plays, that's when we have started centering old words over present humans. And the only thing that matters when encountering a Shakespeare play, in my opinion, is the people connecting with the play right now. What does it mean to you now, in your body, in the specific circumstances of your time and place? We are natural meaning-makers, and the meaning of a play will shift depending on the time in which we live and the people receiving it.

If harnessed through the lens of violence prevention, Shakespeare's plays can provide twenty-first-century audiences with a primer of best practices to not only prevent violence but live in a peaceful way. These four-hundred-year-old plays can be approached by artists and educators to reveal ideas about how to navigate the thorny challenges of violence today, in our present moment, with our present people. We can use these plays as tools to help young people grapple with making their communities, schools, and world safer and healthier.

Shakespeare's plays provide terrific case studies of violence and mistreatment in action, much of which already align with contemporary violence-prevention research. The plays put human behavior on the stage and give us the chance to enact and witness moments of harm, mistreatment, and the cycle of violence. We need these stories, we need these brave actors willing to tell them (even the less likable characters) because they are reminders that we are not alone, that problems have always been around, will always be around, but also that there is great hope in telling these stories, putting our thoughts into words, and putting ourselves into the shoes of others.

Staging a moment is not the same as endorsing it. Staging a moment can also mean putting a situation under a microscope and getting curious about it. It is an opportunity to witness human behavior in all its complicated messiness, but from a safe distance. This critical distance afforded through the metaphor of a story enacted onstage invites audience members to vicariously experience the moments in a play. If educators and artists can also facilitate enriching follow-up experiences to unpack the moments in the play, Shakespeare's work can breathe new life into some of the most pressing findings of violence-prevention research. We can use these plays to shape new narratives, break old cycles, and build healthier climates in which people are valued, respected, and seen.

Acknowledgments

To the year-round staff of the Colorado Shakespeare Festival: Tim Orr, Wendy Franz, Heidi Schmidt, Kurt Mehlenbacher, Jon Dunkle, and Sarah Duttlinger. Thank you for believing in this program. I am honored to call you colleagues.

To the team at University Press of Colorado: Dan Pratt for the initial introduction and endless Shakespeare enthusiasm; Robert Ramaswamy and Rachael Levay for early conversations, support, and thoughtful guidance; Nate Bauer, Skylar Cooper, Darrin Pratt, Laura Furney, Beth Svinarich, Tobin Gold, Chiquita Taborn, Tina Kachele, and Laura Walker for being a wonderful team.

To my collaborators throughout the years on the Shakespeare & Violence Prevention program: Beverly Kingston, Laurie Keith, Lena Heilmann, Kevin Rich, Anne Penner, Tammy Meneghini, Jeff Parker, Rebecca Brown Adelman, Teresa Wroe, Mark Lanning, Susan Payne, Del Elliot, Linda Cunningham, Jane Grady, and Brett Cogswell.

To the actors who have brought this work to life and inspired young people across Colorado: Joan Dieter, Crystal Eisele, Benaiah Anderson, James O'Hagan-Murphy, Erica Johnson, Caroline Barry, Scott Leslie, Alex Demos, Sammie Joe Kinnett, Brendon Milove, Sean Scrutchins, Tessa Nelson, Katie Cross, James Miller, Brittany Handler, David Goldberger, Stephanie Spector, Eddy Jordan, Mackenzie Beyer, Tait Petersen, Sarah Adler, Ben Griffin, Bethany Talley, Elise Collins, Paige

Olson, Satya Chavez, Mehry Eslaminia, Eva Balistrieri, Adrian Egolf, Hannelore Rolfing, Casey Dean, Liz Williamson, Lili Hokama, Royce Roeswood, Anastasia Davidson, Jihad Milhem, Gustavo Marquez, Ashley Frary, Iona Leighton, Katie Medved, Kris Buxton, Maggie Tisdale, Peter Bussian, Rhianna Devries, Adeline Mann, Josue Miranda, Mari Burgos, Sarah Duttlinger, Stephanie Saltis, Brian Bohlender, Tonya Ingerson, Amalia Adiv, Lucinda Lazo, Justin "JPapp" Pappas, Sammie Piel, Claylish Coldiron, Emma Ackerman, and Kenny Fedorko. My gratitude knows no bounds.

To the stage managers and actor managers who have worked magic: Lea Bock, Sarah Baughman, Elia Brovarone, Bianca Gordon, Ana Langmead, Tessa Nelson, Tamarra Nelson, Teresa Gould, Lexi Tompkins, Nellie Speers, and Sarah Duttlinger.

To the directors who guided these productions: Tim Orr, Rand Harmon, Crystal Eisele, Lynn Nichols, Laurie Keith, Wendy Franz, Kevin Rich, Rodney Lizcano, Anne Penner, Heidi Schmidt, and Anastasia Davidson.

To the designers who have brought the plays to life visually: Olivia Allen, Andryn Arithson, Veronica Dewey, Angela Dowdy, Jon Dunkle, Nikki Haabestad, Adrianna Hammack, Katie Horney, Brenda King, Kassandra Kunisch, Ana Langmead, Alika Magas, Ian McMorran, Paige Olson, Sarah Talaba, Dimitriy Yunda, and Misha Zimmerman.

To all researchers who devote their careers to violence prevention. I'm in awe of your work and so grateful you do what you do.

To all actors and teaching artists who devote their careers to theatre and education. I'm in awe of your work and so grateful you do what you do.

To the Office for Public and Community Engaged Scholarship (PACES, formerly the Office of Outreach and Engagement) at CU Boulder for providing thirteen years of funding for this project beginning with our first ever grant, and endless championing of the work, even when funding challenges arise. I'm also grateful to funding from the Boulder Arts Commission, Shakespeare in American Communities, the National Endowment for the Humanities, the Hazel Barnes Flat, the Longmont Metro Grant, and the CU Center for the Humanities and the Arts.

To the individual donors who have contributed to the CSF Education Fund and the CSF Education Endowment Fund—the

Shakespeare & Violence Prevention program would not exist without you. Arts education depends on the generosity of individuals who recognize the positive impact the arts can have on a child's development. You know who you are, and you have my endless gratitude.

To my STA colleagues from across the globe; I'm grateful for our community.

To Kate Wilson, for generously copyediting the manuscript—above and beyond CSF board member duties!

To Kevin Rich, for thoughtful feedback on this manuscript and being a stellar collaborator in Shakespeare & Violence Prevention and Applied Shakespeare.

To Beverly Kingston, for being an open-hearted collaborator who inspires me and motivates me to dream bigger. I'm endlessly grateful.

To Jeanne McDonald for kicking this whole thing off.

To Keri Cahill, who first taught me about Shakespeare, and introduced me to the magic in the plays.

To Kim Strafford, who lives on in every word of Shakespeare.

To all the children who have experienced the Shakespeare & Violence Prevention program. You make this work worth doing.

To my family and my friends, for their patience and support, even when I know they are tired of hearing about Shakespeare this, Shakespeare that. And to my parents, for signing me up for that first Shakespeare camp long ago.

Lastly, to my sweet and supportive crew at home: Jason, Holden, and Baxter. I love you more than word can wield the matter.

Appendix A
Macbeth Materials

POST-SHOW DISCUSSION QUESTIONS

- Research shows that in 81 percent of planned violence, someone other than the perpetrator knew it was going to happen. Which characters in Macbeth knew about Duncan's murder before it occurred? Who could have prevented it?
- *Macbeth* is a play without clear heroes, and the audience is left without a character to root for; just people making mistakes, choosing violence, and getting stuck deeper in violence with every step. What is the value of watching a play in which characters make mistakes? Do you learn more from a play in which characters behave badly or in which characters behave well?
- According to the play, what is "the milk of human kindness?" How does it show up? When is it used, and by whom? When is it explicitly ignored? How is that human kindness (or empathy) connected to a character's ability to harm others?
- What references to masculinity and femininity did you notice in the play? How were gender expectations used by characters in the play as a peer pressure tool? How might casting across gender challenge these messages of gender conformity?
- Who is responsible for the violence in the play? What do you think is the root cause of the violence?

- How do the characters change from the beginning of the play to the end? What causes these changes?
- What happens next? Has Macduff's killing of Macbeth solved the problem? Or does it create new problems under Malcolm's reign?

UPSTANDER ROLEPLAY LESSON PLAN (*MACBETH*)

- "In theatre we rehearse and practice, and in life we need to practice helping people and being an upstander. Today we are going to be practicing upstander behavior."
- "In the play, after Macbeth hears the witches predict he'll be king, he's on the fence about whether or not to kill King Duncan. I'm going to perform this scene for you, in contemporary language, and I want you to listen carefully. Be thinking—if you were overhearing this, what are some ways you might prevent harm?"

> MACBETH: I don't know what to do. If there were no consequences to killing Duncan, I would do it right away. But there are so many reasons not to:
> First of all, killing is wrong.
> Second of all, he is my king.
> And finally, he is staying in my house—I'm supposed to protect him, not murder him.
> I know that violence just leads to more violence—I've seen it thousands of times.
> And Duncan is a really good person. A good friend. A good king.
> But I can't help it. Ever since the witches told me I would become king I haven't stopped thinking about it.
> The only reason I have to do this awful thing is . . . my own ambition. I want to be king.
> I really don't know what to do.

- *Invite students to make observations about what they saw. If you need helpful prompts, use the following:*
  - "What reasons does he give to kill the king? What reasons not to?"
- "I'm going to break you up into small groups, but I want you to consider: immediately after this speech, Lady Macbeth enters and persuades Macbeth to kill the king. What if you were an upstander in this situation? (What do I mean by this?)"

- *In small groups: strategize how you might change this scene to prevent violence.*
- *Students should only roleplay themselves.*
- *The important thing in the roleplays is that students are trying out a wide variety of ideas. Encourage them to think creatively and try out all positive solutions.*
- "This is an extreme situation; what if it were a little less extreme, but happening at your school? For example, you overhear a peer talking about harming someone at your school. What steps would you take as an upstander? What resources are available to you here and now?"

OTHER CLASSROOM ACTIVITIES (MACBETH)

Agree/Disagree/Explain

GUIDING QUESTION: What do you believe about violence, power, and peer pressure?

SKILLS ADDRESSED: Collaborative Meaning-Making, Critical Thinking and Analysis, Self-Awareness

ACTIVITY: In small groups, discuss each statement and ask students to discuss whether they agree or disagree and to explain their decision about the following statements. Follow up with a full group discussion:

- Peer pressure is always harmful.
- Violent words or actions always lead to more violence.
- If you regularly practice empathy, you are less likely to hurt others.
- A planned act of violence always has warning signs.
- A group of people can easily change the opinion of an individual.
- Encouraging someone to commit violence is just as bad as committing violence yourself.
- Power is always a dangerous thing.
- Revenge is sometimes justified.
- When you know that something dangerous is going to happen, you have a duty to try to prevent it.

Look For

SKILLS ADDRESSED: Critical Thinking, Interpreting Creative Work

ACTIVITY: Create a checklist for your class prior to watching the performance (or reading a scene/full play). After the performance, discuss what you noticed from the list:
- A power imbalance
- A planned attack
- Manipulation through peer pressure
- An opportunity to speak up and prevent harm
- Moments of empathy

Adapting Text

GUIDING QUESTION: How do we put existing language into our own words?

SKILLS ADDRESSED: Critical Thinking, Text Analysis, Creative Writing

ACTIVITY: Read the opening speech from act 1 scene 7, and in small groups (or independently) consider the following questions:
1. What decision is Macbeth making?
2. What reasons does Macbeth give himself to take or not take the action he's considering? What is on his pro/con list?
3. What lines do you think are most important to this speech? Which lines are confusing to a contemporary audience?

Independently (or in small groups), create your own version of the speech. Put the ideas into your own words.

Appendix B
Julius Caesar Materials

POST-SHOW DISCUSSION QUESTIONS

- Where did you see examples of violence? Who could have stepped in to prevent the violence?
- Research shows that in 81 percent of planned violence, someone other than the perpetrator knew it was going to happen. Which characters in the play knew about the planned attack on Caesar before it happened? Who tried to step in to prevent it and why/why not?
- What were the warning signs or omens that things were not right in Rome prior to Caesar's assassination? If you were a citizen of Rome, what might have tipped you off that something dangerous was about to happen?
- In the play, we see many examples of persuasive speeches. How is language used to change people's minds? Have you ever been persuaded by someone with a powerful command of language to do something you would not normally do?
- Discuss the terms "herd intoxication" and "mob mentality." Where do we see examples of this in the play? Do people behave differently in a group compared to when they are alone?
- How do the characters change from the beginning of the play to the end? What causes these changes?

- What is the purpose of staging a play that depicts violence? Some people used to think it would encourage similar behavior. What do you see as the role of theatre in understanding violence? How does it shape an understanding of violence when we see it play out in a community that is not ours?

UPSTANDER ROLEPLAY LESSON PLAN (*JULIUS CAESAR*)

- "We're about to watch a scene in which Brutus is approached by Cassius about the plan to assassinate Caesar. I'll perform this scene for you, in contemporary language, and I want you to be thinking—if you witnessed this, what are some ways you might prevent harm?"
- "I'll perform both roles." (*Set up how we'll know which character is which . . . for example, "When I'm standing here, I'm Brutus . . . when I stand here with my arms folded, I'm Cassius"*).

> BRUTUS (*alone*): Caesar is getting so powerful, so fast. Cassius thinks we need to get rid of him. I don't know of a way to deal with this that doesn't involve hurting Caesar. But Caesar's been a really good friend to me.
> CASSIUS: Brutus, buddy! Doing okay?
> BRUTUS: No. I can't sleep. I can't stop thinking about Caesar.
> CASSIUS: Hey. You and me. Right now. Let's swear to do something about this.
> BRUTUS: Oh, come on. We don't need to swear to do anything.
> CASSIUS: Should we just take down Caesar? Or Mark Antony, too?
> BRUTUS: NO! Just Caesar, Cassius.

- "What did you notice about this scene?"
- "This scene takes place *before* Caesar is killed, and we see how the choice to kill Caesar quickly escalates and leads to more violence."
- "Who else in the play knew about the planned attack before it happened?" (*Take several answers; if students need prompting, we have the Soothsayer, Portia, Caesar's gut feeling, Calphurnia's bad dream.*) "Lots of people knew—and yet the violence still occurred."
- "Research shows that in nearly every act of planned violence, someone other than the perpetrator knows it's going to happen."

- "This is an extreme situation—what if we tone it down to a situation you might see at our school?"
- "I'm going to break you up into small groups, and I want you to discuss with your group:"
  - "What if *you* were an <u>upstander</u> in this situation?" (*Review what this means.*) "How could you change the outcome to prevent harm while also keeping yourself safe? Get creative!"
  - "Take a few minutes to share ideas with your group, and be ready to report back to the class."
- *When a student offers an upstander strategy, invite them to play it out with you (if they are willing).*
- *Students should only roleplay the upstander, always as themselves.*
- *The important thing in the roleplays is that students are trying out a wide variety of their own ideas (not the ideas of the teaching artist). Encourage them to think creatively and try out all positive solutions.*
- *Roleplay several scenes, involving as many students as possible, and the classroom teacher, if appropriate.*
- *After each roleplay, debrief:* "What did we appreciate about what ____ just did?"
- *Encourage students to try out indirect and direct ways to help.*
- "If this occurred at school, whom could you approach for help? Share out some ideas about who are your trusted adults."
- "You had so many great upstander solutions! Some were direct" (*reference specific examples from students*) "and some indirect" (*reference specific examples*).
- "Always keep your safety in mind when intervening and consider using other strategies if being direct doesn't feel possible."

OTHER CLASSROOM ACTIVITIES (*JULIUS CAESAR*)

Look For

ACTIVITY: Assemble a list of things to look for in the play. Feel free to use the list below, make your own list, or have the students assemble a list of things to look for. Consider the violence-prevention lens and consider crafting "look-fors" that focus on climate, roles, upstander behavior, and warning signs. After the performance, review the list and share out what the students observed.

SKILLS ADDRESSED: Critical Thinking, Analyzing Texts, Comprehensive Health

> *Suggested List:*
> Warning signs
> A power imbalance
> Someone confiding in another person
> A planned attack
> Manipulation through peer pressure
> An opportunity to speak up and prevent harm
> Moments of empathy
> An angry mob
> A persuasive speech
> Moments of reconciliation
> A character attempting to solve a problem with violence
> Words used as weapons
> A character asking questions or stopping to think before making an important decision

Government and Leaders

GUIDING QUESTION(S): What are the avenues for dealing with a leader you don't respect in a healthy way? In our government, what are the avenues?

SKILLS ADDRESSED: Civic Engagement, Social Awareness, Critical Thinking and Analysis

ACTIVITY: Discuss how characters in the play handled their dissatisfaction with political leaders. What were their strategies when they weren't happy with Caesar's power? Discuss the differences between the play and our own time. Have your students research how to get involved with local, state, and federal policies they disagree with and how to use one's voice to communicate concerns to our leaders. Share ideas and discuss how some of these avenues might have been implemented in *Julius Caesar*. How would those avenues have changed the outcome?

Cutting/Adapting Text

GUIDING QUESTIONS: How would I say what Shakespeare's character is saying if I were in their position? What is essential from the original text and what could be omitted? How does the meaning change when the words are paraphrased or the speech is shorter?

SKILLS ADDRESSED: Critical Thinking and Analysis, Adaptability and Flexibility, Creativity, Perspective-Taking

ACTIVITY: One of the best ways to grapple with Shakespeare is through paraphrasing. How would I say this today? How would I cut it down? Look at a speech and update it to a twenty-first-century context. A good starting point would be Brutus's "It must be by his death" (but you can try this with any of the speeches). Have your students paraphrase the speech in their own words, and then cut the original text down to 50 percent of its original length. Share out the paraphrases and the cut version of the original speech. What do you notice about the different versions?

Disability and the Twenty-First Century

GUIDING QUESTIONS: How does an early modern depiction of disability differ from a twenty-first-century framework? How does Caesar's disability shape perceptions of him?

SKILLS ADDRESSED: Critical Thinking and Analysis, Social Awareness, Creativity

ACTIVITY: Look at the excerpted speech below about Caesar's epilepsy; discuss how disability is framed in this speech. How is disability depicted in this context, and how does that differ from a twenty-first-century representation of disability (in news, literature, film, pop culture)? How might you rewrite this scene with a healthier, more empathetic understanding of disability? Hold a class discussion and share out students' rewrites of the scene. What do you notice about the rewritten versions?

CASCA: [Caesar] swooned and fell down at it. And for mine own part, I durst not laugh for fear of opening my lips and receiving the bad air.
CASSIUS: But soft, I pray you. What, did Caesar swoon?
CASCA: He fell down in the marketplace and foamed at mouth and was speechless.
BRUTUS: 'Tis very like; he hath the falling sickness.
. . . What said he when he came unto himself?

CASCA: When he came to himself again, he said if he had done or said anything amiss, he desired their Worships to think it was his infirmity. Three or four wenches where I stood cried "Alas, good soul!" and forgave him with all their hearts. But there's no heed to be taken of them; if Caesar had stabbed their mothers, they would have done no less.
(*Julius Caesar* I.ii.258–86)

Strategies for Reporting in School

GUIDING QUESTIONS: What tools are available to us to report dangerous behavior? How do we use them?

SKILLS ADDRESSED: Comprehensive Health, Upstander Practice, Critical Thinking and Analysis, Civic Engagement, Self-Awareness, Social Awareness, Creativity

ACTIVITY: As a class, discuss the various tools for reporting available to your community. What situations might warrant which solutions? Come up with a shared list, assign each student one tool to research, and share out the findings. Encourage the findings to be shared in a creative way (maybe a poem, a comic, a rap, a short film). Make the shared findings available to the school.

Perspective-Taking

GUIDING QUESTIONS: Why do characters in the play behave the way they behave? What are the root causes?

SKILLS ADDRESSED: Perspective-Taking, Critical Thinking and Analysis, Creativity

ACTIVITY: Every person in this world has a point of view and behaves the way they do because of their lived experiences. Write a journal entry from one character's perspective (choose any character in the play). Students may exchange their journal entries with a student who wrote from another character's point of view and compare similarities and differences. Practice seeing the play from different points of view and gather the class into "character groups" to share what they learned. Share out the different viewpoints. Discuss the difference between a play (in which there are many competing, conflicting voices) and an argumentative essay, with a single, authorial voice. How do these forms function in different ways?

Appendix C
Romeo and Juliet Materials

DURING THE PERFORMANCE: THINGS TO LOOK FOR

If your students will watch a performance of *Romeo and Juliet*, I recommend assembling a list of "look-fors" prior to viewing the play. You may alternatively assign your students to create a list of what they will watch for in the performance. Below is a suggested list to get you started. You may also use this list as an assignment for your students as they stage portions of the play, with them creating a bingo board of the following moments in their scene:

- Someone confiding in another person
- A trusted adult
- Moments of miscommunication
- A situation where better coping skills could help
- Opportunities to prevent harm
- Moments of empathy
- Moments of reconciliation
- A supportive friend
- Substance abuse
- Lack of sleep
- An unhealthy home life

POST-SHOW DISCUSSION QUESTIONS

The following discussion questions can help students reflect on some of the violence-prevention patterns within the play. I encourage you to use the questions below after watching and/or studying the play. If you wish to create your own questions using the violence-prevention lens, you could encourage students to look at the **climate**, look for the **upstander opportunities**, look at the **roles** involved, and look at what the students' **own strategies** might be in similar situations.

- We never know the source of the grudge between the Capulets and the Montagues. Why do you think Shakespeare made that choice?
- What starts the violence in *Romeo and Juliet*?
- What differences did you observe between the younger generation (Juliet, Romeo, Tybalt, Mercutio, Benvolio) and the older generation (Friar, Nurse, Capulet, the Prince)?
- What kind of behavior were the adults in the play modeling to the young people? Can you think of an example in which an adult influences a young person's behavior?
- Why do you think the friar kept Romeo and Juliet's wedding a secret?
- Why do you think the friar gave Juliet the potion?
- What were some examples of positive, supportive relationships in the play?
- What were some examples of negative, unsupportive relationships?
- How do the characters change from the beginning of the play to the end? What causes these changes?
- What is empathy? Why is it important? How might empathy have changed the outcomes in the play?
- Actors use teamwork to trust one another when they are onstage. How is teamwork useful in school?
- We saw a lot of struggling people in the play. What resources exist in your own school for people who are struggling?

UPSTANDER ROLEPLAY LESSON PLAN (*ROMEO AND JULIET*)

"In the play, after Romeo and Juliet have secretly married, a fight breaks out between Tybalt, Romeo, and Mercutio. I'm going to perform this scene for you, in contemporary language, and I want you to listen carefully, and think about what each character *wants* and what each character *believes to be true*. Be thinking—if you witnessed this, what are some ways you might prevent harm?"

SCENE: *Set up that you'll play three people:*

- ROMEO, *who has secretly married a Capulet, and therefore cannot participate in a fight*
- TYBALT, *who wants to get back at Romeo for crashing the Capulets' party*
- MERCUTIO, *who is trying to be a good friend*

   TYBALT: Romeo, I've been looking for you. You crashed our party, and now we're gonna fight.
   ROMEO: Tybalt, c'mon, man. I'm not going to fight you.
   MERCUTIO: Romeo, what's wrong with you? I'll fight you, Tybalt!
   ROMEO: Guys, remember, the prince said no more fighting. Stop!
   (*The sword fight continues.*)

- *Invite students to make observations about what they saw. If you need helpful prompts, use the following:*
  - "What does Romeo know that the others don't?"
  - "What did (CHARACTER NAME) want? What did (NAME) believe to be true?"
  - "What caused the violence in this scene?"
  - "Who ends up getting hurt?"
- "I'm going to break you up into small groups, and I want you to consider:"
  - "This scene is a *huge* turning point. Mercutio dies, Romeo kills Tybalt in revenge, and Romeo gets banished, then more confusion leads to Romeo and Juliet's suicides. The play ends with lots of hurting people. And the whole community is affected."
  - "What if *you* were an <u>upstander</u> in this situation? (What do I mean by this?) How could you change the outcome to prevent harm while also keeping yourself safe? Get creative!"
- *Play out a variety of strategies, with the students stepping into the scene as themselves, and the teacher/facilitator playing the rest of the roles. It*

is important that students always play themselves and that the students are practicing upstander behavior, rather than perpetuating more harm.
- *After a scenario:* "What did we appreciate about that strategy?"

OTHER CLASSROOM ACTIVITIES (ROMEO AND JULIET)

Activity: Preventing Community Violence

GUIDING QUESTIONS: What strategies might prevent community violence? What kind of leadership might reduce violence in a community?

SKILLS ADDRESSED: Text Comprehension, Perspective-Taking, Collaborative Meaning-Making, Leadership, Civic Awareness

ACTIVITY: In the first scene of *Romeo and Juliet*, a public fight breaks out between the Montagues and the Capulets (two local feuding families). The prince of Verona interrupts the fight, and in a public proclamation to the citizens delivers an edict intended to prevent future violence. Read the prince's speech aloud, dividing the lines among the students.

PRINCE: Rebellious subjects, enemies to peace,
　　Profaners of this neighbor-stainèd steel—
　　Will they not hear?—What ho! You men, you beasts,
　　That quench the fire of your pernicious rage
　　With purple fountains issuing from your veins:
　　On pain of torture, from those bloody hands
　　Throw your mistempered weapons to the ground,
　　And hear the sentence of your movèd prince.
　　Three civil brawls bred of an airy word
　　By thee, old Capulet, and Montague,
　　Have thrice disturbed the quiet of our streets
　　And made Verona's ancient citizens
　　Cast by their grave-beseeming ornaments
　　To wield old partisans in hands as old,
　　Cankered with peace, to part your cankered hate.
　　If ever you disturb our streets again,
　　Your lives shall pay the forfeit of the peace.
　　For this time all the rest depart away.
　　You, Capulet, shall go along with me,
　　And, Montague, come you this afternoon

> To know our farther pleasure in this case.
> Once more, on pain of death, all men depart.
> (from Folger Digital Texts, *Romeo and Juliet* I.i.83–105)

INDEPENDENT WORK: Ask students to reread the speech independently and jot down questions and thoughts about it.

GROUP WORK

- Analyze the speech as a class; ask questions about the meaning of individual words and phrases and attempt to answer those questions as a class. Encourage students to describe, in their own words, what the prince is saying.
- Invite students to describe the prince's strategy to prevent violence in Verona. Why does the Prince believe this is an effective solution?
- Discuss the ripple effects of this strategy. In the play, the prince's edict does not end violence in Verona; the next day, another fight breaks out in which two young people are killed (Mercutio and Tybalt); just a few days later, two more young people (Romeo and Juliet) have died by suicide. Invite students to consider why the violence did not end with the prince's edict.

SMALL-GROUP WORK

- Ask students to discuss in small groups what other options the prince has to prevent further violence. What would *they* do or say if they were in his position? Ask each group to discuss pros and cons of various solutions and pose questions about the reasons for their responses.
- Ask each group to strategize a few ideas about how to cultivate a positive climate at their own school/community. What are things they, as individuals, can accomplish to create a thriving, positive environment?

GROUP WORK: Ask each small group to share out from the discussions.

Activity: Journal

GUIDING QUESTION: What does it feel like to be a citizen of Verona?

SKILLS ADDRESSED: Perspective-Taking, Creative Writing

ACTIVITY: Write a journal entry as a character from the play. What kinds of things are on your mind? What concerns you most about your daily life? What are your hopes for the future?

Activity: Trusted Adults

GUIDING QUESTION: What are the characteristics of a trusted adult?

SKILLS ADDRESSED: Critical Thinking, Social Awareness

ACTIVITY: In small groups, or independently, describe the qualities of a trusted adult. How do you know an adult is trustworthy? Identify a few trusted adults in your community, family, and social network. What might be an example of something you could go to this person about? Share this list with your peers. Do your lists differ? How so?

Rewrite the Narrative

GUIDING QUESTIONS: How might the play have turned out differently?

SKILLS ADDRESSED: Creative Thinking, Textual Analysis

Look at the final scene of the play, in which Romeo and Juliet both die by suicide. Invite your students to explore their own rewrites of the scene, in which the outcome is less harmful. What external conditions would need to change to prevent their deaths? The work can take any form; a short story, a poem, a song, a scene. How might the play have turned out differently?

Appendix D
Much Ado About Nothing Materials

CONTENT WARNING FOR *MUCH ADO ABOUT NOTHING*

Much Ado About Nothing features a character who is targeted by false rumors and fakes her death to escape mistreatment. This content may be triggering to some members of your school community. We encourage you to have conversations with your students prior to the performance, particularly students who may have been personally impacted by rumors, gossip, or the death of a loved one. Please work with your students to make the most appropriate decisions for them regarding viewing the performance and participating in post-show workshops. If you are concerned about a student, below are some resources:

RESOURCES (UPDATE FOR YOUR AREA)

- **AYUDA EN ESPAÑOL** Lifeline ofrece 24/7, gratuito servicios en español, no es necesario hablar inglés si usted necesita ayuda. Cuando usted llama al número 1-888-628-9454, su llamada se dirige al centro de ayuda de nuestra red disponible más cercano.
- **COLORADO CRISIS SERVICES** (confidential and immediate support if you are in crisis or need help dealing with one, or if you are looking for additional resources): 1-844-493-8255; text "TALK" to 38255; www.coloradocrisisservices.org
- **COUNSELING TEAM** at your school

- **CYBERBULLYING RESEARCH CENTER** (resources, research, and presentations about cyberbullying, directed by Dr. Sameer Hinduja and Dr. Justin W. Patchin): cyberbullying.org
- **SAFE2TELL** (anonymous reporting, connects with local law enforcement and other resources): 1-877-542-7233; www.safe2tell.org

POST-SHOW DISCUSSION QUESTIONS
(*MUCH ADO ABOUT NOTHING*)

- What rumors are spread in the play?
- How are the rumors spread?
- Who believes rumors easily? Who questions the rumors they hear?
- Which rumors are harmful to others? Which rumors seem harmless to you?
- What do you think of the reconciliation between Claudio and Hero? Does Claudio deserve forgiveness?
- What were some examples of positive, supportive relationships in the play?
- What were some examples of negative, unsupportive relationships?
- (If appropriate to the production) Did you see characters using phones and devices responsibly? How could you use social media and electronic communication to be an upstander in your community?
- In a healthy community, everyone should feel supported and valued. When people are mistreated, they often mistreat others in return. After watching the play, how could Don John have been more supported? How would that have changed the outcome of the play?

UPSTANDER ROLEPLAY LESSON PLAN
(*MUCH ADO ABOUT NOTHING*)

- Do you know the expression, "Sticks and stones may break my bones, but words can never hurt me"? You just saw a play about how rumors and gossip impact a community—and we see that words *can* actually hurt.
    ▹ Everyone spreads rumors in the play, whether it's Don John, trying to hurt Claudio and Hero, or Beatrice and Benedick's friends, trying to set them up.

- Rumors can be a form of mistreatment, and usually lead to more harm than good.
    - Rumors can spread especially quickly online—we know that we shouldn't believe everything we read on the internet—we have to learn to separate the lies from the truth.
    - Today, we'll use theatre to explore your own ideas about how the harm in the play could have been prevented.
- Theatre is a great way to bring about a better world, because:
    - Theatre is about **teamwork** (you're on the same team as fellow actors!).
    - Theatre is about **empathy** (stepping into someone else's shoes).
    - Theatre is about **change** (just as actors change roles in theatre, so people can choose to change in real life. We all have the ability to change our behavior. That's why we say someone is *acting* like a bully instead of saying they *are* a bully).
- All of the theatre activities we'll do today can actually make for a healthier, stronger community!

ROLEPLAYS

- "In theatre we have to rehearse and practice, and in life we need to practice helping people and being an upstander. Today we are going to be practicing upstander behavior—while still keeping yourself safe."
    - "We have the ability to 'act' when we see something happen that is not okay . . . and that takes practice!"
- "We're about to watch a scene in which Don John spreads a rumor. I'll perform this scene for you, (*if you have a co-teacher, invite them up too*) in contemporary language, and I want you to be thinking—if you witnessed this, what are some ways you might prevent harm?"

SCENE: *Set up which character is which (and how your students will know when you're playing each role. Name tags or specific poses are helpful!):*

- CLAUDIO, *who is in love with Hero and will marry her tomorrow; he knows Don John from the war—they're both soldiers*

- DON JOHN, *who is jealous of Claudio and wants to hurt him . . . so he starts this rumor about Hero*

  > CLAUDIO: Hey, Don John!
  > DON JOHN: Hey, Claudio. Are you marrying Hero tomorrow?
  > CLAUDIO: Yeah, why?
  > DON JOHN: You might wanna rethink that. I heard she's been hanging around with other guys . . . (*show a compromising image on cell phone*).
  > CLAUDIO: I don't believe you.
  > DON JOHN: Don't take my word for it. Come with me and see for yourself.

- "What did you notice about this scene?"
- "This scene takes place *before* most of the mistreatment in the play. Don John stages an encounter at Hero's window to convince Claudio she's cheating. Claudio believes it's true and publicly rejects Hero at the wedding. Although things work out, a lot of people are hurt along the way (including Don John, who is arrested at the end of the play)."
- "What if *you* were an upstander in this situation? (What do I mean by this?) How could you change the outcome to prevent harm while also keeping yourself safe? Get creative!"
  - Additional note: "We don't have to know if the rumor is true to know that spreading rumors can be really hurtful."
- When a student offers an upstander strategy, invite them (or a volunteer) to play it out with the actor.
- Students should only roleplay the upstander, always *as themselves*.
- *The important thing in the roleplays is that students are trying out a wide variety of their own ideas (not the ideas of the teaching artist). Encourage them to think creatively and try out all positive solutions.*
- *Roleplay several scenes, involving as many students as possible, and the classroom teacher, if appropriate.*
- *After each roleplay, debrief:* "What did we appreciate about what _____ just did?"
- Encourage students to try out indirect and direct ways to help.
- "What if this situation took place at your school—who could you go to if you saw something like this happening? If you saw rumors circulating online about a classmate, what could you do as an upstander?"

- "You had so many great upstander solutions! Some were direct" (*reference specific examples from students*) "and some indirect" (*reference specific examples*).
- "Always keep your safety in mind when intervening, and consider using other strategies if being direct doesn't feel possible."

OTHER CLASSROOM ACTIVITIES (*MUCH ADO ABOUT NOTHING*)

Character Analysis

GUIDING QUESTION: How can a character's backstory influence their behavior?

SKILLS ADDRESSED: Empathy, Text Analysis, Imagination, Perspective-Taking

ACTIVITY: In this activity, we'll analyze two different characters and their actions in the play. One critical component of an actor's job is demonstrating empathy by analyzing their character's motivations and understanding the character's perspective.

Actors ask questions like:
- Why does the character say what they say?
- Why does the character do what they do?
- What does the character want?
- What does the character believe to be true?

Characters don't exist within a vacuum; just like real humans, a character is influenced by multiple forces and has a rich inner life. This analytical work leads to more fully realized, believable onstage performances. While this kind of work is vital for live theatre, it's also a key component of preventing violence. When we consider the world from someone else's perspective through empathy, we're more likely to recognize the ways we're connected to that person. Read the following speeches and respond to the reflection questions.

CHARACTER: DON JOHN

CONTEXT: Don John circulates a rumor about Hero in order to get back at Claudio, but first confides in the audience.

INSTRUCTIONS: See handout #1 (reproduced below), a condensed version of several of Don John's speeches. Read the speech aloud;

if you're with others, try dividing the lines among your group members.

REFLECTION QUESTIONS: (respond at first on your own, and then share responses with the group):
- What questions do you have about this speech? Words you'd like clarified, etc.?
- What is Don John saying? How would you express these thoughts in your own words?
- What does Don John want, according to this speech?
- Which line in the speech resonates with you the most and why?
- What might have happened in the past that is influencing Don John's behavior in this moment?
- If a peer shared these thoughts directly with you, what would you say or do to support this person?
- If someone demonstrated empathy, and took the time to understand Don John's experience, how might the play have turned out differently?

Handout #1

> DON JOHN: Why am I thus out of measure sad? There is no measure in the occasion that breeds, therefore the sadness is without limit. I cannot hide what I am. I must be sad when I have cause, and smile at no man's jests; eat when I have stomach, and wait for no man's leisure. I had rather be a canker in a hedge than a rose in their graces, and it better fits my blood to be disdained of all. If I had my mouth I would bite; if I had my liberty I would do my liking. In the meantime, let me be that I am, and seek not to alter me. I have intelligence of an intended marriage. The most exquisite Claudio looks on Hero. This may prove food to my displeasure. That young start-up hath all the glory of my overthrow: if I can cross him any way, I bless myself every way. Let us to the great supper. Their cheer is the greater that I am subdued.

CHARACTER: THE FRIAR

> **CONTEXT:** After Hero and Claudio's wedding grinds to a halt, the friar intervenes to try to repair the harm.
>
> **INSTRUCTIONS:** Take a look at handout #2 below (an abridged, condensed version of Shakespeare's original). Read this scene aloud;

if you're with others, try dividing the lines among your group members.

REFLECTION QUESTIONS (respond at first on your own, and then share responses with the group):
- What questions do you have about this scene? Words you'd like clarified, etc.?
- What is the gist of the friar's argument? How would you express this in your own words?
- How would you describe the friar's strategy to protect Hero? Why does the friar think this is an effective solution?
- If you were in the friar's shoes, what would you do or say? Do you agree with the plan, or would you do something else?
- Consider the line: "What we have we prize not to the worth whiles we enjoy it." What does that line mean to you? Do you agree with this idea? Can you think of an example in your experience when this has been true?
- How is the friar demonstrating empathy in this scene? And for whom?

Handout #2

FRIAR: Pause awhile,
    And let my counsel sway you in this case. Your cousin here has Claudio left for dead.
    Let her awhile be secretly kept in
    And publish it that she is dead indeed.
BEATRICE: What shall become of this? what will this do?
FRIAR: Marry, this well carried shall on her behalf
    Change slander to remorse; that is some good.
    For it so falls out
    That what we have we prize not to the worth
    Whiles we enjoy it, but being lacked and lost,
    Why then we rack the value, then we find
    The virtue that possession would not show us
    Whiles it was ours. So will it fare with Claudio.
    When he shall hear she died upon his words,
    Then shall he mourn,
    And wish he had not so accused her.

Appendix E
Twelfth Night Materials

POST-SHOW DISCUSSION QUESTIONS

After you watch or stage a performance of *Twelfth Night* with your students, a class discussion to unpack the mistreatment and patterns of violence is likely to be fruitful. Here are some suggested guiding questions:

VIOLENCE PREVENTION CONNECTIONS:
- What examples of mistreatment or miscommunication did you notice in the play?
- Which characters took action to try to prevent the harm or mistreatment? (Discuss upstander behavior.)
- What does upstander behavior look like in our community?

ANALYZE THE CHARACTERS:
- Why did the characters in the play behave the way they behaved?
- What motivates Malvolio to quiet down the household when the revelers are partying late at night? What might it feel like to be Malvolio in that moment?
- What motivates Toby and team to plan the trick on Malvolio? What might it feel like to be Toby, Andrew, or Maria in that moment?

ANALYZE THE CLIMATE:
- What kind of behavior is acceptable in Illyria (where the play takes place)?

- What kind of behavior is rewarded?
- Is this the kind of environment in which you'd thrive? Why or why not?

CONSIDER WHAT'S NEXT:
- After Malvolio learns he was tricked, his final line is "I'll be revenged on the whole pack of you." What does Malvolio mean by this? (Important to emphasize that a line in a play does not have a single, correct meaning but rather many possible interpretations.)
- What do you think Malvolio will do next?

UPSTANDER ROLEPLAY LESSON PLAN (*TWELFTH NIGHT*)

- *Discuss the concept of rehearsing (or practicing) behavior.* "When do we practice things? Why is it important to practice?"
- "It's important to practice how we might respond if we see other people doing unsafe or unkind things. So we are going to practice upstander behavior together."
- "In the play, Toby and some friends decide to prank Malvolio, and Malvolio ends up getting really hurt by the prank."
- "I'll (*we'll, if you have a co-teacher*) perform this scene for you, in contemporary language, and I want you to be thinking—if you witnessed this, what are some ways you might prevent harm?"
- "I'll perform both roles." (*Set up how we'll know which character is which, e.g.,* "When I'm standing in this spot, I'm Andrew, but when I am over here, I'm Toby").
  - *Alternatively, you can watch the scene again (if it's a film version) or look at the text of the scene on the overhead projector or have a couple of students play the roles.*
  - *It's most important that students embody upstander behavior (rather than playing Toby/Andrew/Malvolio).*

> TOBY: Hey, Andrew.
> ANDREW: Yeah?
> TOBY: You know Malvolio?
> ANDREW: Yeah?
> TOBY: We should play a trick on him.
> ANDREW: Yeah?
> TOBY: I think we should send Malvolio some messages from Olivia, and trick him into thinking Olivia is in love with him.

And the messages will also tell Malvolio to wear yellow socks. He's going to look ridiculous!
ANDREW: Yeah?
TOBY: Let's do it!
ANDREW: Yeah!

- "What did you notice about this scene?" (*Take a few responses.*)
- "When you watched this scene, how many of you wanted to take action to prevent Malvolio getting hurt? Why or why not?"
- "I'm going to break you up into small groups, and I want you to discuss with your group:"
  ▷ "What if *you* were an <u>upstander</u> in this situation? What do I mean by this? How could you change the outcome to prevent harm, while also keeping yourself safe? Get creative!"
  ▷ "Take a few minutes to share ideas with your group and be ready to report back to the class."
  ▷ *Divide students into groups of three or four, checking around on group progress. Call them back after a few minutes and invite groups to share ideas.*
- **ROLEPLAY:** *When a student shares a strategy, invite them to play out the scene with the teacher, with the student enacting the upstander strategy. The teacher improvises to roleplay the scene with the student. After roleplay, unpack with the class: "What did we appreciate about _____'s strategy?"*
- *Try to play out multiple strategies, and name when you see a direct strategy, an indirect strategy, or a distraction strategy.*
- *When a student tries out an upstander approach like "hey, that's not cool," tie in the upstander stat:*
  ▷ *57 percent of the time, bullying ends in ten seconds or less when a bystander becomes an upstander.*
- *Emphasize there is no single strategy that will solve all the problems all at once, no perfect solutions, just what feels right for you.*
- "What resources exist in our community for upstanders? Are there anonymous reporting tools? Trusted adults we can go to?"

   SOME TIPS FOR ROLEPLAYS:
- *Students should only roleplay the upstander, always as themselves.*
- *Roleplay several scenes, involving as many students as possible. The goal is to get students practicing behaviors.*

- *Emphasize that there are many ways of participating. Some days, participating fully looks like getting up and practicing a roleplay; other days, your best participation is watching, listening, and supporting. Do what feels right for you today.*
- *After each roleplay, debrief: "What did we appreciate about what _____ just did?" If students try to critique the strategy, encourage them to stick with appreciation. It can be scary and hard to try new things in front of our peers, so we want to make sure our peers feel our appreciation when they try hard.*
- *When questions come up? Turn to the students for answers. Be curious; you are not the expert in this. Emphasize that we are working together to figure things out and that our solutions often will come from connecting with our peers.*

OTHER CLASSROOM ACTIVITIES (TWELFTH NIGHT)

Empathy Building

GUIDING QUESTION: What can we learn when we adopt the perspective of another person?

SKILLS ADDRESSED: Perspective-Taking, Creative Writing

ACTIVITY: Write a journal entry from the point of view of Malvolio, Sir Toby, Olivia, Feste, or any character of your choice and share with the class. Reflect on any discoveries you had when writing the journal entry (or hearing it read aloud).

Future Planning

GUIDING QUESTION: How can we make our school safer?

SKILLS ADDRESSED: Comprehensive Health, Civic Engagement, Community Awareness, Resource Awareness, Text Analysis

ACTIVITY: What kind of practices can you put in place in your school to make it okay to speak up when we see mistreatment? As a class, make a list of the resources at your school. Identify a moment in *Twelfth Night* in which one of these resources could have helped the characters in the play.

Connectedness

GUIDING QUESTION: What does it feel like to be connected to others?

SKILLS ADDRESSED: Social Awareness, Text Analysis, Perspective-Taking

ACTIVITY:

- Form a circle in the class and assign each student a character in the play (you can also assign a clump of students to represent a single character). Suggested characters include Viola, Olivia, Orsino, Malvolio, Feste, Toby, Andrew, and Sebastian, depending on the cutting of the play you're working with.
- Tell the students we are going to visually represent how the characters are connected to the others. Invite each character (or character group) to make a statement about their connection to another character. It can be a neutral statement like "I am Viola's twin brother" or a charged statement like "Malvolio made me really angry" or "I love Olivia." With a skein of yarn, link the characters with each new statement (ask a student to hold the yarn). Pretty soon you'll develop an intricate web. Invite students to reflect on how this feels to visualize the connectedness between characters.

Appendix F
The Comedy of Errors Materials

POST-SHOW DISCUSSION QUESTIONS

After you watch or stage a performance of *The Comedy of Errors* with your students, have a class discussion to unpack the mistreatment and patterns of violence. Here are some suggested guiding questions:

VIOLENCE PREVENTION CONNECTIONS:
- What examples of mistreatment or miscommunication did you notice in the play?
- Where in the play did you see characters receiving unequal or unfair treatment?
- Where did you see examples of characters behaving impulsively (without thinking)?
- Which characters took action to try to prevent the harm or mistreatment? (Discuss "upstander" behavior.)
- What does upstander behavior look like in our community?

ANALYZE THE CHARACTERS:
- What motivates each character?
- If you were in Antipholus and Dromio of Syracuse's shoes, how might you feel when you arrive in a foreign land? How would you stand? How would you walk around? How might you talk with strangers?

ANALYZE THE CLIMATE:
- What kind of behavior is acceptable in Ephesus (where the play takes place)?
- What kind of behavior is rewarded?
- Is this the kind of environment in which you'd thrive? Why or why not?

CONSIDER WHAT'S NEXT:
- After the twins are reunited, what do you think the relationship between both Antipholuses and Dromios will be like?
- After the play ends, what kinds of conversations might occur between each boss and employee?

ADDITIONAL QUESTIONS

- What is empathy? Why is it important? Was there ever a time when you "stepped into someone else's shoes"? What did it teach you?
- Actors use teamwork to trust one another when they are onstage. How is teamwork useful in school?
- How do the characters change from the beginning of the play to the end? What causes these changes? Have you ever noticed a change in your own behavior?
- Think of a moment in the play when two characters were equals. How about a moment in the play when two characters were NOT treated equally? What did you notice about the difference between these two moments?

UPSTANDER LESSON PLAN (*THE COMEDY OF ERRORS*)

- "In theatre we have to rehearse and practice, and in life we need to practice helping people and being an upstander. Today we are going to practice upstander behavior."
- "In the play, we have two sets of twins—and usually, without realizing it, the people in the play are talking to the *wrong twin*, so this creates a lot of misunderstanding. In this scene, watch how Antipholus and Dromio respond to the misunderstanding."
- "I'll perform this scene for you in contemporary language, and I want you to listen carefully."
- "Be thinking—if you overheard this, what are some ways you might prevent harm?"

SCENE: *Establish what's happening and how they'll know which character you're playing (name tags could work here!):*

- ANTIPHOLUS of *Ephesus is about to be arrested but sends* DROMIO *off to get some money for bail.*
- *The other* DROMIO *returns from an errand and presents a rope to* ANTIPHOLUS*. Let's see what happens.*

  > DROMIO: Hey boss! Here's the rope you asked me to buy!
  > ANTIPHOLUS: Dromio, where is my money?
  > DROMIO: Uh... I gave the money to the store, and the store gave me the rope.
  > ANTIPHOLUS: Five hundred dollars for a ROPE??? You idiot! (*Begins smacking Dromio.*)
  > DROMIO: Ow, boss! Stop it! (*Turns to the audience.*) You see what I have to put up with?

- "What did you notice about this scene?"
- "When you saw Antipholus hitting Dromio, how many of you wanted to help? Why or why not?"
- "Imagine that you witnessed this moment between Dromio and Antipholus. What if *you* were an <u>upstander</u> in this situation? What do I mean by this? How could you change the outcome to prevent harm while also keeping yourself safe? Get creative!"
  - *Option to break students into small groups to discuss their upstander strategies before a group share-out.*
- **ROLEPLAY:** *When a student shares a strategy, invite them to play out the scene with the teacher, and with the student enacting the upstander strategy. The teacher improvises to roleplay the scene with the student. After roleplay, unpack with the class:* "What did we appreciate about _____'s strategy?"
- *Try to play out multiple strategies, and name when you see a direct strategy, an indirect strategy, or a distraction strategy.*
- *When a student tries out an upstander approach like "hey, that's not cool," tie in the upstander stat:*
  - *57 percent of the time, bullying ends in ten seconds or less when a bystander becomes an upstander.*
- *Emphasize that there is no single strategy that will solve all the problems all at once, no perfect solutions, just what feels right for you.*

- "What resources exist in our community for upstanders? Are there anonymous reporting tools? Trusted adults we can go to?"

OTHER CLASSROOM ACTIVITIES (*THE COMEDY OF ERRORS*)

There are so many ways to deepen a younger person's connection to *The Comedy of Errors*. I know that you will have plenty of creative, imaginative, and enriching activities in mind. Here are a few ideas to get you started.

Journal Entries

GUIDING QUESTIONS:
- What is it like to travel?
- What does it feel like to be separated from the people you love?

SKILLS ADDRESSED: Empathy, Critical Thinking, Creative Thinking

ACTIVITY: Imagine that you are Dromio of Syracuse or Antipholus of Syracuse. Your journeys have been long and difficult as you search the world for your missing twin. Write a journal entry from the perspective of this character. What do you write about? What's on your mind? What are your days like? What do you write in your journal that you don't say aloud to others?

VARIATION: Do this activity for any character in the play (Emilia, Egeon, the Ephesus twins, Adriana, the jeweler, etc.). Assign one character to each student (or have them pick their favorite character) and ask them to journal as this character for one journal entry . . . or daily for a week.

Back Story

GUIDING QUESTIONS:
- How do our memories affect our present behavior?
- How might past experiences shape the way we behave today?

SKILLS ADDRESSED: Perspective-Taking, Critical Thinking and Analysis, Creativity

ACTIVITY: Invite your students to consider the following questions.
- What does each twin remember about the shipwreck that separated their families?

- What memories does each twin have about their missing twin? Their missing parent?
- What dreams do the characters have about their past?

Write (or discuss in small groups) a short description of each character's memory of their past. Do these memories line up, or do some characters remember the events differently? Each student could pick one of the characters (Antipholus of Ephesus, Dromio of Ephesus, Antipholus of Syracuse, Dromio of Syracuse) and answer the following questions, and then share with their peers. Alternatively, each student could answer these questions about all four characters (which encourages them to think like a director, considering the various perspectives of all the characters).

- This is what I remember about the shipwreck.
- This is what I remember about my twin.
- This is what I remember about my parent(s).
- These are the dreams I have about my past.

Breathing through the Text

GUIDING QUESTIONS:
- How does breath impact our emotions and our energy?
- What is the relationship between breath and violence/harm?

SKILLS ADDRESSED: Social and Emotional Learning (SEL), Mindfulness, Critical Thinking and Analysis

ACTIVITY: Introduce a bit of text from the play (perhaps a scene with some anger/mistreatment baked into it). For example: "When I am cold, he heats me with beating. When I am warm, he cools me with beating. I am waked with it when I sleep, raised with it when I sit, driven out of doors with it when I go from home, welcomed home with it when I return." (IV.iv)

Try reading the text aloud, and jot down a few words to describe how you feel and describe the energy of this speech. Now read the text aloud, but this time, with a deep breath in through the nose and a deep breath out through the mouth. Don't rush this part. Coach your students to really take a slow, deep breath. You may model this, and then guide your students through trying it on their own. In unison at first, then you may want to hear from a few volunteers. How does the energy/emotion change when you slow down? Discuss how breath and emotion are related. What about breath and violence?

Interrupting the Harm

GUIDING QUESTIONS:
- How do we recognize harm in the moment?
- What is happening with power dynamics in a moment of harm?

SKILLS ADDRESSED: Critical Thinking and Analysis, Social Awareness, Comprehensive Health

ACTIVITY: Before reading the script of *The Comedy of Errors*, discuss a convention for recognizing moments of harm (a bell students ring, or they snap their fingers, or place their hands on their hearts). Read through the script as a class, starting with one scene. With each moment of harm, ask the class what they noticed, who is being harmed, and who is in power. Have them pay attention to whether the power shifts throughout the play. Discuss the relationship between power and harm/mistreatment/violence.

Given Circumstances

GUIDING QUESTION:
- How do your surroundings impact your thoughts, feelings, and behavior?

SKILLS ADDRESSED: Critical Thinking, Perspective-Taking, Imagination, Self-Awareness

ACTIVITY: In the theatre, actors must analyze the given circumstances of a scene. The given circumstances are the who/what/why/when/where of a play. They are the basic facts about the truth of the moment. If one character says something about the rain outside, then we know one set of given circumstances: it's raining. The given circumstances of a scene are usually outside the control of a character; you usually can't change them, so you need to act within the confines of your given circumstances. Characters will respond differently to the given circumstances, but they are generally not something anyone can change. Try speaking the following lines of text from *The Comedy of Errors*:

When I am cold, he heats me with beating. When I am warm, he cools me with beating. I am waked with it when I sleep, raised with it when I sit, driven out of doors with it when I go from home, welcomed home with it when I return. (IV.iv)

Next, try the scene with different given circumstances.

- You are outdoors in freezing weather without a coat, and you've been locked out of your house.
- You are about to be arrested, and you don't know why; the arresting officer won't give you a reason.
- You are having a really bad day.
- You are having a really great day.
- You are really hungry.
- You have been traveling all week; you are really jet lagged and tired and grumpy and you just want to snuggle up in your PJs and go to bed.
- You are calm, well rested, and really listening to the people around you.

DISCUSSION: What thoughts did you have after playing out this set of given circumstances? How did it feel? How did the circumstances affect your behavior?

VARIATION: You can pick any section of text from the play (or have students write their own text) and introduce additional given circumstances. The students may want to write their own given circumstances and try out their ideas with the text. Discuss how the circumstances impact the person speaking the text. How do they impact the people listening to the text? Were some circumstances more fun to perform than others? What is the relationship between our given circumstances and our thoughts, actions, and behavior?

Graphic Organizer

GUIDING QUESTIONS:
- What kinds of situations will we see in the performance?
- How do mistreatment and miscommunication impact the people in the play?
- How does this play relate to our school?

SKILLS ADDRESSED: Critical Thinking and Analysis, Creativity, Perspective-Taking, Social Awareness

ACTIVITY: Before sharing the play with your students, invite them to answer the following questions:

- In the play, Antipholus of Syracuse comes to a new land where he doesn't know anyone. When characters in the play mistake Antipholus for his twin brother he doesn't know lives there, he becomes confused and angry, and takes his anger out on his sidekick, Dromio. How do you think Dromio feels when he is mistreated?
- We have all felt angry or confused, and sometimes when we are angry we act or speak before we think. What if Antipholus took a moment to stop and think before reacting in anger? Imagine what could happen differently and draw a picture of it.
- If you were standing nearby when Antipholus was mistreating Dromio, what is one way you might be able to help prevent harm? If I saw Dromio being mistreated, I would help by _____. I would do this because _____.
- As a class, discuss the following questions:
  ▷ Can we create some class agreements about how to be upstanders (people who help prevent mistreatment) and look out for one another?
  ▷ How do we react to mistreatment in our community? Remember that when we hurt other people, it's often because we're hurting, too. How do we include both the person being mistreated and the person who is doing the mistreating?

Appendix G

The Taming of the Shrew Materials

POST-SHOW DISCUSSION QUESTIONS

- What do you think of the title? What is a shrew? Who is the shrew in the play?
- Who in the play had the chance to prevent harm? If they had taken action, how would that have impacted what occurred?
- What do you think is next for Kate and Petruchio?
- How would you describe the world of this play? What kind of behavior is tolerated and celebrated? Is this what you want for your community?
- What kind of action can you take in your community to build a positive environment, in which people are able to be themselves?

UPSTANDER ROLEPLAY LESSON PLAN (*THE TAMING OF THE SHREW*)

- "In theatre we have to rehearse and practice, and in life we need to practice helping people and being an upstander. Today we are going to be practicing upstander behavior while still keeping yourself safe."
- "We saw a lot of really harmful treatment in the play. We don't want to see that kind of mistreatment and violence in our world."
- "We're about to watch a scene in which Petruchio shares a plan to 'tame' Kate, and his plan includes starvation and sleep depri-

vation. I'll perform this scene for you, in contemporary language, and I want you to be thinking—if you witnessed this, what are some ways you might prevent harm?"

> PETRUCHIO: Okay, friends, my wife Kate is really headstrong, so I have a great plan to transform her into a better person. I'm not letting her eat any food, I'm not letting her sleep, and I'm making her think I'm doing it all for love. I think it's working! But if anyone has a better idea, lemme know...

- "What did you notice about this scene? What questions might you have for Petruchio? What do you find concerning about his behavior?"
- *Breakout discussion:* "In small groups, discuss if *you* were an upstander in this situation. What do I mean by this? How could you change the outcome to prevent harm while also keeping yourself safe? Get creative!"
- *When a student offers an upstander strategy, invite them (or a volunteer) to play it out with the actor.*
- *Students should only roleplay the upstander, always as themselves.*
- *The important thing in the roleplays is that students are trying out a wide variety of their own ideas (not the ideas of the teaching artist). Encourage them to think creatively and try out all positive solutions.*
- *Roleplay several scenes, involving as many students as possible, and the classroom teacher, if appropriate.*
- *After each roleplay, debrief:* "What did we appreciate about what _____ just did?"
- *Encourage students to try out indirect and direct ways to help.*
- "What if this situation took place at your school—who could you go to if you saw something like this happening? If you saw rumors circulating online about a classmate, what could you do as an upstander?"
- "You had so many great upstander solutions! Some were direct" (*reference specific examples from students*) "and some indirect" (*reference specific examples*).
- "Always keep your safety in mind when intervening and consider using other strategies if being direct doesn't feel possible."

OTHER CLASSROOM ACTIVITIES (*THE TAMING OF THE SHREW*)

Anticipation Guide

Have students complete the following worksheet prior to watching the play.

> **SKILLS ADDRESSED:** Critical Thinking, Perspective-Taking

- In the play, people talk about a character named Katherine (Kate for short) behind her back. They call her a "shrew," which is a nasty word for a woman who is mean, headstrong, or has a "scolding tongue." Draw a picture of what you think Kate might look like based on what's said about her.
- Kate has a sister named Bianca. Imagine you are Bianca. How would you react if you heard someone saying mean things about your sister? If I heard someone saying mean things about my sister, I would _____. I would do/say this because _____.
- Petruchio decides to "tame" Kate by disagreeing with her, telling her she's wrong, taking away things she likes, and playing tricks on her. Imagine you are Petruchio's friend and he tells you his plan. Would you try to stop him? I would tell him _____. I would say this because _____.
- Kate's dad agrees to have Kate marry Petruchio, even though she doesn't want to. When your parents make decisions you don't agree with, what you *want* to do isn't always the best way to handle a situation. Think about what you *want* to do or say when you disagree with your parents, then think about the *best* way to respond. When my parents make decisions I don't think are fair, I *want* to do/say _____. I want to do/say this because _____. The *best* way to respond the next time my parents make a decision I don't think is fair is _____. This is the best response because _____.

Indicate agree, disagree, or it depends, then explain your answer in a full sentence.

- Sibling rivalry is/can be a form of bullying.
- Changing your personality makes it easier to fit in.
- True friendship requires compromise.
- Controlling someone's behavior is a type of bullying.
- Changing your appearance changes the way people treat you.

- People usually need to act cruelly or aggressively to raise their status, popularity, or power.
- Violent words or actions always lead to more violence.
- Parents have the right to make decisions about their child's social life.
- I treat people the same regardless of their gender.

Appendix H
The Tempest Materials

POST-SHOW DISCUSSION QUESTIONS

After you watch or stage a performance of *The Tempest* with your students, a series of class discussions can be a useful way to unpack the mistreatment and patterns of violence. Here are some suggested guiding questions, although, as always when working with Shakespeare, it is important to emphasize that a line in a play does not have a single, correct meaning but many possible interpretations.

SHAKESPEARE QUESTIONS:
- What moments were most memorable in the play?
- Why do you think actors are still performing the plays of Shakespeare? What do the stories have to teach us today?

VIOLENCE PREVENTION CONNECTIONS:
- What examples of mistreatment or violence did you notice in the play?
- Which characters took action to try to prevent the harm? (Discuss upstander behavior.)
- What does upstander behavior look like in our community?
- What is empathy? Why is it important? Was there ever a time when you "stepped into someone else's shoes"? What did it teach you?
- Actors use teamwork to trust one another when they are onstage. How is teamwork useful in school?

- This play has a history of being interpreted through the lens of post-colonialism (a theory that explores the impact of colonization), particularly when we explore Prospero's role in colonizing the island, with Caliban as a colonized islander. How might an understanding of colonization shed light on this production of *The Tempest*?

ANALYZE THE CHARACTERS:
- Why did the characters in the play behave the way they behaved?
- What motivates Prospero to seek revenge on his brother and enemies? What might it feel like to be Prospero when he learns his brother will be sailing near his island?
- What motivates Caliban to plot to harm Prospero when he meets Stephano and Trinculo? How might it feel to be Caliban in that moment?
- For most of the play, Prospero is focused on getting even with his brother, Antonio. By the end of the play, Prospero changes his mind. What do you think makes him change his mind and choose to forgive his brother?
- Prospero realizes he has to make a choice between "virtue" and "vengeance." What do those words mean to you? When have you had to choose between them?

ANALYZE THE CLIMATE:
- What kind of behavior is acceptable on the island (where the play takes place)? How is this different from life in Milan, where Prospero used to live?
- What kind of behavior is rewarded on the island? What kind of behavior is punished?
- Is this the kind of environment in which you'd thrive? Why or why not?

CONSIDER WHAT'S NEXT:
- After Prospero forgives his enemies, what do you think life will be like for him when he leaves the island?
- After Ariel is freed, what do you think the character will do next? What will life be like for Ariel?
- After Prospero leaves the island, what do you think Caliban will do next? What will life be like for Caliban?

UPSTANDER ROLEPLAY LESSON PLAN (*THE TEMPEST*)

This production had a female Prospero, so the pronouns reflect that. Feel free to adapt.

- "In theatre we have to rehearse and practice, and in life we need to practice helping people and being an upstander. Today we are going to be practicing upstander behavior."
- "Early in the play, Prospero creates a magical storm that brings her enemy to the island. Although no one gets physically hurt in the storm, it's a really scary experience for lots of people."
- "Let's back up a bit (before the play even begins) and look at the moment Prospero introduces this plan to Ariel."
- "I'm going to perform this scene for you, playing both roles, in contemporary language, and I want you to listen carefully."
- "Be thinking—if you overheard this, what are some ways you might prevent harm?"

SCENE: *Set up that you'll play two people (if you have a co-facilitator, you can both perform):*

- PROSPERO, *who was really hurt by her brother and is now hatching a plan to get revenge through magic*
- ARIEL, *Prospero's servant, who is trying to do a good job*

> PROSPERO: Ariel, my favorite servant! I've got a great idea!
> ARIEL: Whatcha thinking, boss?
> PROSPERO You know my brother Antonio?
> ARIEL: The one who was super mean to you twelve years ago, and stole your dukedom? You may have mentioned him once or twice.
> PROSPERO: Well, get this. He is sailing near our island pretty soon, and I'm planning to cook up a magical storm to magically wreck his boat on our magical island, and then I can finally punish him for the way he treated me! But I need my favorite magical servant to help me. Pretty please?
> ARIEL: Sounds like a solid plan, boss. Count me in!

- "What did you notice about this scene?"
- "Later in the play, Prospero talks about choosing virtue (choosing goodness) over vengeance (choosing to hold a grudge and get back at someone). In this moment, which is she choosing?"

- "When Prospero was sharing the plan to hurt her brother, how many of you wanted to help prevent harm?" (*If lots of kids raise hands*) "Look at how many potential helpers we have in this class!"
  - "Why do you want to help? Let's hear from a few people about why your hands are up."
- "I'm going to break you up into small groups, and I want you to discuss with your group:"
  - "What if *you* were an <u>upstander</u> in this situation? What do I mean by this? How could you change the outcome to prevent harm while also keeping yourself safe? Get creative!"
  - "Take a few minutes to share ideas with your group, and be ready to report back to the class."
  - *Divide into groups of three or four and check around on group progress. Call them back after a few minutes and invite groups to share their upstander ideas with the class.*
    - *When a student offers an upstander strategy, invite them (or a volunteer) to play it out with the facilitator.*
    - *Students should only roleplay the upstander,* always *as themselves.*
    - *After each roleplay, debrief:* "What did we appreciate about what _____ just did?"
    - *When a student tries out an upstander approach like "hey, that's not cool," tie in the upstander stats:* "What if the next time you saw someone being bullied you said 'That's not cool' to the person acting as the bully? Fifty-seven percent of the time, bullying ends in ten seconds or less when a bystander becomes an upstander."
    - *Encourage students to also try out indirect ways to help (e.g., take target away from the situation, talk to the person being mistreated afterward to let them know you're here for them, approach a teacher).*
    - *The important thing in the roleplays is that students are trying out a wide variety of ideas. Encourage them to think creatively and try out all positive solutions.*
    - "You had so many great upstander solutions! Some were direct" (*reference specific examples from students*) "and some indirect" (*reference specific examples*).

- "Safety first! Always. Your safety is most important—if you don't feel safe, you can't help someone else."
- "You can always seek a trusted adult to help. Who might that be?"
- *Invite students to visualize that trusted adult. If there's time, ask volunteers to share their answers aloud.*

OTHER CLASSROOM ACTIVITIES (*THE TEMPEST*)

Look For

Assemble a list of "look-fors" for your students, while they watch the play, view the film, or read the play together as a class.

VARIATION: after reading the play, have your students craft their own lists of look-fors for when they watch the performance. Below is a suggested list to get you started, ideas that will prime the students to consider the climate of the play. I encourage you to create your own list.

SKILLS ADDRESSED: Climate Awareness, Text Analysis

- A power imbalance
- An instance of bullying
- Someone being mean because someone else was mean first
- Someone choosing to harm instead of help
- Someone choosing to help
- An act of kindness
- Someone who changes

Imagination Activity, Part 1

GUIDING QUESTION: What are the ingredients of a healthy, safe, and happy community?

SKILLS ADDRESSED: Imagination, Empathy, Perspective-Taking, Problem Solving, Conflict Resolution

Soon we will watch a play called *The Tempest*. In the play, Prospero finds himself stranded on an island with his daughter, Miranda. He has to start a new life in a new place. What if you found yourself stranded in an unfamiliar place? How would you start over, and what would you need to make your new home a healthy, happy community?

1. Who's stranded with you? (*Pick one person.*)
2. Draw a picture of yourself and your buddy on your new island home. What supplies do you have with you?
3. When you and your buddy arrive at the island, you meet other people who already live there who are very different from you. How do you create a healthy, happy community with them? What are three most important rules you would agree on and why?

    Rule 1. _____
    Why? _____

    Rule 2. _____
    Why? _____

    Rule 3. _____
    Why? _____

4. If another person on the island hurt my feelings, here are three healthy ways I could respond:

    1. _____
    2. _____
    3. _____

Imagination Activity, Part 2

GUIDING QUESTION: What does a society need to thrive?

SKILLS ADDRESSED: Empathy, Leadership, Text Analysis, Perspective-Taking

The speech below is from *The Tempest*. In this speech, when a group of people are stranded on the island, a man named Gonzalo imagines what he would do if he were the ruler of the island. Shakespeare, the writer, uses some words that might not be familiar to you in this speech. As a class, review what these words mean, then read the speech out loud, dividing the lines among the students.

> Had I plantation of this isle, my lord,
> And were the king on it, what would I do?
> In the commonwealth I would by contraries
> Execute all things, for no kind of traffic
> Would I admit; no name of magistrate;
> Letters should not be known; riches, poverty

And use of service, none; contract, succession,
Bourn, bound of land, tilth, vineyard—none;
No use of metal, corn, or wine or oil;
No occupation, all men idle, all;
And women, too, but innocent and pure;
All things in common nature should produce
Without sweat or endeavor; treason, felony,
Sword, pike, knife, gun, or need of any engine
Would I not have; but nature should bring forth
Of its own kind all foison, all abundance,
To feed my innocent people. (*The Tempest* II.i.157–180)

VOCAB WORDS

commonwealth: community/nation
contraries: not the usual way things are done
traffic: business, commerce
magistrate: a person who administers the law
bourn, bound of land: both terms refer to land boundaries/property lines
tilth: farming labor
engine: machinery
foison: plenty, abundance

As a class, discuss the following questions, and ask thoughtful follow-up questions after each person shares.

1. What would Gonzalo keep out of this new community? Why?
2. What would this community be like to live in?
3. If you were the ruler of a new community, what would be most important to you? Would you ban any items? Would you require anything of your citizens?
4. Now imagine you're a citizen of this new community instead of its leader. Do you still like the way you've set up the community? Would you change anything?

Now, write your own version of the speech:

YOUR VERSION

Had I plantation on this isle, my lord,
And were the leader on it, what would I do?

References

Ahmed, Eliza, and Valerie Braithwaite. 2006. "Forgiveness, Reconciliation, and Shame: Three Key Variables in Reducing School Bullying." *Journal of Social Issues* 62 (2): 209–438.

Banks, Fiona. 2014. *Creative Shakespeare: The Globe Education Guide to Practical Shakespeare*. London: Bloomsbury.

Bate, Jonathan. 1998. *The Genius of Shakespeare*. New York: Oxford University Press.

Blueprints for Healthy Youth Development. n.d. "Program Search." Accessed January 16, 2025. https://www.blueprintsprograms.org.

Boal, Augusto. 2019. *Theatre of the Oppressed*. London: Pluto Press.

Brown, Brené. 2020. "Brené Brown on Power and Leadership." Accessed December 18, 2022. https://brenebrown.com/resources/brene-brown-on-power-and-leadership/.

Center on the Social and Emotional Foundations for Early Learning. n.d. "What Is Emotional Literacy?" Accessed August 31, 2023. http://csefel.vanderbilt.edu/resources/wwb/wwb21.html.

Centers for Disease Control and Prevention. 2022. "Timeline of Violence as a Public Health Problem." Last modified January 18, 2022. https://stacks.cdc.gov/view/cdc/103248.

Centers for Disease Control and Prevention. 2024a. "About Adverse Childhood Experiences." Last modified October 8, 2024. https://www.cdc.gov/aces/about/index.html.

Centers for Disease Control and Prevention. 2024b. "About Community Violence." Last modified May 16, 2024. https://www.cdc.gov/community-violence/about/.

https://doi.org/10.5876/9781646427246.c021

Centers for Disease Control and Prevention. 2024c. "About Intimate Partner Violence." Last modified July 7, 2024. https://www.cdc.gov/intimate-partner-violence/about/index.html.

Centers for Disease Control and Prevention. 2024d. "About Sexual Violence." Last modified January 23, 2024. https://www.cdc.gov/sexual-violence/about/index.html.

Centers for Disease Control and Prevention. 2024e. "About Youth Violence." Last modified February 15, 2024. https://www.cdc.gov/youth-violence/about/index.html.

Centers for Disease Control and Prevention. 2024f. "Bullying." Last modified October 28, 2024. https://www.cdc.gov/youth-violence/about/about-bullying.html.

Centers for Disease Control and Prevention. 2024g. "Fast Facts: Firearm Violence Prevention." Last modified July 5, 2024. https://www.cdc.gov/firearm-violence/data-research/facts-stats/index.html.

Centers for Disease Control and Prevention. 2024h. "The Public Health Approach to Violence Prevention." Last modified April 9, 2024. https://www.cdc.gov/violence-prevention/about/about-the-public-health-approach-to-violence-prevention.html.

Centers for Disease Control and Prevention. 2024i. "Risk and Protective Factors: Youth Violence Prevention." Last modified March 12, 2024. https://www.cdc.gov/youth-violence/risk-factors/index.html.

Centers for Disease Control and Prevention. 2024j. "Risk Factors for Intimate Partner Violence Perpetration." Last modified February 8, 2024. https://www.cdc.gov/intimate-partner-violence/risk-factors/index.html.

Centers for Disease Control and Prevention. 2025. "Teen Dating Violence." Last modified January 14, 2025. https://www.cdc.gov/intimate-partner-violence/about/about-teen-dating-violence.html.

Collaborative for Academic, Social and Emotional Learning (CASEL). n.d. "Fundamentals of SEL." Accessed February 6, 2024. https://casel.org/fundamentals-of-sel/.

Colorado Department of Public Health and Environment (CDPHE). n.d.a. "Healthy Kids Colorado Survey." Accessed February 15, 2024. https://cdphe.colorado.gov/hkcs.

Colorado Department of Public Health and Environment. n.d.b. "Mental Health and Suicide Prevention: How to Talk to Children and Youth." Office of Suicide Prevention. Accessed December 8, 2022. https://cdphe.colorado.gov/suicide-prevention/youth-and-young-adult-suicide-prevention.

Cyberbullying Research Center. n.d.a. "Cyberbullying Identification, Prevention, and Response." Accessed February 15, 2024. https://cyberbullying.org/Cyberbullying-Identification-Prevention-Response-2024.pdf.

Cyberbullying Research Center. n.d.b. "What Is Cyberbullying?" Accessed August 31, 2023. https://cyberbullying.org/what-is-cyberbullying.
Daoud, Nihaya, Ayelet Carmi, Robert Bolton, Ariadna Cerdan-Torregrosa, Anna Nielsen, Samira Alfayumi-Zeadna, Claire Edwards, Fiachra O Suilleabhain, Belen Sanz-Barbero, Carmen Vives-Cases, and Mariano Salazar. 2022. "Promoting Positive Masculinities to Address Violence Against Women: A Multicountry Concept Mapping Study." *Journal of Interpersonal Violence* 38 (9–10): 6523–52.
DeGruy, Joy. 2017. *Post Traumatic Slave Syndrome*. Portland, OR: Joy DeGruy Publications.
Detmer, Emily. 1997. "Civilizing Subordination: Domestic Violence and *The Taming of the Shrew*." *Shakespeare Quarterly* 48, no. 3 (Fall): 273–94. https://doi.org/10.2307/2871017.
Dunn, Esther Cloudman. 1939. *Shakespeare in America*. New York: The Macmillan Company.
Fitzgerald, F. Scott. 1995 (1925). *The Great Gatsby*. New York: Simon and Schuster.
Foakes, R. A. 2003. *Shakespeare and Violence*. New York: Cambridge University Press.
Folger Shakespeare Library. n.d. "Shakespeare's Complete Works." Accessed August 31, 2023. https://www.folger.edu/explore/shakespeares-works/all-works/.
Garber, Marjorie. 2004. *Shakespeare After All*. New York: Pantheon.
Gillions, Anna, Rachael Cheang, and Rui Duarte. 2019. "The Effect of Mindfulness Practice on Aggression and Violence Levels in Adults: A Systematic Review." *Aggression and Violent Behavior* 48:104–15.
Gini, Gianluca, and Tiziana Pozzoli. 2013. "Bullied Children and Psychosomatic Problems: A Meta-Analysis." *Pediatrics* 132, no. 4 (October): 720–29.
Goldfarb, Alia. 2017. "Colorado Shakespeare Festival's Shakespeare & Violence Prevention Program—Form & Implementation Analysis: Insights and Recommendations." Thesis, University of Colorado.
Hawkins, D. Lynn, Debra J. Pepler, and Wendy M. Craig. 2001. "Naturalistic Observations of Peer Interventions in Bullying." *Social Development* 10 (4): 512–27.
Hinduja, Sameer, and Justin W. Patchin. 2022. "Bias-Based Cyberbullying among Early Adolescents: Associations with Cognitive and Affective Empathy." *Journal of Early Adolescence* 22 (9): 1204–35.
Hübl, Thomas. 2020. *Healing Collective Trauma: A Process for Integrating our Intergenerational and Cultural Wounds*. Boulder, CO: Sounds True.
Hunt, Maurice. 1997. "Slavery, English Servitude, and *The Comedy of Errors*." *English Literary Renaissance* 27, no. 1 (Winter): 31–56.
Kang, Kyung-Ah, Shin-Jeong Kim, SoRa Kang, and JungMin Lee. 2022. "Effects of a Violence Prevention Education Program Using Empathy

(VPEP-E) on Fifth-Grade Students in South Korea." *The Journal of School Nursing* 40 (4): 361–71.

Karcher, Michael. 2004. "Connectedness and School Violence: A Framework for Developmental Interventions." In *Handbook of School Violence*, edited by E. Gerler, 7–42. Binghamton, NY: Haworth Press.

Kingston, Beverly, Sabrina Arredondo Mattson, Allison Dymnicki, Elizabeth Spier, Monica Fitzgerald, Kimberly Shipman, Sarah Goodrum, William Woodward, Jody Witt, Karl G. Gill, and Elliott Delbert. 2018. "Building Schools' Readiness to Implement a Comprehensive Approach to School Safety." *Clinical Child and Family Psychology Review* 21: 433–49. https://doi.org/10.1007/s10567-018-0264-7.

Kingston, Beverly E., Marc A. Zimmerman, Monica L. Wendel, Deborah Gorman-Smith, Erin Wright-Kelly, Sabrina Arredondo Mattson, and Aimée-Rika T. Trudeau. 2021. "Developing and Implementing Community-Level Strategies for Preventing Youth Violence in the United States." *American Journal of Public Health* 111, no. S1 (May 1, 2021): S20–S24. https://doi.org/10.2105/AJPH.2021.306281.

Klimecki, Olga M. 2019. "The Role of Empathy and Compassion in Conflict Resolution." *Emotion Review* 11 (4). https://doi.org/10.1177/1754073919838609.

Kyd, Thomas. 2009. *The Spanish Tragedy*. London: Bloomsbury.

Linklater, Kristin. 1992. *Freeing Shakespeare's Voice*. New York: Theatre Communications Group.

Malone, Toby, and Aili Huber. 2021. *Cutting Plays for Performance*. London: Routledge.

Menakem, Resmaa. 2017. *My Grandmother's Hands: Racialized Trauma and the Pathway to Mending our Hearts and Bodies*. Las Vegas, NV: Central Recovery Press.

Morley, Richard H., Paul B. Jantz, and Cheryl Fulton. 2019. "The Intersection of Violence, Brain Networks, and Mindfulness Practices." *Aggression and Violent Behavior* 46: 165–73.

National School Climate Center. 2021. "How Do We Define School Climate?" https://schoolclimate.org/school-climate/.

National Threat Assessment Center. 2019. "Protecting America's Schools: A U.S. Secret Service Analysis of Targeted School Violence." US Secret Service, Department of Homeland Security.

Not in Our House Chicago Theatre Community. 2017. "Chicago Theatre Standards." https://notinourhouseorg.wordpress.com/wp-content/uploads/2022/03/chicago-theatre-standards-12-11-17-2.pdf.

Oxford English Dictionary. n.d. "violence, n." Accessed July 2023. https://doi.org/10.1093/OED/4998467199.

Right to Be. n.d. "The Five Ds of Bystander Intervention." Accessed February 12, 2024. https://righttobe.org/guides/bystander-intervention-training/.

Scharmer, Otto. 2023. "2023 in Eight Points: Meditating on Our Planetary Moment." *Field of the Future Blog.* December 30, 2023. https://medium.com/presencing-institute-blog/2023-in-eight-points-meditating-on-our-planetary-moment-3081cf51ed5d.

Scott, Kim. 2021. *Just Work.* New York: St. Martin's Press.

Search Institute. n.d. "Sparks and Thriving." Accessed August 31, 2023. https://www.search-institute.org/our-research/youth-development-research/sparks-and-thriving/.

Selman, Robert L., Lynn Hickey Schultz, Michael Nakkula, Dennis Barr, Caroline Watts, and Julius B. Richmond. 1992. "Friendship and Fighting: A Developmental Approach to the Study of Risk and Prevention of Violence." *Development and Psychopathology* 4: 529–58.

Smith, Emma. 2020. *This Is Shakespeare.* London: Pelican.

Staub, Ervin. 1989. *The Roots of Evil: The Origins of Genocide and Other Group Violence.* New York: Cambridge University Press.

Staub, Ervin. 2003. *The Psychology of Good and Evil: Why Children, Adults and Groups Help and Harm Others.* New York: Cambridge University Press.

Staub, Ervin, Laurie Anne Pearlman, Alexandra Gubin, and Athanase Hagengimana. 2005. "Healing, Reconciliation, Forgiving and the Prevention of Violence after Genocide or Mass Killing: An Intervention and Its Experimental Evaluation in Rwanda." *Journal of Social and Clinical Psychology* 24: 297–334.

Stopbullying.gov. 2023. "What Is Bullying." Last reviewed October 7, 2024. https://www.stopbullying.gov/bullying/what-is-bullying.

Suicide Prevention Resource Center. n.d. "Suicidal Thoughts and Suicide Attempts." Accessed August 31, 2023. https://sprc.org/about-suicide/scope-of-the-problem/suicidal-thoughts-and-suicide-attempts/.

Thompson, Ayanna, and Laura Turchi. 2016. *Teaching Shakespeare with Purpose: A Student-Centred Approach.* London: Bloomsbury.

United States Secret Service and United States Department of Education. 2004. "The Final Report and Findings of the Safe School Initiative: Implications for the Prevention of School Attacks in the United States." June 2004. https://www.govinfo.gov/app/details/GOVPUB-HS9-PURL-gp0147767.

Van der Kolk, Bessel. 2014. *The Body Keeps the Score.* New York: Penguin Books.

Wilkins, Natalie, Benita Tsao, Marci Hertz, Rachel Davis, and Joanna Klevens. 2014. *Connecting the Dots: An Overview of the Links among Multiple Forms of Violence.* Oakland, CA: Centers for Disease Control and Prevention and Prevention Institute.

Winfrey, Oprah, and Bruce D. Perry. 2021. *What Happened to You? Conversations on Trauma, Resilience, and Healing.* Unabridged. New York: Macmillan Audio.

Woodward, William, and Sarah Goodrum. 2016. *Report on the Arapahoe High School Shooting: Lessons Learned on Information Sharing, Threat Assessment, and Systems Integrity.* https://cdpsdocs.state.co.us/safeschools/Resources/AHS-reports/CSPVExSummary.pdf.

Youth.gov. n.d. "Teen Dating Violence and Gender." Accessed August 31, 2023. https://youth.gov/youth-topics/teen-dating-violence/gender.

Youth Risk Behavior Survey System. n.d. "YRBSS Results." Last modified October 31, 2024. https://www.cdc.gov/healthyyouth/data/yrbs/results.htm.

Index

abuse: child, 14; domestic, 149; elder, 14; experiencing, 152; parental, 76; physical, 127; sexual, 145; verbal, 7
activity: adapting text, 205; agree/disagree/explain, 204; anticipation guide, 240–41; back story, 233–34; breathing through the text, 234–35; character activity (Don John), 222–23; character activity (the friar), 223–24; connectedness, 228–29; content warning, 218; cutting/adapting text, 209–10; disability and the twenty-first century, 210–11; empathy building, 228; future planning, 228; given circumstances, 235–36; government and leaders, 209; graphic organizer, 236–37; imagination, 246–48; interrupting the harm, 235; journal entries, 233; look for, 205, 208–9, 212, 246; perspective-taking, 211; post-show discussion questions, 202–3, 206–7, 213, 219, 225–26, 230–31, 238, 242–43; resources, 218–19; strategies for reporting in school, 211; upstander roleplay lesson plan, 203–4, 207–8, 213–15, 219–22, 226–28, 231–33, 238–39, 244–46; vocabulary words, 248
actor, 11; audience, 173, 174, 197; breathe, 137; character's back story, 93; costumes, 175; depict a climate, 118; empathetic, 28, 184; exercise, working, 12; experience, 135; interactive roleplays, 121; multiple roles, 23, 49, 172, 173; professional, 22, 47, 121; rehearsal, 11, 100, 109, 182, 192, 195; safety concerns, 151; slow down speech, 182; storytelling, 50, 198; training, 19; youth suicide prevention, 65, 79
African American, 13
aggression, 41, 57, 143, 158, 166
Ahmed, Eliza, and Valerie Braithwaite: "Forgiveness, Reconciliation, and Shame," 163
anger, 75, 97, 132, 148, 194
antisemitism, 195–96
Applied Suicide Intervention Skills Training (ASIST), 79
approach, interdisciplinary, xii, 3, 189
Arapahoe High School Shooting, 60
artist, teaching, 3, 22, 25, 28, 84–85
assassination, 45, 50, 54–70
audience: Brutus, 66–68; Christopher Sly, 140–41; contemporary, 96, 198; content warning, 99; Don John, 99–100; Dromio, 130, 132; elementary school, 98–99, 114, 122, 133, 141; fights, staged, 83; high school, 37, 82, 98, 141;

256 | Index

involvement, 23, 84, 110, 114, 117, 120, 130, 132, 133, 135, 141; Macbeth, 44, 46; marginalized, 26; middle school, 37, 82, 98, 141; multilingual, 49; Petruchio, 149; real, 152; rumors, 100

Banks, Fiona: *Creative Shakespeare*, 31
Bate, Jonathan: *The Genius of Shakespeare*, xi, 104
Black, Indigenous, and People of Color (BIPOC), 26, 27
Boal, Augusto, 7–8, 24
Body Keeps the Score, The (Van der Kolk), 7
boundaries, 143, 146, 150–51, 152
Braithwaithe, Valerie. *See* Ahmed, Eliza
Brown, Brené, 44
bullying: aftermath, 158–60; climate, 118–19; criteria, 111; cyberbullying, x, 12, 96, 103, 104–26; gulling (bullying), 96, 107–8, 110, 111, 112, 119, 120, 122; inner causes, 17, 94; *Much Ado About Nothing*, 94; protective factors, 117, 162–63; risk factors, 111–15, 116–17; roleplay exercise, 122–24; root causes, 108–10, 158–60; statistics, 13, 103, 107; targets, 12, 106, 110, 112–13, 114, 115, 120; *Twelfth Night* theme, 104–26; upstanders, 119–21, 136

cast (actors), 23, 48, 133, 172, 173, 195
casting, 27, 48, 66, 113, 133, 149, 173, 202
CDC. *See* Centers for Disease Control and Prevention
Center for the Study and Prevention of Violence (CSPV): Colorado Shakespeare Festival, ix–xi, 22; CU Boulder, 4, 16, 22; Del Elliot, ix; director Beverly Kingston, 16, 20, 32, 80; Jane Grady, ix; Laurie Keith, 32; Linda Cunningham, ix; meetings with Colorado Shakespeare Festival, ix–xi, 98; research center, 4, 49; Shakespeare & Violence Prevention program, x, 3–4, 19–20, 22; upstander behavior, 122–23
Centers for Disease Control and Prevention (CDC): community violence, 81; definition of youth violence, 8; Division of Violence Prevention, 14; expertise, 16; online resources, 18, 39

choreographers, 151
classroom: classmate, 56; complexity of violence, 163; connectedness, 4, 184–85; conversations, 127, 144; creative space, 188; critical distance, 11; CSF method, 24–25; direct involvement, 174; discussion, 58, 61, 120; exploration, 143; interactive approach, 15; live performance, 51, 172; multipurpose, 23; performance-based approach, 3, 179; performance review, 135; play selection, 29; practice, 87; roleplaying, 153, 189, 193–94; school climate, 3; setting, 109, 123; Shakespeare's plays, xi–xii, 31; student performances, 47, 121; students, 153; teacher, 25; upstander behavior, 55, 125, 189; violence-prevention curriculum, 4; violence-prevention lens, 105; word pronunciation, 105
class, (societal): differences, 113; insult, 114; power imbalance, 132; struggles, 56; violence factors, 190
climate: bullying, 156–62, 168; community violence, 80–81, 96, 118; culture of secrecy, 118–19; cycle of violence, 156–62, 168; forgiveness, 156–57, 162–63, 167–72, 178; inequality of women, 138–48, 154; language, 45–46, 95; miscommunication and misunderstanding, 132; music, 119, 174; non-consent, 138–48, 154; power and violence, 44–45; power imbalances, 131–32, 138–48, 158; reconciliation, 156–57; relationship violence, 138–48, 153–54; school, 19–20; targeted violence, 43–44, 59–61
Colorado Shakespeare Festival (CSF): birth of Shakespeare & Violence Prevention, ix–xi, 32; Colorado Office of Suicide Prevention, 77, 79; comedies, 90; *The Comedy of Errors*, 133–85; dismantling racism, 26–27; foundational beliefs, 27; *Julius Caesar*, 64–66, 69; meeting with Center for the Study and Prevention of Violence, ix–xi; *The Merchant of Venice*, 150, 195–97; method, 24–26; *Much Ado About Nothing*, 98–101; performances, 23; rehearsals, 182; *Romeo and Juliet*, 82–85, 87; Spanish, 150; staging *Macbeth*, 47–51; surveys,

190; *The Taming of the Shrew*, 142, 149–50; *The Tempest*, 172–75; *Twelfth Night*, 121, 122
comedies: *The Comedy of Errors*, 126, 130; errors, 136; human behavior, 90; *The Menaechmi* (Plautus), 130; *Much Ado About Nothing*, 90, 91, 93, 99; physical mistreatment, 130–31; *Romeo and Juliet*, 85; *The Tempest*, 30, 89, 156; tragedies compared, 34; violence, 5, 30, 33, 89–90; violence-prevention, 89–90
communities of color, 14, 81, 144. See also African American; Black, Indigenous, and People of Color
community. *See under* violence: attitudes, 130; bonds, 42; climate, 19, 59, 88, 90, 96, 118, 121; collective, 32; connected, 37, 38, 42, 43, 185; forgiveness, 171; gender, 66; gossip and rumors, 96; interconnected, 43, 129; leader, 99, 192; *Macbeth*, 38; mass shooting, 192; partners, 22; reporting tools, 136; risk factors, 18, 40, 116; support, 93; theatre's role, 7, 90, 154, 194; upstander action, 86; values, 19; war, 38, 40
content warning, 65, 84, 99
costumes: character differences, 175; character transformations, 23, 83, 173, 175; death depiction, 83; perceived power, 113; simple design, 23, 121; social climate, 118; storytelling device, 23, 173
COVID-19 pandemic, 42, 82, 192
crimes: assassination, 56; contributing factors, 38; hate, 14; violent, 57
CSF. *See* Colorado Shakespeare Festival
CSPV. *See* Center for the Study and Prevention of Violence
curriculum: diverse languages, 26–27; empathy, 40–43; gender violence, 143; *Macbeth*, 47; *Much Ado About Nothing*, 98–99; racism, 26; relationship violence, 143; roleplay, 66–67, 122; *Romeo and Juliet*, 83; Shakespeare's canon, 28, 85; *The Taming of the Shrew*, 142–43; *Twelfth Night*, 104–5, 121, 124; upstander, 50; violence prevention, 3, 4, 12, 13, 22, 121, 192–93
cutting: Colorado Shakespeare Festival, 82–83; *The Comedy of Errors*, 133–34; critical thinking, 83; *Cutting Plays for Performance*, 31; Folger Shakespeare Library website, 122; *Macbeth*, 48; multiple roles, 172; small productions, 22; teacher or students, 121–22
Cutting Plays for Performance (Malone), 31
cyberbullying: Cyberbullying Research Center, 96, 115; Justin Patchin, 96, 115; risk factors, 115; Sameer Hinduja, 96, 115; statistics, 96, 103; *Twelfth Night* theme, x, 12, 104–26

dating violence, 145
Davidson, Anastasia, 121
Davis, Claire, 60
DeGruy, Joy: *Post Traumatic Slave Syndrome*, 17, 194
Dunn, Esther Cloudman: *Shakespeare in America*, xi

Eisele, Crystal, 121
Elizabethan theatre: all-male companies, 149; audience participation, 152; England, 54–55; London, 147; music, 174; playhouse, 23; scaffold, 7; version of cyberbullying, 115
Elizabeth I, 36, 154
Elizabeth (wife of Edward IV), 10
England: early modern, 8; Elizabethan, 54, 152; Elizabeth I, 143; James I, 36; street fighting, 8

family, 26, 139, 150, 163. See also parent
fight: among groups, 81; *The Comedy of Errors*, 130; high school students, 13; *Julius Caesar*, 69; *Much Ado About Nothing*, 100–101; physical, 14, 17, 131; roleplaying, 84, 86; *Romeo and Juliet*, 72–76, 81, 83, 84–87; shooting in public places, 81; staging, 83, 85, 100; street, 8, 81, 85; *The Taming of the Shrew*, 142, 148; *The Tempest*, 166; *Twelfth Night*, 117, 122
Fitzgerald, F. Scott: *The Great Gatsby*, 197
Foakes, R. A.: *Shakespeare and Violence*, 6
Folger Shakespeare Library, 29, 122
forgiveness, 7, 30, 90, 156–78
Franz, Wendy, 32, 64, 133
Freeing Shakespeare's Voice (Linklater), 182

Garber, Marjorie, 156
gender: character casting, 23, 29, 66, 113, 133, 149; equity, 144; expectations, 139; identity, 144; minority youth, 145; norms, 143, 144, 147; roles, 145, 149; rules, 147; secret, 118; *The Taming of the Shrew* theme, 138–55; treatment of people, 66; underlying concepts, 143, 147; violence, 14, 30, 139, 143, 190; violence-prevention, 66, 143, 144
generation: Capulets, 74; future, 194–95; intergenerational legacy, 17; older, 71, 87–88; trauma passed on, 17, 81, 194–95; younger, 75, 83, 87–88
The Genius of Shakespeare (Bate), xi, 104
genocide, 162
gossip, 91–103, 195
Great Gatsby, The (Fitzgerald), 197
grief: *All's Well That Ends Well*, 10; humanity, 7; intergenerational legacy, 17; *Julius Caesar*, 59; *Macbeth*, 10, 45; spoken, 45; *Twelfth Night*, 108, 116, 118
group: attentional violence, 15; audience, 11; breakout, 24, 31; collaborators, x; community violence, 81; differing perspectives, 184; direct violence, 14; distinct, 172; empathetic, 162; middle and high school, 34, 122; offending, 162; peer, 18; sexual and gender minority youth, 145; storm sound effects, 173; structural violence, 14–15; students treated differently, 131
gulling. *See* bullying

Handbook for School Violence (Karcher), 42–43
Harmon, Rand, 172
Healing Collective Trauma (Hübl), 17, 129, 135, 137
health, mental: bullying, 160; challenges, 14, 39, 42, 159, 190; COVID-19 pandemic, 42; crisis, 76; factors, protective, 42; friend's intervention, 64; issues, 47; professionals, 40, 163; risk factor in violence, 39, 108, 116, 160
Heilmann, Lena, 77
Hinduja, Sameer, 96, 115
histories, 6
Howarth, Carolyn, 182

Huber, Aili. *See* Malone, Toby
Hübl, Thomas: *Healing Collective Trauma*, 17, 129, 135, 137

Induction, 139–41, 147
intervention: Applied Suicide Intervention Skills Training, 79; cause for, 57; earlier, 56, 111; intensive, 20; opportunity for, 23, 52, 64, 84; rehearsing, 187; targeted, 20; unhealthy relationships, 145; upstander, 81, 132–33, 186–87
Intimacy Directors and Choreographers (IDC), 150–51

Jewish Studies, 195
Just Work (Scott), 21

Karcher, Michael J.: *Handbook for School Violence*, 42–43
Keith, Laurie, 32, 149, 172
Kent, Geoffrey, 135
Kingston, Beverly, 16, 19–20, 32, 80, 180
Kyd, Thomas: *The Spanish Tragedy*, 19

language: Arabic, 49; connectedness, 27, 37, 45, 50, 193; connection to violence, 10; contemporary, 114, 135; conversations, 47, 79; dehumanizing, 44; harmful, 27, 89, 95; healing force, 10; information, 73; insults, 95, 109–10; lack of skills, 66; non-confiding, 46; path out of violence, 10, 45–46; play dominated by, 100; power, 37, 95; racist, 27; rhythmic, 36; skills, 26; Spanish, 26–27, 49, 65–66, 150; violence-prevention, 27, 37, 45, 125, 186; warn, 119
leaders: community, 99, 192; dangerous, 55; daring and transformative, 44; decision making, 62; empower people, 44; frustrated, 71; inspire people, 44; leadership, 44–45, 52; new, 35; overthrow, 56; political, 54; "power over" framework, 44–45, 55; present, 55; response to, 54, 55, 56, 59, 66; share power, 44, 45
legal rights, 153
lesbian, gay, bisexual, transgender, and queer (LGBTQ+), 105

lesson plan, 29, 51–52, 69, 86, 103, 124, 137, 152, 176
Linklater, Kristin: *Freeing Shakespeare's Voice*, 182
Living Works, 79
Lizcano, Rodney, 121

Malone, Toby, and Aili Huber: *Cutting Plays for Performance*, 31
Marlowe, Christopher, 8
marriage: arranged, 73, 74; consent, 150; contract, 59; family ties, 85–86; forbids, 141; forced, 75, 76, 141, 147, 150–51; hasty, 73; peace in, 141; proposes, 106; rules about, 148; secret, 72, 77, 86; unwanted, 82
Mean Girls, 32
Menakem, Resmaa: *My Grandmother's Hands*, 17
mindfulness: *The Comedy of Errors*, 126; develop, 183; emotional regulation, 128; practices, 127; reduce violence, 12, 127; theatre's reinforcement of, 11, 190
misogyny, 138–39, 196
multitiered system of support (MTSS), 20, 94
music: "Freedom Hey Day," 174; "Full Fathom Five," 174; live, 23; singing and instruments, 23; *The Tempest*, 174; *Twelfth Night*'s climate, 119; "Where the bee sucks," 174
My Grandmother's Hands (Menakem), 17

National Suicide Prevention Hotline, 79. *See also* suicide; violence prevention
Nichols, Lynn, 121
non-Hispanic Black, 13

Office of Suicide Prevention, 65, 77, 79, 84. *See also* suicide; violence prevention
offstage: Benedick, 101; Brutus, 59; conversations, 121, 188–89; murders, 38; offstage characters, 159; suicide, 65
online: anonymous, 21, 115, 136; interactions, 99; mistreatment, 96, 115; parental concern, 146; reporting tool, 21; resources, 18, 39; rumors, 96, 103. *See also* Cyberbullying

onstage: address audience, 174; audience connection, 185; character transformations, 48, 83, 133, 173, 183; empathy, 184; fictional world, 197; gender representation, 66; intimacy, 146–47; kiss, 100; Macbeth soliloquy, 50; Malvolio's final line, 120; metaphor of a story, 198; power imbalances, 131; risk and protective factors depicted, 138; scene of harm, 197; self-reflection, 67–68; several roles, 110; Sly as audience member, 150; struggle and conflict, 5; suicide, 65; vicarious audience, 7
Orr, Timothy, 32, 98, 121

parent: abusive relationship, 139; authoritarian, 18; children's online life, 146; helicopter, 146; low parental involvement, 18; poor supervision of children, 18; *Romeo and Juliet*, 73, 74, 76, 80, 81, 86; Sycorax, 159. *See also* family
Patchin, Justin W., 96, 115
peer: antisocial, 18; aware of planned school attacks, 43–44, 69, 94, 186; connectedness, 18–19, 185; different from, 145; emotional state, 4; group, 18; personal grievance, 56, 120; power dynamics, 131; pressure, 39; prosocial, 18; protective factor, 97; red-flag behavior, 70; roleplay upstander behavior, 190; rumors, 102–3; Spanish speaking, 26; threat, 125; upstanders, 21, 98; watching and listening, 86, 153
Penner, Anne, 150, 195
performance: abridged, x, 48, 121; actor changes role, 169; actors interrupt, 150; audience participation, 84, 114, 120, 196; catharsis, 7; content warning, 65, 99; elementary audience, 22; four versions of a scene, 186; full-length, 22; Induction, 139; kiss, 100–101; live approach to plays, 3, 12, 22, 47, 108, 172, 179, 197; music, 23; "nowness," 11; post-play reflection, 23, 25; roleplaying, 122–23, 135, 190; Shakespeare & Violence Prevention, 4; Sly watches, 141; Spanish-speaking characters, 23, 26; stage slap, 100; suicide, 65, 84, 99;

260 | Index

venues, xi, 23; witness problematic behavior, 3, 121, 179
Perry, Bruce D. *See* Winfrey, Oprah
protective factors: access to trusted adults, 18, 78, 97–98; connectedness to community, 18, 27, 185; connectedness to family, 18, 79; connectedness to peers, 18, 83, 185; empathy and connectedness, 40–43, 58–59, 78, 117, 162, 185; forgiveness, 162–63; prosocial attitudes, 18, 46, 80, 83; reconciliation, 162; rehumanization, 162; social and emotional learning skills (SEL), 10, 18, 131; suicide prevention, 78–79; theme, 16; understanding causes of genocide, 162; understanding trauma symptoms, 162; violence-prevention lens, 28, 56
public health: approach to violence, 194; comprehensive approach, 14, 16, 18–19; intimate partner violence, 143; multidisciplinary approaches, xii; suicide prevention, 77; youth violence, 13, 14

racism, 26–27
resources, 79; contemporary, 44, 58; content warning, 84; dating violence, 145; emergency lifesaving, 194; friends, 46; lack of, 58; local, 65, 79, 84, 99; national, 65, 79, 84; National Suicide Prevention Hotline, 79; online, 18, 39, 41; phone number 988, 79; risk factors, 18, 39; suicide, 58, 65, 78, 79, 84, 99; Suicide and Crisis Lifeline, 79; theatre books, 31
Rich, Kevin, 48, 82, 121, 133, 172
risk factors: absence of trusted adults, 74; antisocial behavior, 57; antisocial peers, 18, 40, 117; belief in male dominance, 145; belief in strict gender roles, 145; bullying, 94, 111, 160; community, 18; cyberbullying, 115; disconnection, 40, 57, 58, 75, 116; early childhood trauma, 116; economic stress, 14; family, 14, 18; gossip and rumors, 96; high emotional distress, 39, 116; hostile attitudes toward women, 145; individual, 18; lack of communication, 58; lack of healthy conflict skills, 145; miscommunication, 131; online resource, 18, 39; past hurt, 94; physical abuse, 129; repeated violence, 145; secrecy, 116, 119; sleeplessness, 57, 58, 77; social isolation, 14, 40, 57, 75; steady exposure to violence, 58; substance abuse, 75, 116; unemployment, 146; war trauma, 40
roleplaying activities, 122, 152, 179, 190; *The Comedy of Errors*, 134–37; *Julius Caesar*, 66–69; *Macbeth*, 50–53; *Much Ado About Nothing*, 102–3; *Romeo and Juliet*, 84–87; *The Taming of the Shrew*, 151–53; *The Tempest*, 175–78; *Twelfth Night*, 122–24
roles. *See* actors; roleplaying
romances, 30, 156, 170
root causes: bullying, 17, 94, 104–25, 157–62; childhood trauma, 129; class struggles, 56; control, manipulation, inequality of women, 138–55; cyberbullying, 96, 115; cycle of violence and trauma, 157–62; generational collective trauma, 17; grudges, 56, 73–74, 157; home life, 108; insulting language, 95, 108–9; mental health issues, 108; physical fights, 13, 73–74, 100, 130; poverty, 17, 100; power imbalance, 157–62; public humiliation, 96; rumors and gossip, 93, 95; social inequality, 56; social isolation, 99, 118, 129; structural racism, 17, 108; suicidal ideation (thoughts), 17, 99; violence against women, 138–49, 151–52; violent acts, 38; war, 38, 56, 93
rumor, 91–103
Rwandan genocide, 162

Safe2Tell, 21, 136, 194
scaffold, 7
Scharmer, Otto, 15, 148
Schmidt, Heidi, 32, 84
school: assembly period, 22, 122; attacks, 20–21, 120, 186; bullying, 94, 115; bus, 115; climate, 19, 71, 118, 131, 166, 187, 197; Colorado students, 32; content warning, 65, 84; counselors, 163; curricula, 181; drama department, 172; *Handbook for School Violence*, 42; matinees, 47; positive climate, 16,

19–20, 94–97, 132; *Twelfth Night*, 121; violence-prevention researchers, 197
school, elementary: *The Comedy of Errors*, 30; lesson plan suggestions, 90; *The Taming of the Shrew*, 30, 139, 141; *The Tempest*, 156, 178; thirty-minute performance, 22; *Twelfth Night*, 30, 122; upper-elementary-age students, 126–27
school, high: Arapahoe High School shooting, 61; forty-five-minute-performance, 22; *Julius Caesar*, 30, 34, 55, 56, 70; *Macbeth*, 30, 34, 37, 47; *Much Ado About Nothing*, 30, 90, 91–103; plays about real life, 34–35; *Romeo and Juliet*, 30, 34, 72, 82; *The Taming of the Shrew*, 139, 141; *The Tempest*, 156; *Twelfth Night*, 122; violence, 13, 130
school, middle: forty-five minute-performance, 22; *Julius Caesar*, 5, 30, 34, 55, 56, 70; *Macbeth*, 30, 34, 37; *Much Ado About Nothing*, 30, 90, 91–103; plays about real life, 34–35; *Romeo and Juliet*, 30, 34, 72, 82; *The Taming of the Shrew*, 139, 141; *The Tempest*, 156; *Twelfth Night*, 122
Scotland, 36, 37, 38
Scott, Kim: *Just Work*, 21
script, 64, 121–22, 134, 169, 172
sexual violence, 143, 149
Shakespeare and Violence (Foakes), 6
Shakespeare in America (Dunn), xi
shooting, 17, 60, 81, 192–93
Smith, Emma: *This is Shakespeare*, xi, 138
social emotional learning (SEL), 10, 18, 131
social media, 99–100
South Korea, 41
Spanish (language), 23, 26, 49, 65–66, 133, 150
stage (acting platform): element of safety, 7; empty, 11; plays work best, 172; scaffold, 7; whose stories belong, 66
staging: abstract, 65; actor, 184, 189; audience as performers, 174; audience connection, 185; climate, 80; *The Comedy of Errors*, 131, 133, 135; creating scenes, 182, 185; diverse languages, 27; doubling actors as characters, 48; fictional world, 197; interpreting a play, 138; *Julius Caesar*, 64; kiss, 100–101; *Macbeth*, 46, 47, 51, 53; manager, 100–101, 174; manipulating reality, 141; *The Merchant of Venice*, 150, 195, 196; *Much Ado About Nothing*, 98; onstage, 65, 66, 83; onstage intimacy, 146, 151; onstage transformation, 173; prologue, 48; scenes of harm, 197, 198; setting, 73; soliloquy, 50; stage slap, 100; student, 31, 32, 47, 69, 190; suicide, 65, 78; *The Taming of the Shrew*, 142, 149, 150; *The Tempest*, 172; thoughtful and present, 197; *Twelfth Night*, 114, 118, 120, 121; violence, 5, 78, 83; violence prevention, 158; workshop, 177
storytelling, 23, 50, 66, 110, 173, 174, 180
suicide: Applied Suicide Intervention Skills Training (ASIST), 79; attempts, 78, 98; Colorado Office of Suicide Prevention, 65, 77, 79; firearm-related deaths, 13; ideation (thoughts), 17, 65, 77, 78, 98; *Julius Caesar*, 30, 35, 55–70; prevention, 65, 77, 78, 84, 98–99; reasons, 78; *Romeo and Juliet*, 57, 71–88; Shakespeare Violence & Prevention program, 77, 79; staging, 78; Suicide Prevention Resource Center, 78, 79; terms, 78
Suicide and Crisis Lifeline, 89

teacher, 53, 104, 149, 154, 180–81, 183; Colorado Office of Suicide Prevention, 65; *Creative Shakespeare*, 31; *Cutting Plays for Performance*, 31; discussion tools about suicide, 65; gender violence, 139; professional certification in applied Shakespeare, xii; relationship violence, 139; roleplay, 124; Shakespeare, 31–32; Shakespeare & Violence Prevention program, 24–25; student reporting, 21, 94; study guide, 65, 84, 195; *Teaching Shakespeare with Purpose*, 31; violence prevention, 4, 24
Teaching Shakespeare with Purpose (Thompson), 31
theatre: Aristotle, 7; art form, 11, 190, 194–95; audience, 7, 11, 152, 154, 185; Augusto Boal, 7–8; author's background, 16; Bessel van der Kolk, 7; Colorado Shakespeare Festival, 4, 22;

company, xii, 47, 169, 172; consent in the workplace, 146, 151; early modern audiences, 6; Forum Theatre, 8; live, 21, 134, 172; part of a community, 7; plays, 5, 124, 190, 197; portrays unhealthy realities, 35; reducing costs, 22–23; school climate, 20; teaches social and emotional skills, 3, 190, 194; Theatre of the Oppressed, 8; violence, 7; violence-prevention, xi, 12–13, 194

theatre company: character genders, 23; Colorado Shakespeare Festival, 4, 22, 175; four-actor, 98; local schools, 172; local theatre, 172; reduce costs, 22–23; Spanish speaker, 26; stolen script, 169; three-actor tour, 82

This is Shakespeare (Smith), xi, 138

Thompson, Ayanna, and Laura Turchi *Teaching Shakespeare with Purpose*, 31

threat: community violence, 81; humans seen as, 61, 194; *Julius Caesar*, 59, 61, 68; *Macbeth*, 37, 45; *Much Ado About Nothing*, 101; physical, 131; *Romeo and Juliet*, 72, 75, 80, 81; targeted school attacks, 20; *The Tempest*, 160; *Twelfth Night*, 107, 111, 124; violence definition, 34; violent crimes, 57; youth violence definition, 8

tragedies: *Julius Caesar*, 30, 54–70; *Macbeth*, 30, 36–53; *Romeo and Juliet*, 30, 71–88; *The Spanish Tragedy*, 10; *Titus Andronicus*, 34; violence, 33–35, 38, 59, 89; violence prevention, 33–35

trauma: adverse childhood experiences (ACES), 76, 116; childhood, 128, 129; collective, 17, 194; *The Comedy of Errors*, 128, 129; content warning, 65, 84; expert Bruce D. Perry, 17; generational, 17; Joy DeGruy (*Post Traumatic Slave Syndrome*), 17, 194; *Julius Caesar*, 65; *Macbeth*, 10, 39–40, 45; past, 12; Resmaa Menakem (*My Grandmother's Hands*), 17, 194; *Romeo and Juliet*, 74, 76, 82, 84; symptoms, 162; systemic racism, 194; *The Tempest*, 158, 159, 160, 161, 162, 170; Thomas Hübl (*Healing Collective Trauma*), 17, 129, 194; *Twelfth Night*, 116; violence, 15, 116, 158, 159, 194; war, 40; *What Happened to You? Conversations on Trauma, Resilience, and Healing*, 17

troupe, 4, 22, 25, 32, 140, 174, 175

Turchi, Laura. *See* Thompson, Ayanna

University of Colorado Boulder (CU Boulder): Center for the Study and Prevention of Violence, 4, 16, 22; Colorado Shakespeare Festival, 4, 22; Del Elliot, x; Jeanne McDonald, x; professional certificate in applied Shakespeare, xii; Program in Jewish Studies, 195

upstander (defender): Augusto Boal, 24; bystander, 20, 21, 25; *The Comedy of Errors*, 128–29, 132–33, 134–37; *Julius Caesar*, 55, 61, 64, 66–69; *Macbeth*, 46–47, 50–53; *Much Ado About Nothing*, 92–93, 96–98, 99, 102–3; practice, 25–26, 28, 125, 187–89; *Romeo and Juliet*, 81–82, 84–87; *The Taming of the Shrew*, 138, 145, 147–49, 151–53; *Twelfth Night*, 105, 107–8, 119–21, 122–24, 125; violence prevention themes, 16, 20–21

US Capitol, 55, 64, 70

US Secret Service, 19–20, 43, 56, 120

Van der Kolk, Bessel: *The Body Keeps the Score*, 7

violence: attentional, 15, 19, 148; community, 18, 54–70, 71–88, 130, 144, 192; direct, 14–15; domestic, 14, 34, 40, 76, 149, 182; gender, 14, 30, 138–55, 190; homicide, 13–14, 34, 36–53, 54–70, 71–88, 91–103, 157, 167; mass, 17, 192–93, 194; patterns, 6, 14, 16, 30, 56, 128–29, 156–78; perpetual, 81, 95, 129; physical, 8–9, 13–14, 34, 42, 81, 126–37, 143, 163; planned attack, 43–44, 47, 55, 60, 65, 69, 70, 186, 193; psychological, 143, 146; racial, 13–14, 15, 17, 26–27, 108, 166, 194; relationship, 39, 47, 138–55; root causes, 16–18, 38, 56, 73–74, 93–94, 108–10, 129, 143–44, 158–60; structural (indirect), 8–9, 14–15, 17, 19, 93, 146; suicide, 13, 30, 35, 54–70, 71–88, 98–99; war, 9, 37, 38, 40, 55, 56, 70, 91–103. *See also* bullying; cyberbullying

violence prevention: *The Comedy of Errors*, 128–33, 134–37; connectedness, 181, 184–86; further research, 189–90;

have hope, 181, 188–89; *Julius Caesar*, 56–64, 66–69; *Macbeth*, 38–47, 50–53; *Much Ado About Nothing*, 92–98, 102–3; practice empathy, 181, 183–84; *Romeo and Juliet*, 73–82, 85–87; Shakespeare in the Classroom, 179–80, 184; slow down, 181–83; speak up, 181, 186–88; *The Taming of the Shrew*, 142–49, 151–53; *The Tempest*, 158–72, 175–78; themes, 15–21; *Twelfth Night*, 107–21, 122–24. See also violence-prevention lens

violence-prevention lens: *The Comedy of Errors*, 129; *Julius Caesar*, 55; *Macbeth*, 36, 47, 48, 50, 53; *Much Ado About Nothing*, 92–93; *Romeo and Juliet*, 71, 77, 78; Shakespeare's plays, 4, 28–29, 33–34; *The Taming of the Shrew*, 142–43; *The Tempest*, 158, 164–68; themes, 16–21, 36; tragedies, 35; *Twelfth Night*, 104–5

war: *Julius Caesar*, 69; *Macbeth*, 37, 38, 40; *Much Ado About Nothing*, 91, 92, 93, 100; peace after, 9; Shakespeare's plays, 197
warning signs: audience participation, 84; community violence, 72; educate students, 43–44, 61; examples, 57; *Hamlet*, 63; ignore, 62; *Julius Caesar*, 55, 60, 61, 62, 63, 64, 65, 66; *Macbeth*, 43, 44; *Much Ado About Nothing*, 99; real life, 60, 61, 63; recognize, 55, 61; respond, 38; *Romeo and Juliet*, 72, 77, 84; speak up, 43; targeted violent acts, 43, 55, 61; *Twelfth Night*, 124

What Happened to You? Conversations on Trauma, Resilience, and Healing (Winfrey), 17

Winfrey, Oprah, and Bruce D. Perry *What Happened to You? Conversations on Trauma, Resilience, and Healing*, 17

women: differing expectations, 144; early modern attitudes, 143, 144; fictional Padua, 148, 153; historic violence, 149; inequality, 144, 147; inferiority, 144; MeToo movement, 149; reducing violence, 144; sexual violence, 143, 145

workshops: content warning, 84; facilitation, 24; post-show, 47, 65, 84; role-playing exercises, 24, 84, 103, 177, 194; Shakespeare & Violence Prevention performances, 4, 52, 69, 84

About the Author

AMANDA GIGUERE (she/her) holds an MA and a PhD in Theatre from the University of Colorado Boulder. She is the Director of Outreach for the Colorado Shakespeare Festival in Boulder, Colorado, and teaches for CU Boulder's Applied Shakespeare program. Her earlier work includes *The Plays of Yasmina Reza on the English and American Stage* (McFarland 2010).

www.ingramcontent.com/pod-product-compliance
Lightning Source LLC
Chambersburg PA
CBHW060554080526
44585CB00013B/557